POST-FORDISM AND SKILL

This book is dedicated to my father

Post-Fordism and Skill

Theories and perceptions

DENISE THURSFIELD
Leeds Business School
Leeds Metropolitan University

Ashgate

Aldershot • Burlington USA • Singapore • Sydney

HP
8391
.T49
2000

Published by
Ashgate Publishing Limited
Gower House
Croft Road
Aldershot
Hampshire GU11 3HR
England

Ashgate Publishing Company
131 Main Street
Burlington, VT 05401-5600 USA

Ashgate website: http://www.ashgate.com

British Library Cataloguing in Publication Data
Thursfield, Denise
    Post-Fordism and skill : theories and perceptions
    1.Skilled labour - Great Britain 2.Ability - Evaluation
    3.Occupations - Great Britain - Sociological aspects
    I.Title
    331.1'1422'0941

Library of Congress Control Number: 00-134828

ISBN 0 7546 1509 X

Printed in Great Britain by
Antony Rowe Ltd, Chippenham, Wiltshire.

Contents

Acknowledgements

I would like to thank the following individuals for their help during the writing of this book. Paul Bagguley and Sarah Irwin for their comments and advice on early drafts. Watson for his comments, and John, Paul and Olga for their help and understanding. Most of all I would like to thank Alan whose love and encouragement made the book possible.

List of Abbreviations

CA	Cold Area
EETPU	Electrical, Engineering, Telecommunications and Plumbing Union
GMBU	General Municipal and Boilermakers Union
HA	Hot Area
JIT	Just-In-Time
NVQ	National vocational Qualification
TGWU	Transport and General workers Union
TQM	Total Quality Management

1 Introduction

Since the publication of 'Labor and Monopoly Capital' (Braverman 1974), the issue of skill has been the subject of a considerable amount of sociological debate. These debates focus on a range of issues. Sociologists have attempted to define the nature of skill (Braverman 1974, Cooley 1987, Spenner 1990, Attewell 1990, Scarbrough and Corbett 1992), to chart changes in aggregate skill levels over time (Penn 1994, Gallie 1996), to show how, especially from a feminist perspective, definitions of skill are socially constructed and related to the power of groups to define their work as skilled (Dex 1988, Bradley 1989, Steinberg 1990, Wajcman 1991, Coyle 1992, England 1992) and to identify the relationship between technology and skill (Kelley 1989, Lane 1988, Hendry 1990, Scarbrough and Corbett 1992). Little attention has been given, however, to the subjective perceptions of skill held by those directly involved in production. Nor has research been undertaken to explore the ways in which the perceptions of skill held by managers and workers are developed and maintained. Thus, the subjective perceptions of skill held by managers and workers are a neglected area in the sociology of skill. This book aims to redress the general neglect of manager and worker perceptions of skill through the presentation of empirical evidence from three case study organisations. This evidence is used to construct a model through which to explain subjective perceptions of skill and the causal processes that shape them. This approach serves to shift analysis away from definitions of skill constructed by sociologists towards a theory of skill that is grounded in the subjective definitions of those directly involved in production.

Further issues dealt with in the book are as follows. First, it explores the extent to which the causal processes identified as shaping subjective perceptions of skill are explicable in the context of existing theories. Second, perceptions of skill are examined and explained in the context of an alleged shift between Fordist and post-Fordist production paradigms. Third, management and worker perceptions of skill are related back to the wider capitalist system. Finally, comparison is made between workers and managers' perceptions of skill, and sociological definitions of skill. I shall show that managers' and workers' perceptions are more narrowly defined and context dependent than the definitions applied by sociologists. I also show that the causal processes that shape subjective perceptions of skill occur on a variety of levels. That is, at the level of the capitalist structure itself, at the level of organisational structures, and at the level of individual agency. Examination of the above issues is conducted through empirical research in three case study factories, and a description of each factory will be given later in the chapter.

In addition to perceptions of skill, the second theme of the book concerns the perceptions of core and periphery held by workers in two of the three case study factories. The concept of core and periphery was put forward by Atkinson (1984) in his model of the flexible firm, and purports to describe a division between core workers with permanent employment contracts and peripheral workers with non-standard part-time and temporary contracts. This analysis of perceptions of core and periphery aims to explore how the perceptions of workers, whose formal contract of employment could be defined as peripheral, compare with theoretical conceptualisations of the periphery. A further issue, and one that links skill, and core and periphery, is the implicit assumption in Atkinson's model that core workers are more highly skilled than allegedly peripheral workers. I will show that neither workforce skills nor workers' perceptions of skill are patterned around different types of employment contract. I will also show that part-time and temporary workers do not perceive themselves as forming part of a peripheral labour force.

The remainder of this introductory chapter is concerned with delineating the contours of the book. This begins with an an outline of the theories that have informed the construction of a general model to explain perceptions of skill, core and periphery, and an explanation of their relevance. This is followed by a brief description of the realist social theory that underpinned the research and writing of this book, and a short, preliminary description of the three case study firms. The chapter then provides a brief outline of the proposed model before ending with an outline of each subsequent chapter.

The Theoretical Background

The construction of the model to explain subjective perceptions of skill, and the causal processes that shape them, draws on a variety of theories. These theories are discussed in detail in Chapters Two and Three. What follows now is a brief explanation of their relevance to the concerns of this book. In

Chapter Two the discussion focuses on labour process theory and theories of post-Fordism. The applicability of these two broad perspectives to the study of subjective perceptions of skill, core and periphery concerns a number of issues. First, it is from within the labour process and post-Fordist perspectives that the subject of skill has been most widely debated. Second, both perspectives are concerned with explaining processes that have a generative influence on skill formation. For labour process theorists, the main question concerning skill is that of whether the labour process under monopoly capitalism has led to a general deskilling of the workforce. It is argued by Braverman and his supporters that the articulation of Taylorist management strategies and technology serve to separate the conception and execution of work, and that this results in a deskilling of the workforce. It is beyond the scope of this book to examine the extent to which Taylorism remains a feature of industry in general or to consider the deskilling thesis. What I do intend to argue is that in the three case study factories Taylorist or neo-Taylorist managerial strategies prevail. These strategies combine with various forms of technology to generate jobs that are characterised by a deep division between conception and execution of tasks. The outcome in terms of perceptions of skill are perceptions that emphasise practical task related competencies, but which exclude any theoretical understanding of specific production processes. The book also shows, however, that the developments set out by Braverman do not apply to all workers in the three factories. For a small group of workers the separation between conception and execution is less marked, and perceptions of skill are, as a result, less tied to practical task competencies. Thus, the relevance of labour process theory to this book concerns the ways in which Taylorist managerial strategies combine with technology to produce a division between conception and execution of tasks, and the implications of this division on the subjective perceptions of skill held by some workers.

With respect to post-Fordism, the subject of skill is debated in the context of the alleged shift from Fordist mass standardised production to flexible post-Fordist production. This flexible production relates to new flexible technologies (for example Piore and Sabel 1984) and flexible forms of work organisation (for example Atkinson 1984, Atkinson and Meager 1986). The specific relevance of post-Fordist theory to perceptions of skill, core and periphery relates to five issues. First, subjective perceptions of skill are shaped, primarily, by firm specific organisational structural features, which are themselves shaped, in part, by developments in wider capitalist product markets. In each firm, instability in the product market has led to the introduction of some form of flexibility that is explicable in the context of post-Fordist theories. The second issue relates to the particular properties of organisational structural features, and their effects on work characteristics. Although the development of some organisational structural features at each firm accords with those described by variations on the post-Fordist theme, I will attempt to show that organisational structural features themselves cannot be analysed in terms of a Fordist and post-Fordist dualism. Rather, each firm contains an amalgamation of structural characteristics commonly associated with both Fordist and post-Fordist paradigms, specifically an articulation of new flexible production technologies and rigid Taylorist managerial strategies. The perceptions of skill identified are generated, I will argue, by the causal properties contained in the specific articulation of a variety of the organisations' structural features. Thus, the causal processes that shape subjective perceptions of skill are highly contextual, and occur in distinct circumstances at particular points in time. On the other hand, whilst none of the three case study firms corresponds to Fordist or post-Fordist ideal types, and no linear patterns relating to Fordist and post-Fordist work patterns are discernible, the conceptualisation of organisational structural features in relation to Fordist and post-Fordist models does aid the initial investigation into the generative properties of particular features.

The third area of relevance concerns the post-Fordist notion of Japanisation (for example, Murray 1988, Clegg 1990). One of the case study firms is a Japanese electronics transplant. Comparison is made between the organisational features that characterise this firm with those described in the Japanisation literature, and the generative effects of Japanese production strategies are identified. Whilst the whole notion of Japanisation is complex and difficult to define, a number of the organisational characteristics found in this firm are comparable to those described by others (for example, Taylor, Elger and Fairbrother 1993). Examples include a Just-In-Time (JIT) production strategy and Total Quality Management (TQM). I shall argue that JIT and TQM at the firm does signify a shift away from traditional Fordism, for example with respect to the articulation of supply and demand, but that the effect of this shift on work is to intensify Taylorist work patterns. The outcome in terms of skill is to reinforce the separation of conception and execution, and to generate perceptions of skill that are patterned around this separation.

The fourth issue in relation to post-Fordist theory concerns the proposed skill trajectories advanced from particular strands within the overall perspective. Each variant on the post-Fordist theme to be discussed contains specific predictions with respect to developments in workforce skills. Empirical evidence from the three case study factories provides an understanding of how far the subjective perceptions of workers accord with these predictions. I shall show that the persistence of Fordist features at each firm serves to constrain the upskilling and multi-skilling tendencies proposed by some post-Fordist theorists. As a result, the perceptions of skill expressed by the majority of workers bear little or no resemblance to the more optimistic skill trajectories set out by theorists such as Piore and Sabel, and Atkinson.

The final aspect of post-Fordist theory significant to this book concerns the core and periphery model put forward by Atkinson in 1984. Since the publication of this model the notion of core and periphery, although not without its critics (for example Pollert 1988a, 1988b, 1991, Elger 1991, Casey 1991), has become an accepted concept in the sociology of work. In his model of the flexible firm Atkinson suggested that the workforce, both in terms of labour markets and individual firms, is becoming increasingly polarised into a stable multi-skilled and secure core, and an unstable, insecure and low skilled periphery. Peripheral workers are defined as those with non-standard employment contracts such as part-time and temporary staff. This book explores the perceptions of core and periphery held by workers whose formal employment situation could be described as peripheral, and explains why workers hold the particular perceptions identified.

The exploration of perceptions of skill, core and periphery in the context of post-Fordism does not involve an unquestioning acceptance of the concept. An important conclusion of the book is that it is necessary to challenge the idea that a shift in production paradigms from Fordism to post-Fordism has taken place. This challenge is based on the argument that social processes are complex and cannot be described in terms of dualistic categories. First, the production process, machinery and organisation of work within organisations develop, in part, in response to wider economic and product market pressures. Organisational development is however uneven and results in a complex mix of structural features, some of which can be described as Fordist and others that correspond to notions of post-Fordism. Second, the categorisation of workers into core and peripheral sectors ignores important differences within and between groups. The concept of core and periphery does not provide a useful framework for exploring workers formal position in an organisation. Nor does it provide a model for exploring the patterning of skills amongst workers. The skills required of workers, and the perceptions of skill held by workers, are *not* patterned around formal contract types. Thus, the evidence to be put forward later contradicts Atkinson's model of a multi-skilled core workforce and a low skilled periphery.

In Chapter Three, the theoretical discussion moves away from the more wide ranging considerations of Chapter Two to focus on four specific issues.

These are as follows. First, the definitions of skill advanced from within three ontological and epistemological paradigms: namely, the positivist, Weberian and ethnomethodological paradigms. The aim of this discussion is to highlight how research into skill from within these paradigms would marginalise the subjective perceptions held by workers themselves. Following the discussion of sociological definitions of skill, the theoretical debate turns to two factors that have a significant impact on subjective perceptions of skill: managerial strategies and technology. The theoretical discussion of these factors considers the nature of their generative properties prior to the elaboration, in the case study chapters, of their effects on subjective perceptions of skill. The final topic of the theoretical discussion concerns the issue of gender and skill. I will argue later that gender both is and is not a variable with respect to women's perceptions of skill. Explanation of this seemingly contradictory statement is as follows. The subjective perceptions of skill held by women are, like those of men, shaped by the organisational structural features that characterise their jobs. Women perceive skill in exactly the same way as men, and for exactly the same reasons. Thus, in this respect gender is not a salient issue. However, the jobs performed by women can be understood in terms of the vertical and horizontal gendered division of labour. In the two case study firms where women are employed they are located, in general, in the lower levels of the occupational hierarchy. Thus, it can be argued that in terms of the structural conditions that impact on perceptions of skill, gender is a salient variable.

Realist Theory and Methodology

I have already pointed out (and will discuss in more depth in Chapter Three) that the positivist, Weberian and ethnomethodological perspectives do not provide a suitable ontological and epistemological basis for an investigation of the subjective perceptions of skill held by those directly involved in production. The construction of a model through which to explain subjective perceptions of skill and the causal processes that shape them is best achieved within a realist framework. A description of realist theory and methodology is discussed in Chapter Four prior to delineation of the model. It is not the intention at this stage to give a detailed explanation of why the book is ground in the realist framework. For now I simply wish to highlight the ontological basis of the model, and to point out a number of realist principles that informed the research.

According to Pawson (1996), realist ontology is committed to the notion that "since social events are interwoven between various layers of social reality, then so must any account of them" (Pawson 1996 p. 300). Pawson identifies three key features that are fundamental to social research, and which he argues are well suited to getting to grips with the way the social world is put together:

> The basic task of sociological enquiry is to explain interesting, puzzling, socially significant outcome patterns (O) between events or happenings or social properties. Explanation takes the form of positioning some underlying mechanism (M) which generates these outcomes and thus consists of propositions about how the interplay between structure and agency has constituted these outcomes. Explanatory closure requires that, within the same investigation, there is also an examination of how the workings of such mechanisms is contingent and conditional, and thus are only fired in particular historical or institutional contexts (Pawson 1996 p. 301).

This book explores outcomes in the form of subjective perceptions of skill, core and periphery in the context of underlying generative structure and agency mechanisms, and in the context of particular institutional settings. To achieve these aims, the research draws on the following principles. First, realist social theory is concerned not only with identifying regularities in the social world, but also with explaining the causal processes that link these regularities (Keat and Urry 1982, Pawson 1989). I have already indicated that the book aims to identify perceptions of skill, core and periphery, and also to uncover the emergent properties and causal processes that shape them. Second, some strands of realist social theory are concerned with identifying multi-level processes, that is, processes that occur at the levels of structure, culture and agency (Archer 1997). This concern with the stratified nature of society allows for an investigation of the interplay between processes that occur over time and on different levels of social reality. The causal processes that shape subjective perceptions of skill occur on three levels: at the structural level of the capitalist system, at the level of individual organisations, and at the level of individual agency. Third, from the realist paradigm social reality is viewed as being context dependent. Causal processes occur in relation to particular social conditions and in open social systems, thus rendering positivist claims to prediction problematic (Pawson 1989). The book identifies particular social events, and the causal processes that shape them, in the context of the specific structural conditions within which they occur. A primary assertion is that the subjective perceptions of skill held by workers are context dependent in that they develop in relation to specific organisational formations. The model will also suggest that these perceptions are open to change as individuals move between different social systems. That is, between various organisational structures.

The Case Studies

GlassCo

GlassCo manufactures clear glass containers for the cheaper end of the glass container market. The firm is, however, attempting to shift production away from standardised mass-market products towards speciality products made for more upmarket retailers. The reasons for this shift relate to developments in the glass container industry, for example market saturation and the subsequent polarisation between large firms that can utilise economies of scale, and small firms such as GlassCo that utilise economies of scope. The firm employs around 370 people, 98% of whom belong to the GMBU. It was established in the 1890s and was, for the first 100 years of its existence, owned and run by one family. In 1994 the firm was, along with a second glass manufacturer located nearby, purchased by a British multi-national company. Since the take over a number of changes have been introduced in an attempt to modernise the firm. These changes have taken the form of new flexible technologies designed to facilitate the flexible manufacture of niche market products. The firm has, however, retained its traditional Taylorist hierarchical management structure, rigid division of labour and task fragmentation, and close direct style of supervision. Thus, subjective perceptions of skill at the firm are explored in the context of these conflicting developments. A further issue that will be argued to impact upon the firm's organisational structure, and therefore perceptions of skill, is the poor relations found to exist between management and workforce. This firm also employs what could, in terms of Atkinson's typology (Atkinson 1984, Atkinson and Meager 1986), be classified as peripheral labour.

Electronics UK

The second firm is a Japanese electronics transplant that was established in 1990 in an area with no history of electronics production. The firm chose to locate in the area to take advantage of the ready supply of labour that exists due to the closure of coal mines and textile factories, and the need for the parent company to establish a base within the European Community (Personnel Manager). Electronics UK employs around 800 people and, unlike the two other case study firms, has low levels of trade union membership. Around 40% of the workforce are members of the EETPU. The firm manufactures consumer electronics goods for the middle range mass market, specifically video and audio equipment. Activities are concentrated on the assembly of parts brought in from Japan and South East Asia. All research and development takes place in Japan. The company also performs sub-contract assembly work for other, larger, Japanese consumer electronics manufacturers. In terms of the organisational structure, Electronics UK utilises both modern flexible automated technology and traditional assembly line production. It is also characterised by a hierarchical managerial structure, rigid division of labour and fragmentation of tasks, and a close direct supervisory style that includes oppressive methods of surveillance. The organisational features uncovered at Electronics UK are highly similar to those found in other Japanese transplants, and the labour process at this firm represents an intensification of Taylorist control mechanisms. Perceptions of skill at Electronics UK are examined in the context of these organisational features.

In addition to the features described above, Electronics UK operates what appears to be a deliberate core and periphery strategy. All new recruits at the firm are given temporary contracts of two years duration, a strategy that is said by one British manager to stem from two factors. First is the need for flexibility over staffing levels. During slack periods of demand, temporary workers are more easily discarded than permanent staff. Second, workers deemed to be unsuitable can be discarded more easily during their temporary period of employment.

Chemicals UK

The third case study firm, Chemicals UK, was established in 1917 and employs around 900 people. Like GlassCo it was, at the outset, a family owned firm but became a limited company in the 1930s. The firm manufactures chemical intermediate products which are sold to other chemicals companies who make finished consumer products. Chemicals UK makes, for example, the optical brightening agents that are used in washing powders and paper. Like GlassCo, Chemicals UK is attempting to shift its product base away from mass standardised goods towards niche market areas. One research plant manufactures products made to the specifications of individual customers, often for the first time. A second research plant manufactures chemical intermediates for the niche pharmaceuticals market. In recent years, and as a partial result of a sharp dip in profits in the early 1990s, the firm has attempted to introduce a number of changes to the organisational structure. In contrast to GlassCo, these changes do not relate to new forms of technology. Rather, changes have been made to the social organisation of work at the factory and have involved the introduction of flexible, empowered teamworking. Thus, subjective perceptions of skill at Chemicals UK are explored in the context of traditional automated continuous process production technology articulated with a flexible social organisation of work.

The Model

The model to be put forward in Chapter Four draws on a range of theoretical influences to explain the empirical evidence generated through the research. The realist ontology and epistemology that forms the basis of the model allows for an explanation of structure and agency level causal processes, and of the interaction between these multi-level processes. I shall argue that the network of causal processes that ultimately shape subjective perceptions of skill originate at the level of the capitalist system. Three structural emergent properties of capitalism will be put forward as causal mechanisms: the unstable product markets in which each firm operates, the necessity for capital to transform the labour power of workers into productive labour, and the stratified capitalist employment structure. A major theme of the post-Fordist paradigm is that unstable product markets result in flexible organisational structures that are better equipped to deal with product market instability than are rigid Fordist structures. It will also be argued that this relationship is not the only explanation. Organisational structures also develop as a result of the strategic choices made by senior managers. These choices are, according to Child (1997), the outcome of managers evaluating information that is both external and internal to the firm.

I shall argue that the combined effects of production systems and technology, and management strategies are to generate particular job characteristics. These characteristics form a salient reference point on which workers draw when considering the subject of skill. For the majority of workers the most salient reference point is current occupation. However, and leading to the third emergent property of capitalism, the capitalist system creates a structural and hierarchical set of educational, training and employment opportunities. In addition to being a property of the capitalist structure, once these opportunities are distributed, consumed and experienced by the individual, the qualifications and/or experience gained is transformed into a property of the individual. As individuals move between structured employment opportunities they take their qualifications and experience with them. Qualifications and work experience are therefore defined as agency mechanisms. The argument that qualifications are inseparable from the individuals to whom they belong is similar to that put forward by Savage, Barlow, Dickens and Fielding (1992) in their theory of middle class assets. They argue that the professional qualifications held by some middle-class groups, such as doctors, lawyers and accountants, are cultural assets that can be exploited by individuals. This is not to argue, however, that qualifications as assets are independent of employing organisations. Whilst qualifications may be owned by individuals, they require an organisational context in which they can be applied in order that their value can be realised. Despite this, qualifications are assets that are transferable between organisations, and allow individuals some freedom of movement between organisations. They can therefore be defined as attributes of individual agency. With respect to experience, this may or may not be an asset that can be exploited by individuals. It does however influence the perceptions they currently hold, and is again defined here as an attribute of agency.

Amongst individuals who have, in the past, held jobs of a similar or lower status, that is those that have moved up or across the occupational hierarchy, the current salience of previous qualifications and experience will be shown to be weak. The structural features associated with the current job generate perceptions of skill amongst this group. Amongst workers who have previously held jobs of a higher occupational status, that is people with downwards employment trajectories, the previous higher status occupation forms the most salient reference point from which to consider skill. Thus, the main assertions to be put forward in relation to subjective perceptions of skill are that these are shaped by the structural features of specific organisations, the position of individuals in relation to those features, and by the routes through which individuals come to occupy their current position. In short, perceptions of skill are shaped by the most complex competencies required of individuals either now or in the past.

The Structure of the Book

Chapters Two and Three elaborate the theoretical context of the research. Chapter Two consists of a discussion of labour process theory followed by theories of Fordism and post-Fordism. In Chapter Three the discussion turns to an examination of the ways in which skill is conceptualised from within various sociological paradigms. It then moves on to a theoretical discussion of two factors that play an important role in generating subjective perceptions of skill, that is managerial strategies and technology. Finally, the chapter moves on to a discussion of gender and skill. The aim of these discussions are to set out the theories that are pertinent to the construction of the model. Following these theoretical discussions, Chapter Four begins with an explanation of the realist framework through which the model to explain subjective perceptions of skill has been constructed. This is followed by a delineation of the model itself.[1]

Chapters Five, Six and Seven move on to the case studies themselves. These chapters begin by describing the relationship between product markets and organisational structures before going on to outline the emergent properties of these structures. This is followed by analysis of each organisation in relation to Fordist and post-Fordist production paradigms. The chapters then go on to describe and discuss the perceptions of skill held by workers and managers. In Chapters Five and Six, this is followed by an examination of perceptions of core and periphery at GlassCo and Electronics UK. The final chapter, Chapter Eight, presents the book's key conclusions.

Note

[1] Presentation of the model prior to the case study evidence does not follow the logic of the development of the model. The model was constructed following the data collection stage rather than prior to it. The reason for presenting the model fist is as follows. Outlining the model before the empirical evidence that informed its construction allows the evidence to be put forward in a more straightforward manner. It is not necessary to continually explain why data is being interpreted in a particular way. This format thus facilitates a clearer reading of the evidence.

2 Labour Process Theory, Fordism and Post-Fordism

Introduction

This chapter addresses the labour process debates that dominated industrial sociology in the 1970s and 1980s, and the post-Fordist theories of the 1980s and 1990s. It is from within these theoretical frameworks that the subject of skill has been most widely debated. During the 1970s and 1980s the skill discourse focused on the question of whether the labour process under monopoly capitalism was characterised by a linear deskilling of the workforce. In the late 1980s and 1990s the debates have largely centered on the extent to which the alleged shift towards post-Fordism and flexibility has facilitated an up-skilling, or multi-skilling, of the workforce. The subjective perceptions of skill held by workers in the three case study factories are influenced primarily by firm specific structural organisational features, which are themselves related, in part, to wider processes at work in the capitalist system of production.

Both labour process theory and post-Fordist theories promote models of organisational structures, and relate these back to developments within the capitalist system. From the labour process perspective, the main issue of debate is that of whether the fundamental capitalist need to secure profit leads to the sole use of a Taylorist management strategy and division of labour. From the post-Fordist perspective, increasing uncertainty in product markets, due to changing consumer demand patterns and technological change, is assumed to have led to a need for flexibility in organisations and a resulting change in organisational structures and patterns of work. The issues that are crucial to an in-depth understanding of perceptions of skill, core and periphery, and the causal processes that shape them are as follows. First, to analyse the extent to which the oganisational structural features of each case study firm accord with thetheoretical models advanced by these theories. Second, to identify the extent to which these theoretical paradigms provide a useful framework through which to examine the processes that shape subjective perceptions of skill.

The third reason for grounding the book in the context of post-Fordist theory is the assumption that the workforce is increasingly divided into a stable core and an unstable periphery. Two of the three case study firms have adopted strategies that correspond to the theoretical representation of the periphery. The subjective perceptions of so called peripheral workers in relation to their position within the company are explored in later chapters. The chapter thus begins with a discussion of labour process theory, which takes Braverman's deskilling thesis as its starting point. It then goes on to give an account of Fordism and post-Fordism containing sections on Fordism, regulation theory, flexible specialisation, the flexible firm and Japanisation.

Labour Process Theory

The labour process debates of the 1970s and 1980s provide an effective theoretical framework through which to understand the subjective perceptions of skill held by workers in the three case study factories, particularly with respect to the distinction between conception and execution of work set out by Braverman (1974). This relevance relates to the proposed relationship between management strategies, technology, and deskilling. Although the book is not concerned with presenting an objective assessment of deskilling at the three firms, I will show that there is a strong relationship between management strategies, technology and perceptions of skill. I will also show that many of the ideas put forward by theorists of the period concerning the processes that lead to deskilling, remain pertinent to an understanding of some of the processes that generate subjective perceptions of skill.

The labour process refers to the means by which workers' labour power is articulated to material aspects of production, such as machinery and raw materials, in order to secure capital accumulation. The capitalist system of accumulation requires the creation of surplus value through the conversion of raw materials into exchange goods by labour. This surplus value is appropriated by capital in the form of profits, and the process is referred to by Marx as valorisation (Marx 1976). It is from within labour process theory that much of the debate and discourse around the subject of skill has been conducted. This debate has centred on Braverman's theory of deskilling, with various sociologists putting forward conflicting evidence in response to Braverman.

The main thrust of Braverman's argument is that the process of valorisation requires increasing capitalist control over the labour process. The exchange relationship between capitalist and worker is characterised by the capitalist purchasing the worker's labour power for a specific period of time. It is essential for capitalism that this labour power is transformed into productive labour, thus giving rise to the need for managerial strategies to control the labour of workers. Control is achieved through the application of Taylorist or scientific management techniques, and the appropriation of knowledge by management from skilled workers. This process results in an intensification in the division of labour and fragmentation of tasks. The separation of conception and execution precipitates the deskilling of craft work and other formerly skilled occupations. For Braverman, scientific management is the sole managerial strategy possible in the era of monopoly capitalism. Human relations management techniques do not represent a break with Taylorism, rather they are viewed as an alternative means of controlling and intensifying the labour process in order to ensure that valorisation occurs. A further tenet of the deskilling thesis is the indivisibility of technology from the imperative for managerial control. Technology is not a neutral or autonomous entity, rather it is interwoven with management strategies, and mechanisms of control are built into its application and functions. According to Braverman the technological drive towards deskilling cannot be divorced from the prevalence of Taylorism. He argues that:

> in the capitalist mode of production, new methods and new machinery are incorporated within a management effort to dissolve the labour process as a process conducted by the worker and reconstitute it as a process conducted by management. In the first form of the division of labour, the capitalist disassembles the craft and returns it to the workers piecemeal, so that the process as a whole is no longer the province of any individual worker. Then, as we have seen the capitalist conducts an analysis of each of the tasks distributed among the workers, with an eye toward getting a grip on the individual operations. It is in the age of the scientific-technical revolution that management sets itself the problem of grasping the process as a whole and controlling every element of it (Braverman p. 170-171).

Thus, Braverman argues that the division of labour and subsequent deskilling engendered by Taylorism is intensified by the application of technologies which allow for greater managerial control over workers' activities. Braverman does not allow for a conception of skill built around the notion of task complexity, rather the separation of conception and execution underpins and defines deskilling. The deskilling process is seen as a linear and unified trend resulting from the current phase of capitalism termed 'monopoly capitalism.' The increasing size of firms under late capitalism, and the ensuing centralisation of production, facilitates departmental specialisms, developed divisions of labour and hierarchical management structures. This results in a loss of control and knowledge over work on the part of labour and, as a consequence, a process of deskilling. According to Braverman this process is inevitable. Even where new production processes give rise to new skills, management will eventually appropriate these skills and the linear processes of deskilling will continue. Writing in relation to the growth of new occupations in late capitalism, Braverman argues that:

> In this manner, short term trends opening the way for the advancement of some workers in rapidly growing industries, together with the ever lower skill requirements characteristic at the entry level where large masses of workers are being put to work in industrial, office and marketing processes for the first time simply mask the secular trend towards the incessant lowering of the working class as a whole below its previous conditions of skill and labour (Braverman 1974 p. 129).

The assertion that management strategies and new technology lead to an inevitable and linear process of deskilling was widely debated in the labour process literature of the 1970s and 1980s. Cooley (1987), for example, suggests that new computerised technologies can be applied in such a way as to enskill workers. He argues however, that the current application of technology serves to produce an electronically controlled division of labour which facilitates deskilling (Cooley 1987). Cooley suggests that five stages are necessary to the acquisition of skill. These are novice, advanced beginner, competent, proficient and expert, and it is by moving through these five stages that workers develop skills through experience. Cooley also argues that new design technologies deny workers the 'deep situational involvement' necessary for experiential skill development. Finally, Cooley suggests that deskilling occurs when technology replaces the analytic and interpretative skills held by humans. The reason for this replacement lies in the ability of capital to increase control over the labour process through the elimination of the subjective will of humans (Ibid.).

A number of criticisms have been developed which question both the theoretical and empirical basis of Braverman's deskilling thesis. First is the questioning of whether the labour process is necessarily antagonistic. The relationship of dependency between capital and labour is mutual; capital relies on labour in order to secure accumulation, and this is best achieved through co-operation rather than conflict. Thus, it is in the interests of capital to assume managerial strategies which engender co-operation (Littler and Salaman 1982).

A second criticism relates to Braverman's conceptualisation of knowledge in terms of a zero-sum model. That is, the assertion that knowledge held by management is automatically lost to the worker. The notion that managerial appropriation of knowledge must necessarily reduce workers' knowledge is argued to confuse the acquisition of knowledge with monopoly of knowledge (Wood and Kelly 1982, Wood 1987). It can be argued that the zero sum model makes no allowance for the possibility that knowledge may be shared between management and workforce. It can also be argued that the conceptualisation of knowledge in terms of the zero sum model is predicated on the real subordination of labour. The theory of the real subordination of labour was first put forward by Marx (1976), and refers to the way in which the development of the factory system enabled capital to intensify the mechanisms of control over workers' labour power through science and technology. Through this process the subjectivity and will of the worker was subjugated to the control of capital.

Two particular criticisms of the real subordination of labour, particularly as theorised by Braverman, have been advanced. The first relates to the need for capitalism to develop the co-operation of the workforce in order to secure valorisation, not just in the immediate term but also in the future. It is also necessary for capital to conceal its appropriation of surplus value (Cressey and MacInnes 1980). I will argue later in the book that the perceptions of workforce skill held by managers in the three factories are associated with the need to secure worker co-operation. Second, struggles by workers against capitalist control have resulted in various forms of workplace resistance (Beynon 1975, Nichols and Beynon 1977, Edwards 1988, Thompson and Ackroyd 1995). Thus, although I will show that some of the processes described by Braverman provide a useful framework for understanding the processes that shape subjective perceptions of skill held by the majority of production workers in the case study factories, I am not suggesting that these processes lead to a real subordination of labour.

A third criticism of Braverman stems from his conceptualisation of skill itself. The notion that real skill involves both conception and execution is argued to fail to recognise skills which signify competence in the execution of tasks. Elger suggests that "specialised expertise may be embedded in the complex structure of collective labour" (Elger 1982 p. 29). Although this expertise is subordinate to capital it can be regarded as skill (Ibid.). In relation to technology, the conceptualisation of skill in terms of a conception-execution dichotomy serves to ignore the level of complexity in machine-human interaction. Scarbrough and Corbett suggest that computerisation goes hand in hand with abstract knowledge regardless of whether craft (skilled) work or detail (unskilled work) is under consideration. Abstract knowledge is an intellectual skill at the higher end of the skill spectrum, and is historically the domain of management (Scarbrough and Corbett 1992). In addition, it is not possible to objectively read skill off from technology. Although technology may shape the tasks, it does not determine who carries them out, and the definition of tasks as skilled or unskilled depends on who does them. Tasks carried out by women are, for example, often defined as unskilled regardless of complexity (Walker 1989).

A final criticism relates to Braverman's assertion that deskilling represents an all embracing linear trend. Critics have provided empirical evidence to show that deskilling/enskilling trajectories are uneven and complex. Penn's compensatory theory of skill suggests, for example, that whilst direct production occupations have been subject to deskilling, other occupations such as installation, maintenance and programming of automated machinery involve increasing levels of skill (Penn 1990, 1994).

In defence of Braverman, Hyman and Streek (1988) accept his conceptual division between conception and execution, and argue that wherever management devised training schemes fail to impart the knowledge necessary for the re-amalgamation of conception and execution, reskilling remains a myth. Enhanced ability to carry out production tasks which do not involve meaningful decision making fail to represent a real shift towards enskilling. They further argue that many empirical studies carried out to test the deskilling thesis have focused upon the stage of development following the introduction of new technology and production techniques. These changes may lead to higher levels of skill in the short term, but examination of the long term effects may show a reversion to deskilling (Hyman and Streek 1988). This argument is supported by Cockburn's research in the printing industry. She puts forward evidence to show how changes in composition tasks in the newspaper printing industry have led to deskilling, and that this deskilling is felt acutely by the workforce (Cockburn 1983).

The relevance of these labour process debates to workers' and managers' subjective perceptions of skill concerns a number of issues. The first relates to Braverman's assertion that Taylorism is the only form of managerial strategy available under monopoly capitalism. It is not a concern of this book to present arguments for and against this assertion. It is concerned, however, with analysing the nature of managerial strategies at each case study firm. Case study evidence reveals that in each of the firms Taylorism remains the dominant management strategy. In addition to this, although Littler and Salaman (1982) may be correct in suggesting that it is in the interests of capital to employ managerial strategies that engender co-operation, it will be demonstrated that this does not exclude the use of traditional Taylorist strategies. It will also be shown that where human relations strategies are adopted, for example at Chemicals UK, the differences between these and Taylorist strategies are largely superficial.

The second point relates to Cooley's assertion that computerised technology has traditionally been applied in a way that facilitates deskilling. The application of both computerised and automated technology reduces the analytical and interpretative aspects of many of the production jobs examined here. Although many of the jobs performed by interviewees require some analytical and interpretative competencies, these are low level and confined to monitoring tasks and the identification of irregularities. Once identified, these irregularities are dealt with by others. Involvement in the overall production process is, furthermore, restricted to the latter stages. That is, to the execution of narrowly defined tasks, thus denying workers the deep situational involvement that Cooley argues is necessary for experiential skill development. The outcomes in terms of subjective perceptions of skill are perceptions that focus on task performance, and which exclude a detailed understanding of the principles that underpin these tasks.

The third point concerns Braverman's alleged zero sum conceptualisation of knowledge. That is, the argument that knowledge appropriated by management is necessarily lost to the worker. Evidence from the three case studies indicates that all workers possess some form of knowledge in relation to their work. However the type and level of knowledge differs between groups, and the evidence suggests that for the majority of production workers, higher-level forms of abstract knowledge are appropriated by management or are built into machinery. The outcomes in terms of perceptions of skill are, again, narrowly defined perceptions that focus on task competence, but which exclude theoretical knowledge of the wider production process.

Fourth, it is argued by Penn (1990), in his compensatory theory of skill, that aggregate changes in skill levels over time have led to a dichotomy between maintenance workers and production workers. New complex forms of technology have resulted in an increase in the skills required of workers responsible for maintenance and repair. Production workers, on the other hand, are susceptible to deskilling as the more complex aspects of production worker are taken over by machinery. Evidence from the three factories indicates that the dichotomy proposed by Penn is reproduced in relation to the perceptions of skill held by these two groups. I will demonstrate that the perceptions of skill held by craft maintenance workers, and workers responsible for planning functions do differ from those of other production workers with no such responsibilities. A fifth, and very important, issue concerns the division between the conception and execution of work. I will show that this division is an extremely important factor in shaping subjective perceptions of skill, and that evidence from the three factories highlights distinctions between those workers with conceptual responsibilities and those with responsibility for execution only. Whilst Scarbrough and Corbett may be correct to assert that computerisation can lead to an increase in abstract forms of knowledge required for the execution of tasks, evidence to be put forward in Chapters Five, Six and Seven suggests that this outcome is not inevitable. Production occupations in the three case study factories that are characterised by computerisation, and/or automation, are also characterised by an absence of abstract knowledge. Practical knowledge of the tasks associated with a particular stage of production is the main form of knowledge required of direct production workers.

Finally, no attempt has yet been made to understand and explain the subjective perceptions of skill held by actors in relation to the various issues covered. Although a large body of research exists which purports to explain the relationships between managerial strategies, technology, and resulting skill trajectories, little knowledge exists as to how actors experience and perceive these relationships. The evidence to be advanced later suggests that workforce perceptions of skill do not, in general, include explicit notions of deskilling in relation to management strategies and technological developments. The only individuals to explicitly articulate perceptions of having been deskilled are a small number of apprentice qualified craft workers who are now employed as chemical process operatives.

Structures and styles of management, and constraints built into various types of technology are extremely influential factors in the generation of perceptions of skill. The perceptions of skill articulated by production workers whose jobs are highly constrained by technology, and/or exclude proactive actions, differ from the perceptions expressed by workers who are less constrained by technology, and whose jobs involve a level of proactive planning. It will also be shown that rigid Taylorist management strategies and divisions of labour generate hierarchically structured and task specific perceptions of skill. Flatter managerial structures, on the other hand, generate factory wide perceptions of skill, although when broken down through more detailed questioning these factory wide perceptions do contain qualitative differences between particular groups of workers, differences that again reflect the specific tasks performed by interviewees.

In summary, the arguments put forward by Braverman, Cooley, and Hyman and Streek provide a useful framework through which to examine the processes that generate subjective perceptions of skill. This relevance relates to the effects of Taylorist management strategies and technology on the division between conception and execution of work. However, I part company with these authors with respect to the argument that the processes they describe are applicable to all occupations. The effects of management strategies are variable and uneven, and although it will be demonstrated that the dominant management strategy in each firm is fundamentally Taylorist, it will also be shown that some workers, namely craft maintenance workers and a small number of production workers at Chemicals UK, retain some responsibility for conception. This responsibility takes the form of mental planning and decisions relating to the manipulation of work. The perceptions of skill held by these two broadly defined groups display important differences that reflect the variations in production processes.

This outline of labour process theory has concentrated on the position of workers in the capitalist system of production. According to Braverman, however, the deskilling process is also applicable to the work of middle and junior managers. This assertion is rejected by Armstrong (1989), who suggests that that the position of managers cannot be viewed in terms of conventional labour process analysis, that is the labour of managers cannot be seen as comparable to that of subordinates. Rather, agency is a fundamental feature of the capitalist-management relationship:

> Management, in the present sense of the term, cannot be regarded as a
> pre-defined set of tasks and functions, which are then controlled from

above. Instead it is a matter of acting (or appearing to act) as to further
the aims of more senior managers (and ultimately ownership) as these
appear to the manager (Armstrong 1989 p. 311).

Whilst the roles of managers in the capitalist enterprise may be varied,
and whilst they may not be concerned solely with control over workers, it
cannot be denied that one feature of the managerial role is the direction and
co-ordination of labour. I shall show, in Chapters Five, Six and Seven, that
the perceptions of workforce skill held by managers across the three case
studies are shaped by the need for managers to procure the co-operation
and consent of the workforce. This is not to argue that managers are
simply agents of capital whose actions are shaped entirely by the needs of
the firm. The perceptions of managers are influenced by interaction
between their formal position in the organisational structure and by their
own interests.

The position of junior and middle managers in the capitalist
organisation is described by Savage, Barlow, Dickens and Fielding (1992)
in their theory of middle-class formation in contemporary Britain. These
authors put forward a realist model to explain the historic processes that
have shaped the development of the various groups that make up the
contemporary middle-class. They argue that the middle-class consists of
various groups who have access to, or own, different types of assets. These
variable assets affect the ability of individuals to protect their position in
the capitalist labour market.   Savage and his colleagues delineate the
historic processes that led to the development of a professional middle-
class and a managerial middle-class. For the professional middle-class, for
example accountants, lawyers and doctors, a growth in credentialism in the
19th and 20th centuries underpinned their social and labour market position.
The professional qualifications held by this group, whilst dependent on an
organisational context in which their value can be realised, are assets that
are transferable between organisations.   The development of the
managerial middle-class occurred as a result of an increase in the size of
firms and the bureaucratisation of control. As firms grew in size,
bureaucratic and hierarchical chains of command became necessary, and
were staffed by a new managerial middle class. Unlike the professional
class, whose assets are their professional qualifications, the managerial
middle-class owes its social and economic position to the organisation.
Such individuals could, in the past, work their way up the organisational
hierarchy through patronage and loyalty to the firm. According to Savage
et al, however, a shift away from centralised bureaucratic organisations,

and a corresponding delayering of managerial hierarchies has led to a decline in the value of organisational assets.

Two particular trends are identified by these authors as facilitating this decline. First, there has been a growth in the number of professionals, for example accountants and financial specialists, who have moved into senior management posts. Savage et al point out that an increasing professionalisation of managerial occupations has not occurred through an improvement in the qualifications held by junior and middle management. They argue that the rise in the number of managers with a degree qualification has been slow and unspectacular and that, given the increase in the number of degrees awarded since the 1950s, managers are now proportionately less well qualified than in the past (Ibid.). Second, a delayering of managerial hierarchies has resulted in the removal of middle management layers. Both these trends have served to block the career paths of junior and middle managers and to devalue their organisational assets.

Drawing on the model set out by Savage, Barlow, Dickens and Fielding, it can be argued that the position of junior and middle managers is contradictory. On one hand the group appear to be subject to a process of proletarianization in that their marketable assets are comparable to, and in some cases worse than, those of subordinates. An example of this is found at GlassCo where a small number of interviewees had, in the past, been middle and junior managers in other glassworks. Following redundancy, the opportunities open to these men were limited to low level production jobs in remaining glassworks. They had no marketable assets in the form of qualifications to substitute for the loss of their organisational assets. In contrast to this, a number of redundant British coal apprentice qualified craftsmen had found skilled jobs in each of the three case study factories. Their apprenticeship credentials appear to be a more marketable asset than the organisational assets of junior and middle managers.

On the other hand, as Armstrong points out, a fundamental feature of the managerial role is the exercising of agency on behalf of more senior managers. It can also be suggested that junior and middle managers are likely to exercise agency on their own behalf. Because the assets of this group are tied to the organisation in which they are employed, they need to strengthen their position in the firm. Thus, by attempting to secure valorisation managers are exercising agency not only on behalf of the firm, but also to secure their own position. This process is made easier if workers adopt co-operative attitudes and are competent to perform their work.

A final and brief point concerns the introduction, in recent years, of Foucault into labour process debates. This development has led to a shift of emphasis away from debates around skill towards a focus on methods of discipline and surveillance in the workplace (for example, Knights and Willmott 1985, 1989, Knights 1990, Deetz 1992, Sakolosky 1992, Clegg 1994, Collinson 1994, Knights and Vurdubakis 1994). A particular aspect of this theoretical development is a concern with the ways in which new methods of work organisation, such as Just-In-Time production and teamworking, have shifted control away from direct managerial forms of discipline and surveillance towards self and peer group discipline (Sewell and Wilkinson 1992, Barker 1993, McKinlay and Taylor 1996). With respect to the concerns of this book, one particular issue arises from the current dominance of Foucauldian analysis in labour process theory, an issue that relates specifically to Chemicals UK. It will be argued in Chapter Five that the neo-human relations management strategy at the firm has strong practical and theoretical links with traditional Taylorist forms of control. It will also be suggested that this link arises from the fundamental similarities between Taylorist and alleged non-Taylorist methods of work. Associations between Taylorism and Weber's theory of bureaucracy, and between human relations management strategies and Foucauldian methods of workplace discipline will be outlined. I will also argue however, that practical and theoretical links can be drawn between Weberian and Foucauldian methods of workplace disciple. The impact of this link in terms of perceptions of skill is that the perceptions generated by overt Taylorist strategies, and those generated by the forms of discipline described by Foucault are, in reality, indistinguishable.

Fordism and Post-Fordism

During the 1980s and 1990s, debates on the subject of skill have been conducted largely within the context of an alleged shift between the Fordist system of production and the post-Fordist system. The term post-Fordism does not signify a unified theoretical approach, but contains distinct theories that each emphasise differing aspects of the alleged shift between Fordism and post-Fordism. What these theories do have in common is that each portrays Fordism and post-Fordism as distinct phases in capitalist development, and all assume that post-Fordism has arisen in response to an inherent crisis of Fordism (Aglietta 1979, Piore and Sabel 1984, Murray 1988). The first theory to be considered is regulation theory as exemplified by the work of Aglietta (1979). Aglietta concentrates on the durability of capitalism in terms of its inherent tendencies towards crisis, and its ability to overcome crises and sustain long periods of relative stability (Amin

1994). The approach attempts, therefore, to identify the crisis tendencies of Fordism and the contrasting properties of post-Fordism. The relevance of regulation theory to this book concerns the ways in which the methods of overcoming the crises of Fordism adopted by capital have led to developments in the regulation of the labour process. It will be shown in the case study chapters that the effects on the labour process predicted by Aglietta are in evidence in the three case study factories, and are important factors in shaping subjective perceptions of skill.

A number of other theoretical approaches within the post-Fordist perspective are relevant to the concerns of this book. These are Piore and Sabel's flexible specialisation theory, Atkinson's model of the flexible firm and theories of Japanisation. The applicability of the first and second relates to three sub-issues. First the relationship between product markets, unstable consumer demand, and ensuing organisational structures and labour processes. The contention of this book, that the most salient factors to shape workforce perceptions of skill are firm specific structural features which are themselves engendered, in part, by environmental factors such as product markets and industrial sector trends, suggests that the generation of perceptions of skill can be traced back to developments in the wider capitalist system. An important question is whether the processes that have shaped organisational structures in the three firms are consistent with post-Fordist theories. Second, flexible specialisation and the flexible firm provide ideal type models through which the structural features of case study firms can be analysed, for example, in terms of the nature of flexible technology and the development of work organisation. Third, both these theories contain explicit assumptions with respect to trends in workforce skill trajectories, and thus provide a theoretical context with which perceptions of skill can be compared. That is, how far the perceptions of skill held by workers accord with post-Fordist assumtions regarding trends in workforce skills. Finally, the relevance of Japanisation theories relates to one case study company, Electronics UK. This firm is a Japanese owned and managed UK transplant that displays strong similarities with other Japanese transplants discussed in the literature.

The view that western capitalism has entered into a new post-Fordist era is not universally accepted and a number of criticisms of post-Fordist theories have been advanced, both with respect to their theoretical coherence and their empirical basis. It is beyond the scope of book to examine evidence for and against the purported general shift towards post-Fordism. However, I will show in the case study chapters that within individual firms the shift between Fordism and post-Fordism is uneven and complex. All three firms contain elements of Fordism and post-Fordism, and rigid Taylorist management strategies are found alongside flexible production technology. Additionally, it will be argued that the flexible machinery employed in the firms does not fit neatly into Fordist or post-Fordist models.

Fordism

The term Fordism was conceived by Gramsci (1971) to describe trends in American capitalism during the 1920s. He argued that the American system of capitalism was flourishing due to the smaller number of social classes in America than in to Europe. In particular the absence of classes not engaged in production, classes that Gramsci termed "useless idlers who live on the 'inheritance' of their ancestors" (Gramsci 1971 p. 281). He argued that American capitalism was able to retain surplus profits because there was no parasitic class to support. Gramsci also argued that Fordism resulted from an inherent need to achieve a planned economy, and that a prerequisite for the system was the development of a new type of worker. Throughout the history of industrialism there has been a "continuing struggle against the "animality" in man" (Op-Cit. p. 298). In the past this struggle had been conducted by superior classes, under Fordism however, the struggle was conducted through persuasion. Finally, Gramsci saw Taylorism as an important and integral component of the Fordist system.

Since Gramsci the term Fordism has generally been applied to descriptions of the dominant system of production from the 1930s to 1970s. According to Aglietta (1979), the advent of Fordism signified a new stage in the regulation of capitalism in which the process of production is articulated with the mode of consumption. Goods that were mass produced in the Fordist factory were consumed by wage labourers who had themselves become part of the Fordist system. The principle of mass production was also underpinned by Keynesian economic demand management and the Beveridgian social security system. With respect to perceptions of skill however, the most salient features of the Fordist system are those that occur at the level of the organisation, and their impact on the labour process of workers.

The first characteristic of the Fordist labour process put forward by Aglietta (1979) is the development of the semi-automatic assembly line used to manufacture standardised consumer goods and intermediate products. Second, the alignment of mechanisation with the principles of Taylorism. This alignment of Taylorism and assembly line technology serves to fix workers to jobs, the nature of which are determined by mechanisation. Workers lose control over the pace of work to the machine, and the resulting loss of autonomy makes possible the further simplification and fragmentation of tasks. The Fordist labour process results, therefore, in an intensification of work and a separation of mental and manual labour. The Fordist system of accumulation was argued by Aglietta to have reached its limits in the 1970s. These limits occurred both in relation to social conditions and at the level of the system itself. In terms of social conditions, Fordism required increasing consumer demand to match the increases in productivity made possible by mechanisation. The need to increase demand is crucial due to the constraints that are built into the assembly line process. Namely, the limits reached in terms of the fragmentation of tasks, and the rigidities inherent in the technology rendered it ever more costly to achieve increases in output. Any rise in productivity could only be achieved through higher levels of investment, and thus rendered the expansion of markets essential. The internal limits to Fordism include delays in production caused by imbalances on the assembly line, the negative effects of intensification of work on the physical and mental capabilities of workers, for example as manifested in fatigue and absenteeism, and the eradication of the link between individual effort and collective output. According to Aglietta, these limitations led to a crisis of Fordism, and the subsequent need for capitalism to protect itself against crisis. The outcome was a transformation of the labour process into what he terms neo-Fordism (Aglietta 1979). It will be demonstrated that the changes in the labour process predicted by Aglietta are, to some extent, evident in the three case study factories. The theory provides, therefore, a useful context in which to examine the processes that generate subjective perceptions of skill. A description of Aglietta's account of neo-Fordism will be given following a brief digression to discuss two criticisms of Fordism.

The first criticism concerns the alleged standardisation and inflexibility of Fordism. According to Clarke (1992) the form of Fordism associated with Ford himself, that is the production of one standardised model, died in the 1920s. The key to the Fordist revolution was not standardisation of product, but standardisation of the components used to manufacture various models and goods (Op-Cit. p. 18). Fordism is therefore characterised by flexibility rather than inflexibility (Kumar p. 60), an assertion that renders questionable the association of Fordism with inflexibility and post-Fordism with flexibility. The significance of this issue with respect to skill in the workplace concerns the efforts of each case study firm to introduce flexibility of some form into the labour process, and the impact of these various forms of flexibility on perceptions of skill. In order to locate perceptions of skill in relation to flexibility within the context of Fordist and post-Fordist organisational structures, it is necessary to first consider whether particular forms of flexibility can be defined as either Fordist or post-Fordist. It will be argued, however, that to label particular forms of flexibility as Fordist or post-Fordist is problematic. At Chemicals UK, for example, similar types of process technology are used in different ways on different plants. That is, to produce both a high volume standardised product for the mass market, and low volume speciality chemicals that are flexibly manufactured to meet the needs of individual customers. Similarly, at Electronics UK typically Fordist assembly line technology is closely articulated with flexible automated technology to produce a highly integrated flexible system of production. Thus complications and contradictions occur when attempts are made to apply rigid Fordist or post-Fordist labels to complex production systems. The question of how this issue relates to each case study firm will be dealt with in the case study chapters.

A second criticism of the Fordist orthodoxy, again advanced by Clarke, relates to the equation of Fordism with Taylorism. According to Clarke these systems are not synonymous, and Taylorism is just as easily applied to small scale batch production as to mass standardised production (Clarke quoted in Kumar 1995 p. 60). Clarke argues that 'Taylorism decomposes tasks and assigns those tasks to individual workers, while Fordism recomposes the tasks by welding the individual labours into the human machine' (Clarke 1992 p. 19). In terms of skill formation, these criticisms can be countered with the argument that the decomposition of tasks and subsequent deskilling of the worker remains regardless of whether this decomposition relates to small batch production or to mass standardised production. In addition, the effects of task decomposition on workers will remain salient regardless of whether or not they are recomposed into a collective whole through the introduction of Fordist machinery. Thus, whilst Taylorism is not necessarily synonymous with Fordism, the Fordist labour process is supported by the Taylorist division of labour, hierarchical management structures and close supervisory systems. In support of Clarke, on the other hand, it will be shown that Taylorism is not confined to the typical Fordist organisation. Taylorism may underpin the Fordist labour process, but it is also compatible with the flexible forms of production associated with post-Fordist theory. I will demonstrate that both GlassCo and Electronics UK utilise flexible production technology, but that this technology is closely allied to Taylorist management strategies.

Aglietta and Neo-Fordism

Aglietta argues that the new organising principle of the labour process under neo-Fordism centres on automation and the reconstruction of tasks. Under the Fordist system the flow of work remained, to some extent, dependent on the worker. Under automation however, all stages in the production process are integrated and reconstituted into a single process, a development made possible by automated machinery that controls its own operations. This new system facilitates flexibility in that the process can be adapted to both mass and batch production, and long and short production runs. Aglietta predicted that the impact of automation on the labour process would be radical. First, it would deskill the workforce due to the suppression of complex tasks by machinery. All that will be required of workers is machine supervision. Second, work in the automated factory will become homogenised, thus enabling the rotation of labour between jobs. Whilst this will require some polyvalence amongst workers, it will not result in enskilling due to the simplification of tasks that results from automation. Third, responsibility for production programming will be given over to skilled technicians, thus facilitating an increase in the separation of conception and execution. Fourth, the new system will change the way in which workers are controlled, and no longer will they be subject to personalised hierarchical supervision. Rather, control will result from collective constraints built into the production process itself. Finally, the development of semi-autonomous work teams, who are collectively responsible for the preparation of work, regulation of the machinery and execution of tasks, will not result in job enhancement. This is because automation strips these functions of any qualitative content.

Although Aglietta was describing conditions that pertain to completely automated factories, that is where the whole production process is allied to centralised control, the effects with respect to the labour process can also be argued to be applicable to factories where automation is less extensive. I shall show that the effects on the labour process predicted by Aglietta are highly relevant to the case study factories, and that the developments envisaged by Aglietta are important factors in the generation of subjective perceptions of skill.

Flexible Specialisation

Flexible specialisation is argued to be at the heart of post-Fordist theory and is exemplified by the work of Piore and Sabel (Amin 1994). Two equally important and related developments form the basis of the theory:

changes in consumer demand patterns and technological innovations. It is argued that post war demand for standardised consumer durables reached saturation in the 1970s. This resulted in a shift in demand away from uniform products towards diverse and differentiated products. Markets became unstable and uncertain, which in turn engendered a need for flexible patterns of production. Such flexibility is provided by new flexible manufacturing technologies that can produce, and easily transfer production between, a variety of goods. This contrasts with the dedicated specialist machinery producing the standardised uniform goods that characterised Fordism.

According to Piore and Sabel, the shift from Fordism to flexible specialisation is underpinned by new flexible production technologies, and is associated with the possibilities for economies of scale that exist in relation to particular product markets. Where demand is stable and plentiful, production can be centralised in large units operating in accordance with the principles of economies of scale. This system is supported by Taylorist forms of work organisation where tasks are fragmented and workforce skills are substituted by machines. However, where stability breaks down and markets splinter into niche areas, economies of scale become impossible. Firms respond by organising production around flexible technology and economies of scope. That is by flexibly manufacturing a range of goods geared towards niche market areas. The organisation of work involves the reconstitution of fragmented tasks and a reskilling of the workforce (Piore and Sabel 1984).

The shift towards economies of scope is argued to favour small innovative firms often located in particular geographical regions. Relations between these firms are characterised by horizontal integration and mutual co-operation (Sabel 1994). Flexible specialisation is not however limited to smaller production units and multi-nationals are shifting towards more flexible production where subsidiaries manufacture goods for niche markets (Kumar 1995). With respect to individual companies, the move towards flexible specialisation is argued to eradicate inflexible hierarchical Taylorist management structures in favour of flexible flatter looser structures. Work itself is transformed as Taylorist division of labour and task fragmentation gives way to a more humane organisation of work. Under flexible specialisation work is organised around craft principles, the separation of conception and execution is rescinded, workers are given more responsibility and autonomy, and workforce skills are restored. This optimistic view of the future of work is premised on the argument that computerisation represents a break with Fordist forms of technology. Piore and Sabel argue that:

Efficiency in production results from adapting the equipment to the task in hand: the specialisation of the equipment to the operation. With conventional technology, this adaptation is done   by physical adjustments in the equipment: Whenever the product is changed the specialised machine must be rebuilt. In craft production this means changing tools and the fixtures that position the workpiece during machinery. In mass production, it means scrapping and replacing machinery. With computerised technology, the equipment (the hardware) is adapted to the operation by the computer program (the software): therefore, the equipment can be put to new uses without physical adjustments - simply by reprogramming (Piore and Sabel 1984 p. 260).

Piore and Sabel go on to argue that the computer is comparable to Marx's definition of the artisans tool in that it responds to, and extends the production capabilities of, the user. It also restores operator control over the production process, and machinery is subordinated to the operator rather than the operator subordinate to the machine (Op-Cit. p. 261).

Various criticisms of flexible specialisation have been put forward, and some are directly relevant to the arguments to be advanced in this book. First, the theory is constructed around a dualism between production eras (Amin 1994, Elam 1994). It can be suggested that the tendency to view production in terms of a dualism ignores the complexities and contradictions found in industrial organisations. A second set of criticisms relate to the emphasis placed on technology. The theory is argued to be technologically deterministic in that technology alone is responsible for changing work patterns (Amin 1994). The theory also overestimates the extent of flexibility inherent in new technologies (Tomaney 1994), and to overestimate the extent to which flexible specialisation has been applied in the UK (Jones 1988). The case study evidence presented here provides some support for the first and second of these criticisms.

This evidence indicates that flexible production technology alone is not responsible for shaping patterns of work. Whilst technology is important, its effects depend upon the configuration of machinery with the social organisation of work. In addition, the flexibility inherent in new technology does not necessarily correspond with its age. Chemicals UK, for example, has adopted Fordist continuous process technology to the flexible manufacture of batch chemicals aimed at new niche market areas. Finally, flexible specialisation is criticised for its optimistic assumption that the shift towards flexible manufacturing systems results in increased workforce skills. Empirical evidence suggests that new forms of work associated with the shift towards post-Fordism represent an intensification of work and/or the reconstitution of previously demarcated unskilled and semi-skilled tasks (Pollert 1988a, 1988b, 1991, Garrahan and Stewart 1992).

Data from this research indicates that the skill trajectories generated by flexible production systems are uneven, and depend on the alignment of technology with other factors. For a small group of workers, the introduction of flexible production systems has led to the reconstitution of mental planning (i.e. conception) and operation (i.e. execution). For this group, perceptions of skill will be shown to focus on a theoretical knowledge of the whole production process. For others, however, the introduction of computerised flexible technology has done nothing to reduce the rigidly demarcated, semi-skilled nature of work. It will be suggested in Chapter Seven that computerised continuous process production in the chemicals industry, rather than returning control to the workers as predicted by Piore and Sabel, removes what control workers held prior to computerisation. For this group perceptions of skill focus on a knowledge of the practical tasks necessary to machine monitoring.

In summary, each of the three firms has introduced machinery that could, to some extent, be described as flexible specialisation. This flexible machinery has been adopted in response to instability and uncertain market conditions. At this point, however, comparisons between the case studies and theories of flexible specialisation break down. The effects of flexible technology in transforming the labour process is limited to the small number of workers mentioned above. For the majority of workers, flexible technology is aligned with rigid Taylorist management techniques, and the combined effects of these two factors is to constrain the optimistic upskilling trajectories proposed by Piore and Sabel.

The Flexible Firm

The third post-Fordist theory relevant to this research is Atkinson's model of the flexible firm[1] (Atkinson 1984). Whereas flexible specialisation emphasises the role of technology in facilitating flexibility, the flexible firm focuses on the organisation of work and employment patterns within firms. It is argued to synthesise three distinct yet key theoretical perspectives. The first is labour market segmentation theory which divides the labour force into specific labour market categories. Second is the labour law perspective which is concerned with the contractual arrangements of particular jobs, for example, contract duration and employment rights, and benefits such as occupational pensions and sickness benefits. Finally, the industrial relations perspective focuses on the labour process and relations between management and workers (Hakim 1990). These theoretical perspectives are synthesised into two key themes: core and periphery, and flexibility. Like flexible specialisation the flexible firm is argued to have developed in response to changeable consumer demand patterns, and ensuing market uncertainty and instability. According to the model, this results in a necessity for firms to embrace flexible work and employment patterns in order to achieve flexibility of production. The core workforce provide functional flexibility in the sense that they are multi-skilled and able to transfer between a variety of tasks. The peripheral workforce, on the other hand, provide numerical flexibility in that they are less skilled and more easily hired and discarded. This group consists of unskilled and semi-skilled full-time workers, part-time, seasonal and temporary workers, or those on short term contracts.

It is suggested by Hakim that the model of the flexible firm provides a simplified and successful interdisciplinary means of studying the various forms of flexibility within individual firms (Hakim 1990). This argument is questionable and Pollert, for example, has sought to demonstrate that rather than simplifying the issues, the flexible firm and core and periphery fail to capture the complexities of real workplace relations. The tendency to view all developments in workplace organisation as a drive towards flexibility imposes a false conceptualisation of a variety of processes. The model can also be criticised for its propensity to slot workers into rigid categories which may not be so clear cut in practice. Pollert argues that the flexible firm, by promoting a dualism around the notion of a stable core labour force and an unstable periphery, conceals conflict and inequality in relations to production, and issues surrounding intensification of effort and job enlargement in the core are largely ignored (Pollert 1991). Hakim anticipated these criticisms by suggesting that the flexible firm model is not intended as a factual representation of any specific organisation. Rather, it is an ideal-type framework through which to study the various aspects of core and periphery, and flexibility (Hakim 1990). A further criticism of the model is that it portrays changes in the organisation of work and employment patterns as recent developments associated with a shift to post-Fordism. Pollert argues that these developments do not represent a radical break with the past, but rather an intensification of existing exploitative employment practices (Pollert 1991).

The relevance of the flexible firm to this book relates to two broad issues. First, to what extent do the assertions advanced in the core and periphery model adequately describe employment patterns in the two case study firms that employ non-standard labour. In addition, how salient are these theoretical assumptions to worker perceptions of their position in relation to the core and periphery dichotomy. Second, to what extent do the skill trajectories explicit in this theory describe those in each case study factory. Is there, for example, any evidence of multi-skilling amongst full time core workers, and if so do workers perceptions of skill include notions of multi-skilling? Consideration of how this theoretical approach can be used as a basis for understanding the formation of perceptions of skill, core and periphery in the case study factories will be made during discussion of the main strands of the theory. Namely, core and periphery, and numerical and functional flexibility.

Core and Periphery

The core and periphery model applies to both macro-level employment structures, and to an alleged polarisation between the core and peripheral labour force within firms. The theory draws heavily on labour market segmentation theories that stress the division between primary and secondary labour markets. From this perspective, the labour force divides into those with access to better paid, more highly skilled and secure occupations, and those located in the low paid, low skilled, insecure peripheral sector. Core and periphery at the macro-level can be criticised on the grounds that segmentation of the labour force has been a feature of capitalism from the outset. The division of the labour force into distinct categories was first applied by Marx in his theory of the reserve army of labour (Marx 1976), divisions that are repeated in segmented labour market models. On the other hand, core and periphery can be argued to represent a distinct development in the labour process; labour market segmentation occurs as a result of structural labour market conditions and labour market supply, whilst core and periphery represents a 'deliberate, ideological and political division of the nation' (Pollert 1991 p. 14). Thus, labour market segmentation is a characteristic of the market for labour whilst core and periphery is the result of a deliberate strategy pursued by UK governments in the 1980s.

At the level of individual firms, core and periphery is seen to represent employer strategies to increase flexibility in order to cope with changeable product markets. Full-time core workers are essential to the production process, and provide firms with functional flexibility. They are rewarded with relatively secure employment contracts, stable earnings and various occupational benefits. Peripheral workers, on the other hand, are marginal and easily dispensable in that they can be discarded when no longer required by firms. A particular criticism of core and periphery at the level of the firm is that the model is underpinned by notions of dualism

(Pollert 1988a, 1988b, 1991). Although Atkinson puts forward a number of peripheral categories, it can be argued that the primary division in terms of core and periphery implies an overall dualism between two groups of workers. The imposition of a dichotomous conceptual framework serves to detract from the intensity of differences within the two categories, and to ignore the consequences in terms of workers experiences of work. According to Atkinson's model, for example, part-time workers on fixed term contracts would be placed within the same peripheral sector as those on short-term contracts and public subsidy trainees. The degree of exploitation to which these different types of worker are subjected may differ markedly, and their different concrete circumstances should be considered separately and not as part of an abstract concept of the peripheral worker. This argument supports that put forward by Gallie and White (1994). They suggest that the various categories of employee that are placed together as an undifferentiated peripheral sector are, in reality, an heterogeneous group in terms of job security.

The classification of part-time workers as forming part of the periphery results from an assumption that they are considered, by management, to be less central to production than are full-time core workers. Part-time workers are, furthermore, generally considered to have less access to occupational benefits such as company pension schemes, and to have fewer employment rights than full-time workers (Hakim 1990). In criticism of this argument, it can be suggested that whilst the employment situation of part-time workers may be less favourable than that of full-time workers, for example in terms of pay and conditions, it does not necessarily hold that the first assumption is true. Certain types of manufacturing industry have relied on part-time female labour to meet production deadlines (Smith 1991), and these firms may well view part-time workers as central to the production process. In a detailed study of part-time work, Tam (1997) found a number of differences in the work situations of part- and full-time workers. First, part-timers are less likely to belong to a trades union. Second, they are more likely to perform jobs requiring no qualifications. Third, they enjoy fewer opportunities for promotion and have less access to occupational fringe benefits. Fourth, they are less likely to use discretion in their work or have supervisory responsibilities. On the other hand, part-time workers are less likely to be subject to close direct supervision and there is little difference between part- and full-time workers in terms of permanence of employment contract (Tam 1997). It can be suggested that part-time workers who have open ended contracts and stable earnings, and who have access to company pension schemes, have more in common with core workers than with temporary or home workers with no access to these benefits. Additionally, it could be argued that to classify part-time workers as peripheral due to their limited access to occupational pension schemes and other similar benefits ignores the fact that a number of full-time workers do not enjoy such benefits.

With respect to the categorisation of temporary workers as a distinct and homogenous peripheral category, again a distinction needs to be drawn between different types of temporary worker. For some employees temporary status can be a first step towards permanent employment (Dex and McCulloch 1997). For others, such as agency and/or seasonal workers, temporary jobs may offer no opportunities for permanent status. It can be argued therefore, that qualitative differences exist within the overall category of temporary employee. Rather than grouping temporary workers together as one peripheral category, consideration should be made of the opportunities associated with different types of temporary contract. Finally, in terms of employment rights, Pollert accepts that the impact of the deregulatory policies of the previous conservative governments (such as increasing the qualifying period for unfair dismissal from six months to two years) have weakened the position of already vulnerable workers. She also accepts that this has led to increased polarisation between the legally protected workforce and the unprotected. Pollert argues however, that attacks by the Thatcher governments on trades unions have also eroded many of the privileges of the so called core workforce (Pollert 1991). This evidence suggests that the core and periphery model does not provide an adequate framework through which to understand the employment situation of various groups of heterogeneous workers. Distinctions within and between so called peripheral groups make it difficult to sustain a dualistic categorisation.

Numerical Flexibility

Intrinsic to the flexible firm and the model of core and periphery is the concept of numerical flexibility. Peripheral workers are argued to provide firms with flexibility over the size of the labour force, and numerical flexibility is viewed as a response to changing and uncertain product markets. In the context of this book two questions arise in relation to numerical flexibility: why do firms utilise a numerically flexible workforce, and how do so called peripheral employees in two of the three case study factories perceive their situation? Previous evidence on the question of why employers employ peripheral labour is contradictory, and studies highlight a number of factors. Survey evidence from McGregor and

Sproull (1992) suggests that few employers report the need for flexibility as the sole reason for employing non-standard labour. The main reasons given for employing part-time workers were the need to employ workers to carry out tasks of a limited duration, and the need to employ workers when demand was high. Two further reasons mentioned were the need to hold onto valued staff, and the demand for part-time work from female workers (McGregor and Sproull 1992). It can be argued that the last two points do not support the view of part-time workers as members of peripheral workforce. The validity of this view is questioned by Hows, Hurtsfield and Holmaat (1989) who argue that the concept of flexibility in relation to female workers ignores their domestic responsibilities which may well constrain their choice over when to work. In terms of temporary work, McGregor and Sproull found that traditional rationales such as the need for temporary cover, for example to cover maternity leave, remain the major determinants behind the use of such labour. However, evidence to support the flexibility thesis was also found, with over 25% of employers reporting using this type of labour as a means of adjusting staff levels to demand for the product (McGregor and Sproull 1992).

Functional Flexibility

Atkinson and Meager (1986) use the concept of functional flexibility to describe changes in the organisation of work amongst the core labour force within firms. Unlike the Fordist system of production, where work is broken down into fragmented and specialised tasks, core workers in the flexible firm perform a variety of functions. Thus, the numerical flexibility provided by the periphery is paralleled by functional flexibility in the core. Integral to functional flexibility is the notion of multi-skilling which, according to Atkinson and Meager, takes a number of forms. First is the horizontal integration of jobs which involves workers deploying the basic skills of other trades. An example of this would be intercraft flexibility where fitters are trained to perform basic welding tasks. Second, and according to these authors less common, is the vertical integration of tasks. This involves workers performing tasks that require a higher level of skill, and which were previously the preserve of a separate group. An example of this would be machine operators taking enlarged responsibility for setting, maintaining and repairing machinery. Atkinson and Meager also suggest that firms have taken one of two general approaches to functional flexibility. First, and most common, is to replace one rigid and pre-defined job classification with another similarly rigid, but wider classification. The second approach does not involve pre-defined grouping of tasks, rather it establishes the principle of flexibility. It demands that workers perform any task for which they are capable as and when required by the company. This form of functional flexibility thus involves the deployment of labour in accordance with the needs of the firm rather than the job description of the incumbent.

A criticism of the concept of functional flexibility is that it is used to describe a variety of contradictory developments within the labour process. On the one hand it implies a shift towards multi-skilling of the core workforce, whilst on the other it implies increased managerial controls over workers' activities. Pollert suggests that a key assumption of the functional flexibility model is that "there is now a new role for enhanced skills which confer on key skill-flexible workers a cardinal role in the reform of production and a core position in the workforce" (Pollert 1991 p. 12). In criticism of this assumption, Elger (1991) argues that evaluation of Atkinson and Meager's survey evidence by Pollert indicates that changes towards multi-skilling have been minimal. In addition, changes which have occurred in the labour process have been more a trend towards reduced staffing levels and job enlargement. The shift towards job enlargement has not however included a shift away from specialisation. Rotation between jobs was viewed by many managers sampled in this survey as causing disruption to the production process. Elger argues that managers were concerned to adjust labour loading more closely to the requirements of production, and in a way which generally implies greater and/or more continuous effort. At the same time efforts are made to retain the advantages of specialisation. The result is a modest but real change in a substantial number of firms, usually involving broadening rather than upgrading of production tasks (Op-cit. p. 51). Further evidence that functional flexibility is a euphemism for task flexibility which does not involve multi-skilling is provided by Garrahan and Stewart. They argue that whilst Nissan promote an impression of multi-skilling amongst its workforce, the reality is somewhat different. Just-in-Time (JIT) production methods and neo-Taylorist work patterns have produced an intensive work process which involves the ability to carry out a number of tasks within one specialised production area (Garrahan and Stewart 1992).

These criticisms of functional flexibility appear to rest on the assumption that the model implies a process of multi-skilling. However, as Bagguley (1994) argues, it is implicit in Atkinson's concept of flexibility that the term refers to "management's enhanced control over the deployment of labour in an attempt to increase productivity" (Bagguley p. 165). From this perspective, functional flexibility does not necessarily imply multi-skilling, but merely implies task flexibility which can be utilised at management's discretion. It also implies that job enlargement and work intensification are part of this process. It can also be argued that some of Pollert's criticisms relate to outcomes rather than the adequacy of the model as a descriptive framework. Pollert herself states that the term functional flexibility allows for the multi-skilled core craft worker "but also the more pliable employee and the removal of demarcations." She goes on to argue that the outcome of both the above strategies is the creation of an employer/employee partnership which weakens labour resistance (Pollert 1988 p. 67). Pollert suggests in much of her work that the flexible firm model is portrayed as a prescription for the future. It can be suggested however, that acceptance of the model as a loose descriptive tool is not to imply unquestioning acceptance of the outcomes. Nor is it to ignore any concealment or distortion of negative developments within the labour process. It is in this context that the concept is used as a framework through which to understand the processes that shape subjective perceptions of skill. Whilst functional flexibility at GlassCo and Chemicals UK is, in general, a euphemism for task enlargement and effort intensification rather than multi-skilling, the concept remains a useful analytical tool through which to explore the organisation of work. It will be demonstrated that the organisation of work amongst craft maintenance workers in both firms, is characterised by horizontal task integration. In both factories skilled craftsmen are given basic training in craft skills other than their own, and are expected to deploy these skills whenever management demands. The approach to flexibility with respect to these workers corresponds to the establishment of principle rather than the imposition of rigid job classification schemes. Horizontal task integration will also be shown to characterise the organisation of work amongst production staff at Chemicals UK, although for many workers at this firm functional flexibility is confined to workers performing an enlarged range of specialised and pre-defined set of daily tasks.

In terms of the criticisms advanced by Pollert, Elger, and Garrahan and Stewart, I shall show how evidence from Chemicals UK indicates contradictory trends. Whilst reduced staffing levels, job enlargement and intensification of effort are features of the organisation of work, there is, amongst one group, evidence of vertical integration and a degree of multi-skilling. For others however, functional flexibility entails horizontal job integration and the rotation of specialist, pre-defined and fragmented tasks between individual workers. It will be suggested that functional flexibility can, in practice, embody both positive and negative elements simultaneously. A degree of vertical task integration can occur in conjunction with job enlargement and effort intensification. The issue of functional flexibility and perceptions of skill is returned to in later chapters. It will be suggested that where functional flexibility involves the rotation of specialist tasks, perceptions of skill focus on practical knowledge of those tasks. Where, on the other hand, functional flexibility involves vertical integration, perceptions of skill focus on more abstract forms of knowledge.

The concept of functional flexibility provides a useful starting point from which to examine some developments in the organisation of work at GlassCo and Chemicals UK and, therefore, the processes that help shape subjective perceptions of skill. Whilst criticisms of the model are valid, there is no necessary dichotomy between the positive and negative aspects of functional flexibility in practice.

Japanisation

Japanisation is often put forward as an example of the shift from Fordism to post-Fordism (Clegg 1990, Murray 1988). However, disagreement exists with respect to the related issues of the meaning of the term and the extent to which it has been applied in the UK. On one level Japanisation refers to a convergence of Western economic, political and social systems with those of Japan. According to Ackroyd, Burrell and Hughes (1988), there is little evidence of this form of Japanisation outside Japan. A second, and more narrow, definition of Japanisation is that it signifies a set of management and production practices adopted by Japanese transplants and UK emulators (For example, Ackroyd et al 1988, Oliver and Wilkinson 1988, Delbridge and Turnbull 1994). Such practices would include just-in-time delivery and production, total quality management, statistical process control, continuous improvement (kaizan), numerical and functional flexibility, employee participation and single status, and single one union agreements. Wood argues that it is the cohesion between these systems and their mutually supportive nature that renders them distinct from indigenous management strategies (Wood 1991), whilst Delbridge and Turnbull suggest that it is at this level that the impact of Japanisation is most keenly felt (Delbridge and Turnbull 1994). Ackroyd and his colleagues, on the other hand, argue that even amongst Japanese transplants there is evidence of only selective application of these features.

A final definition of Japanisation advanced by Wood (1991) also attempts to distinguish between Japanisation at the wider economic and social level, and Japanisation at the level of the firm. He puts forward an analytical separation between Japanisation in the broad sense and

'Toyotaism.' Toyotaism refers to a Japanese management model based on the Just-in Time (JIT) production system that has its origins in Japan's Toyota factory. In simple terms, this is a system that eliminates waste through the eradication of surplus stock and wasted worker time associated with Fordism. JIT stock control and delivery systems dispense with buffer stocks and what Wood terms 'the just in case mentality.' It will be demonstrated in Chapter Four that Electronics UK does not operate a JIT delivery system although it does utilise a JIT production strategy. It will also be shown that this JIT system is a highly important factor in the generation of workforce perceptions of skill.

Comparing Japanese and none Japanese Firms

Japanisation is an ambiguous concept. In practice, definitions generally focus on the distinctive management and production practices said to characterise the Japanese system. The extent to which Japanisation has permeated British industry is, from this perspective, measured in terms of the degree to which British firms and overseas transplants adhere to Japanese methods. Elger and Smith (1993) argue that this method of assessing the extent of Japanisation characterises incomplete adoption of the methods as deviation from the Japanese ideal type. Further criticisms of this strategy are as follows. First, the internationalisation of Capitalism has led to many countries copying the management techniques of others. Quality circles, a management practice now associated with Japan, originated in the USA (Wood 1991). Second, the construction of a Japanese ideal type with which to compare transplants and indigenous UK industries assumes a unified model in Japan. Whilst viewed by some as an innovative model in Japan (Elger and Smith pg. 39), the extent to which Toyotaism has permeated throughout Japanese industry is questioned by Wood. He argues that the spread of Toyotaism in Japan has been uneven. This is especially true of the electronics industry where changeovers in the product cycle are rapid, and component stocks need to be held in order to carry out last minute changes in production schedules (Wood 1991). It is evident that the term Japanisation is used to describe a variety of processes and practices. This leads to the question of how to assess Electronics UK within this broad theoretical context. Whilst it is not possible to create an ideal type Japanese firm with which to compare Electronics UK, it is possible to compare the firm with other Japanese electronics transplants operating in the UK.

Evidence from Japanese Transplants in the UK

Previous research carried out in Japanese transplants indicates commonalities between different firms. This discussion draws on evidence from two such studies, both of which suggest that implementation of practices associated with Japan in the electronics industry is highly selective. This selectivity results from constraints that are common to this industrial sector. One important issue relates to the absence of JIT delivery which characterises both Japanese electronics transplants and the electronics industry in Japan (Wood 1991). It is argued by Delbridge and Turnbull (1994) that whilst JIT delivery and stock control systems are largely absent, JIT production techniques are a significant feature of Japanese electronics transplants.

The first study to be considered took place at 'Terebi', a large Japanese electronics subsidiary in South Wales. This research by Taylor, Elger and Fairbrother (1993) reveals a number of features comparable to Electronics UK. First, similarities exist in respect of the relationships between higher Japanese managers and British middle managers. Taylor and his colleagues argue that Japanese managers at Terebi view British managers with some suspicion, and that the work of British managers is closely controlled by the Japanese. This compares with the attitudes held, according to British Managers, by senior Japanese management at Electronics UK. These managers expressed the view that the Japanese saw themselves as an elite to whom inferior British personnel must defer. Second, and like Electronics UK, production at Terebi consists of an automated insertion area where printed circuit boards (PCBs) are manufactured, and flow line assembly production areas. The automated insertion department contains technician programmers who prepare the sequencing of components and machine operators who perform the routine tasks of loading and minding machines. The flow line production area involves operators performing sequential short cycle tasks such as inserting components, soldering, checking and packing. These workers are watched closely by a technical supervisor, and 80% of the group are female. Women tend to perform what are regarded as unskilled jobs that require manual dexterity whilst men carry out 'skilled' maintenance work. This study also reveals that there are distinct promotion patterns for men and women with men achieving faster promotion and performing more technical jobs.

JIT delivery and production is absent from Terebi due to the changeable batch production process, which requires a steady supply of components. These components are imported from Europe and South East

Asia, thus rendering the utilisation of a JIT delivery strategy impossible. The flexible core and periphery employment patterns often associated with Japan are adopted to suit local conditions, for example, fluctuations in demand are dealt with through overtime and seasonal employment. High levels of labour turnover at the firm make it possible to achieve numerical flexibility; during slack seasons leavers are not replaced whilst in busy periods new staff are recruited. Functional flexibility at the plant is achieved by moving people between assembly lines whenever necessary.

A second study that illustrates the selective nature of Japanese management practices in Japanese UK transplants is provided by Delbridge and Turnbull (Delbridge and Turnbull 1994). These authors draw on their own research carried out at 'Nippon Electric' and secondary evidence from Garrahan and Stewart (1992), Wickens (1997) and Morris and Imrie (1992).   It is argued by Delbridge and Turnbull that within a variety of Japanese transplants there exist a number of manufacturing techniques associated with Japanisation. Examples include JIT, TQM, Kaizan and highly visible monitoring systems. The form of JIT found at these firms' is mediated, and rather than JIT delivery from suppliers, stocks are held in bonded areas and delivered on a JIT basis. Further generic characteristics of the plants surveyed are "the standardisation of work procedures, an inexhaustive attention to detail in respect of both processes and quality performance, and a consistent determination to learn from problems and rectify the causes of these. The pace of work is intense and the nature of work, particularly at the electronics plants, is essentially semi or un-skilled. Workers are also required to follow strict standardised procedures, and flexibility comes from the ability to rotate tasks, not in how those tasks are completed" (Delbridge and Turnbull p. 13). Additional features identified by Delbridge and Turnbull are the constant search for the 'one best way', the recruitment process which attempts to identify recruits with the correct behavioural attitudes, the lengthy probation period, the single union agreement and the requirement for workers to work overtime when demand dictates.

I shall show in Chapter Six that the labour process features found in these firms are very similar to those discovered at Electronics UK. The effects of Japanese management techniques such as JIT and TQM are argued by Delbridge et al to intensify the labour process. They also suggest that this intensification renders Japanese management or Toyotaism distinct from the Fordist labour process. It is in the context of this theoretical framework that the labour process at Electronics UK is analysed. I shall demonstrate that the management practices identified are influential in determining how workers experience their work. I will also show that the specific type of Japanese production system in operation at the firm generates highly job specific workforce perceptions of skill.

Conclusion

This chapter has presented an outline of the theoretical context in which this book is framed: namely labour process theory and post-Fordism. The chapter began with a discussion of some of the issues that were discussed within the labour process debates of the 1970s and 1980s. It was argued that this theoretical paradigm still provides a useful framework from which to analyse the causal processes that shape subjective perceptions of skill in the 1990s. This usefulness relates the proposed relationship between management strategies, technology and skill, in particular Braverman's emphasis on the distinction between conception and execution. I shall argue in later chapters that the division between conception and execution of tasks is a highly important factor in the generation of subjective perceptions of skill. I will also show, however, that whilst the distinction set out by Braverman remains salient in relation to the majority of jobs performed by interviewees it is not a universal trend. For craft maintenance workers, and a small number of production workers at Chemicals UK, the division between conception and execution is blurred. In addition, the perceptions of skill articulated by this group contain significant differences to those expressed by the majority of production workers in all three case study factories.

Following the discussion of labour process theory the chapter went on to discuss Fordism and post-Fordism. The salience of post-Fordism concerns the ways in which changing product markets, and developments in the industrial sectors in which individual firms are located, influence the structural organisational features of firms. A key assertion made later in the book is that firm specific structural features are important factors in the generation of subjective perceptions of skill. By adopting this theoretical perspective, links can be drawn between developments in the wider capitalist system and subjective perceptions of skill. It will be demonstrated, in Chapters Five, Six and Seven that attempts to define firms as either Fordist or post-Fordist ignore the complex nature of organisational structures, and the uneven ways in which they develop. In all three firms some organisational characteristics correspond to the Fordist paradigm, whilst others appear to conform to the new post-Fordist orthodoxy. In addition to this, some organisational features, for example production systems and technology, embody elements of Fordism and post-Fordism simultaneously.

To argue that the perceptions of skill uncovered in this research are generated by either Fordist or post-Fordist organisational structures would be to oversimplify a variety of sometimes contradictory developments within firms. On the other hand, the ideal type organisational formations, and ensuing forms of work, that are described in the post-Fordist literature (for example, Aglietta 1979, Piore and Sable 1984, Atkinson and Meager 1986) constitute a valuable starting point from which to consider organisational features and, ultimately, perceptions of skill. Finally, with respect to the theories of Japanisation outlined in this chapter, one case study firm, Electronics UK, will be shown to display strong similarities to other Japanese UK electronics transplants. These similarities concern the ways in which Japanese transplants selectively apply Japanese production and work methods in the UK.

The effects of developments within organisations, which are described in the labour process and post-Fordist literature, will be returned to during the case study chapters. For now the theoretical discussion continues, in the next chapter, with issues relating to sociological definitions of skill, managerial strategies, technology, and gender.

Note

[1] The inclusion of the flexible firm under the general post-Fordist umbrella is not universally accepted. Proctor, Rowlinson, McArdle and Forrester (1994) argue that the flexible firm needs to be considered on a different level from flexible specialisation theory, and other varieties of post-Fordism. He suggests that whereas flexible specialisation, and post-Fordism in general, imply a strategy for reforming the capitalist system, the flexible firm is best viewed as a managerial strategy for controlling labour. They also suggest that the implications of post-Fordism and the flexible firm differ both in scope and content. The decision to include the flexible firm in the discussion of post-Fordism results from two related points. First, the model is premised on the argument that changing consumer demand patterns have led to qualitative changes in the structures of organisations that represent a break with the Fordist system. That is, to organisational forms which utilise a deliberate core - periphery strategy, and a functionally flexible core workforce. Second, it is implicit in the model that these changes have led to a shift from the Fordist labour process to one that is organised around flexibility. The aim of this book is to examine perceptions of skill in the context of these various forms of flexibility. For this reason the flexible firm is defined here as a strand of post-Fordist theory.

3 Skill, Management Strategies, Technology and Gender

Introduction

To develop a sociological understanding of the subjective perceptions of skill held by individuals and groups in the three case study factories, a discussion of various sociological definitions of the term 'skill' will be carried out. This begins with an account of the various dimensions of skill, and goes on to explore the ways in which skill is conceptualised from three sociological paradigms. The chapter then moves on to discuss two factors that are significant in the generation of subjective perceptions of skill: managerial strategies and technology. The final section of the chapter presents an introduction to issues of gender and skill.

Dimensions of Skill

The concept of skill is ambiguous and a diversity of definitions are found in the literature. The deskilling thesis advanced by Braverman (1974) is a good starting point from which to consider the subject. It is based on the assumption that the labour process under monopoly capitalism has engendered a division between the conception and execution of tasks. Braverman argued that intellectual capabilities necessary to the conception of tasks are utilised by fewer and fewer workers, whilst occupations associated with execution only are expanding. The erosion of intellectual skills has led to a deskilling of large sections of the workforce. From this perspective, varying levels of complexity inherent in tasks are irrelevant. More recent definitions of skill do incorporate notions of task complexity. Spenner (1990), for example, refers to 'substantive complexity' whilst Scarborough and Corbett (1992) position skill on a four point scale that takes account of manual, craft and intellectual dimensions, and proactive and reactive dimensions.

A second dimension of skill refers to the distinction between specific task skills and skills that reside in the individual. These elements do not necessarily sit side by side. Technological innovations may, for example, deskill tasks but not the worker, although workers' skills may be devalued as a result of this process. In addition, although a worker may not possess formal qualifications, he or she may be highly skilled in the task requirements of their particular occupation. A third dimension of skill is the level of autonomy-control over work that is held by workers. Spenner argues that autonomy-control should not be confused with power relations between workers and managers, rather it is a feature of tasks rather than power over the production process (Spenner 1990). It will be shown in later chapters that the level of autonomy-control held by groups and individual workers is a highly significant factor in facilitating or constraining workforce perceptions of discretion and autonomy as skill. Wood (1987) advances a final dimension of skill, tacit skill. Tacit skills develop when conscious actions become internalised leading to unconscious task performance. Skills are learned through experience, are situation specific and are difficult to express in formalised terms. An example of tacit skill would be an instinctive understanding of how particular actions fit into the overall production process.

This brief discussion has highlighted some attributes deemed to signify skill and it is apparent that the concept is conceived of in various ways. The discussion now considers how the concept of skill is approached from three sociological paradigms: the positivist, social constructivist and ethnomethodological paradigms. Each will be assessed in terms of its adequacy as an ontological and epistemological tool through which to examine subjective perceptions of skill.

The Positivist Approach to Skill

From the positivist perspective, skills are quantifiable and measurable attributes found in tasks or individuals, and much research into skill is grounded in this paradigm. This includes studies relating to aggregate changes in skill levels over time (Penn 1994, Gallie 1996), and studies which equate skills with formal levels of training and education (Gallie and White 1993). Previous research by Burchell, Elliot, Rubery and Wilkinson (1994) attempted, from within the positivist paradigm, to uncover the subjective perceptions of skill held by workers. This involved analysis of management and worker responses to identical questions regarding the skill content of employees jobs. Whilst the study aimed to establish how management and worker perceptions differ in relation to this issue, it employed a positivist methodology and predefined concepts relating to choice in performance of tasks, supervision, responsibility and type of skill. Responses were analysed using statistical data analysis (Burchell et al. 1994). Although this research by Burchell and his colleagues was useful in highlighting the perception gap between management and workers, it is not an analysis of subjective perceptions of skill. Managers and workers were asked to evaluate the content of employees jobs in relation to a number of predefined indicators. These included discretion and responsibility, and clerical, organisational, social and physical skills. In contrast to this, the evidence advanced in this book draws on subjects' own definitions of skill.[1] In addition to the use of predefined definitions of skill, Burchell et al's study made no attempt to discover the causal processes that generate the particular perceptions of skill articulated by interviewees. A second study into subjective perceptions of skill by Francis and Penn (1994) attempted to develop a phenomenology of skill based on the understandings of respondents. Survey evidence from 987 individuals between the ages of 20 and 60 living in Rochdale in 1986 suggested that perceptions of skill are influenced primarily by job characteristics. This particular study, whilst shifting the analysis away from definitions of skill applied by sociologists, does not explore the causal processes that shape workers' subjective perceptions of skill.

It can be concluded that from within the positivist paradigm, research into workplace skills tends to focus on measuring quantifiable attributes in relation to predefined categories that marginalise the subjective perceptions held by workers. This type of research is, furthermore, concerned primarily with the search for regularities between distinct variables. Questions of how particular variables generate particular outcomes are ignored. For these reasons, investigation of subjective perceptions of skill and the causal processes that shape them would not be possible using a positivist framework.

The Neo-Weberian Approach to Skill

From the neo-Weberian perspective, skill is a social construct related to the status accorded to particular occupations. Occupational groups are defined as skilled as a result of their members power to impose meaning on their occupational status, and the ability of some groups to protect themselves from market competition and control access into occupations. From within the broad social constructivist paradigm, different levels of emphasis are placed on the role of social determinism in the construction of skilled status. Braverman, for example, argued that real skill reflected workers powers to not only produce goods, but also to create them. Truly skilled workers have control over creation and accomplishment of work. Under late capitalism, however, the creative power of the worker is subordinate to the power of capital. Skills associated with accomplishment such as dexterity, ability to carry out complex procedures, and limited autonomy are not real skills. The labelling of occupations as skilled results from the ability of groups to secure skilled status and exclude other types of worker. In contrast to this strong social deterministic view, Penn (1982) and More (1982) argue that occupations require varying levels of competency which are not the result of a simple arbitrary definition. However, these competencies alone are not responsible for skilled status, rather skilled status is established through interaction between the power of occupational groups to impose meaning, and the actual competencies required for particular jobs (Attewell 1990).

A number of issues arise in relation to the neo-weberian perspective and research into subjective perceptions of skill. First, if a strong constructivist position were adopted, perceptions of skill would be assumed to be shaped by workers position in relation to the power struggle between capital and particular occupational groups. From a weaker constructivist position, skill would be seen as resulting from interaction between specific task content and socially constructed meanings. I shall demonstrate that the perceptions of skill held by apprentice qualified craft workers at GlassCo and Chemicals UK can to some extent, although not exclusively, be seen in terms of status claims. For these men perceptions of skill are closely related to their experience of the apprenticeship system. However, their perceptions are also shaped by concrete characteristics of their work, and perceptions of skill amongst the group can be partially understood in terms of the weak social constructivist perspective. Nevertheless, adoption of a purely neo-Weberian perspective would negate the main argument of this book: that workforce perceptions of skill are shaped primarily by the concrete characteristics of particular jobs which are themselves generated by firm specific organisational structural features.

Ethnomethodology and Skill

From the ethnomethodological perspective, all human activity requires skill no matter how mundane this activity appears (Attewell 1990). Because skills are a part of everyday existence they are hidden from view, and real skills require little conscious effort. The necessity to engage in conscious thought in order to successfully complete tasks is evidence of defective knowledge, and only when skills are internalised is knowledge complete. Research into skill from the ethnomethodological perspective would aim to uncover the tacit skills involved in seemingly simple tasks (Attewell 1990). This conceptualisation of skill is, however, highly questionable as no account is taken of the conscious effort needed to deal with unfamiliar tasks. In terms of research aimed at uncovering and explaining subjective perceptions of skill, the adoption of a purely ethnomethodological epistemology would create two insurmountable problems. First, once skills are internalised by workers, they would not recognise their own skills as skills. Thus, research to uncover workers' perceptions of skill would be seen as inconsequential. A second problem concerns ethnomethodology's preoccupation with description rather than explanation (Hammersley and Atkinson 1983, May 1993). Interpretation and explanation of the causal processes that shape subjective perceptions of skill, rather than simple description, is the central objective of this book.

Sociology and Subjective Perceptions of Skill

The above sociological perspectives have an in-built tendency to neglect the subjective perceptions held by workers. This is due to the ways in which they define and measure the concept. This book sets out to widen the sociological understanding of skill by uncovering workers own perceptions and the causal processes that shape them. In order to do this, the above paradigms have been rejected in favour of the qualitative realist approach outlined in the book's introduction.

Management Strategies

It will be demonstrated in the case study chapters that management strategies are a highly influential factor in the generation of workforce perceptions of skill. This discussion thus provides a theoretical context through which to understand the nature of management strategies at each firm, and to explain their generative effects with respect to perceptions of skill. For Marx, the fundamental problem for management in the capitalist mode of production is the transformation of workers labour power into productive labour in order to secure valorisation. An important task for management is to achieve control over the labour power of workers. Whilst it is recognised that managerial strategies are concerned with aspects of valorisation other than control over the workforce, for example finance and marketing, it is the control imperative that ultimately influences subjective perceptions of skill.

According to Braverman the sole managerial strategy in the era of monopoly capitalism is Taylorism or scientific management. Strategies promoted as alternatives are, in reality, variations of Taylorism. For others Taylorism is not the only method for achieving control over the labour process, and managerial strategies that emphasise worker autonomy and discretion do represent real alternatives (Burawoy 1985, Friedman 1990).

In later chapters, an assessment of the case study firms' management strategies in comparison to the Taylorist model is made. I also analyse the extent to which workforce perceptions of skill differ in relation to various management strategies. The final objective in relation to this issue is to identify the causal mechanisms that emerge from these various management strategies to generate workforce perceptions of skill. The discussion begins with a brief outline of Taylorist, human relations and neo-Taylorist management strategies. This is followed by a summary of management strategies, and their effects on subjective perceptions of skill in each case study factory. The ultimate aim is to provide a framework through which to interpret the evidence to be presented in Chapters Five, Six and Seven.

Taylorism

The most logical place to begin a typology of managerial strategies is with the alleged dichotomy between the Taylorist and human relations approaches. Taylorism is often presented as an ideal type with which other management approaches can be compared. Burns and Stalker, for example, identify mechanical (i.e. bureaucratic, Taylorist) and organic (flexible, adaptable) systems of management (Burns and Stalker 1961). Friedman identifies direct control, which is an example of Taylorism, and responsible autonomy, which is viewed as an alternative to Taylorism (Friedman 1990). It can be suggested that these dichotomous typologies contain similarities to the Fordist and post-Fordist organisational dichotomies outlined in Chapter Two, for example, the equation of Fordism with Taylorism, and post-Fordism with functional flexibility. There are, however, possible alternatives to this twofold typology. Neo-Taylorism, for example, retains some aspects of Taylorism, yet also embodies features of the human relations approach.

Taylor developed the practice of scientific management in the 1890's during his employment as a supervisor at the Bethlehem Steelworks. Taylor aimed to develop a job design which would facilitate the most efficient production methods. The essence of Taylorism was the decomposition of tasks into their simplest constituent parts, and the subsequent division of labour into specialised jobs. This involved the separation of conception and execution of tasks, a reduction in the skill requirements of particular jobs, and target setting and performance measurement by management. Taylorism thus intensified the degree of control that management could exert over workers. Taylor also stressed the importance of financial incentives in relation to work performance and motivation, and developed the piece rate system of financial rewards. The adoption of the Taylorist system requires a clearly defined and hierarchical style of work organisation in which individual workers are closely supervised, and work effort strongly determined by management. Workers are left with no discretion in the execution of tasks, and are reduced to following the instructions of direct superordinates.

The development of mechanisation and the introduction of Fordism represents an advancement on Taylorism. Under Fordism production is centralised into large production units. The decomposition and specialisation of tasks, and strict Taylorist division of labour is enhanced by the assembly line. Increased intensification of work effort and control is made possible by management's ability to set the speed of the assembly line. The centralisation of production in large units and the Taylorist division of labour is assumed to generate a uniformly semi-skilled and homogenous group of workers with a strong collective consciousness. However, Burawoy suggests that the effect, in reality, is the fragmentation and individuation of workers, and creation of 'skill hierarchies that pit workers against one another' (Burawoy 1985 p. 33).

The extent to which Taylorism has been a feature of UK manufacturing industry is the subject of much dispute. Issues relating to the impact of worker resistance and the need to cultivate worker co-operation, the applicability of Taylorism and Fordism to specific production processes, and problems of co-ordination within production have been cited as limits to the advancement of Taylorism (Littler and Salaman 1985). One particular criticism of Taylorism, advanced by Cressey and MacInnes (1980), relates to Taylor's belief that it should not be possible for workers to improve on the labour process, and that this 'represents the appropriation by capital of *all* the workers subjectivity and skill, to prevent the exercise of their own initiative frustrating the valorisation process' (Cressey and MacInnes 1980 p. 17). These authors point out however, that if labour is to have any value to capital, capital must harness workers' power to create surplus value. They argue therefore that "to abolish dependence on the workers subjective force is to abolish any dependence on their labour as value creating activity: it is to subordinate labour by eliminating it" (Op-Cit. p. 13). It is argued by Littler and Salaman, however, that after taking these limits into consideration 'the direct and indirect influence of Taylorism on factory jobs has been extensive' (Littler and Salaman 1985 p. 90-91). It can be suggested that in order to understand Taylorism in practice, it is necessary to distinguish between the ideal type advanced by Taylor himself and weaker versions that consist of elements of this ideal type. Thus, future references to Taylorism allude to the weaker version. I am not suggesting that, by adopting a Taylorist approach, the case study firms have succeeded in achieving the real subordination of labour. That is, that all the subjectivity and skills of workers have been appropriated. Rather, what I am arguing is that for the majority of workers, skill has been reduced to that which is required for the execution of tasks that vary in levels of complexity. After taking these points into account evidence from the three case study factories shows that the influence of Taylorism in the weaker sense remains pervasive. It will also be shown that the fragmentation of labour and hierarchy of skills suggested by Buroway are evident at GlassCo and Electronics UK, and are reflected in perceptions of skill at the firms.

Human Relations Theory

In contrast to Taylorism, which views workers as mere cogs in the production processes motivated solely by economic rewards, human relations theorists emphasise social factors and human needs as the dynamics which motivate workers. The theory was developed by Elton Mayo and his associates during their research at the Hawthorne works, Chicago between 1927 and 1932. The Hawthorne studies challenged the traditional emphasis on the physical conditions of work and the focus of research was shifted to two further factors. These were work group cohesiveness and solidarity, and relations between foremen and workers. It was found by the Hawthorne researchers that these factors led to the development of behavioural norms which appeared to contradict Taylorist assumptions. For example, the application of group sanctions on workers who exceeded set production targets. Although the subject of later criticism (for a review, Smith 1987, Thompson and McHugh 1995), the outcome of the Hawthorne studies was to stimulate research into the social dimension of production in relation to worker participation, morale and job satisfaction. One particular example is the work of Herzberg who identified two sets of factors that influence worker motivation. The first 'hygiene' relates to the job environment, for example, work conditions and pay. The second, 'motivators' or 'growth factors' is concerned with job content and achievement. If either of these factors is absent, the result will be worker dissatisfaction leading to reduced motivation (Herzberg 1968).

A further strand of the human relations approach is Maslow's theory of human needs (Maslow 1943). Maslow developed a hierarchy of needs consisting of physiological needs (i.e. food, shelter, warmth), safety, love, esteem and finally self actualisation. The majority of people, once they have satisfied the lower level needs, desire a high evaluation of themselves, that is a desire for self-esteem and the esteem of others. The need for self-actualisation can be viewed in more abstract terms and alludes to a desire for self-fulfilment, and a striving to 'become all that one is and everything that one is capable of becoming' (Vroom and Deci 1992 p. 44). A number of incentives appear to have their origins in the human relations framework. Increased autonomy and discretion, and flexibility over task performance and within job design are put forward as moves towards skill enhancement and increased job satisfaction. An assumption that can be argued to be implicit in these initiatives is that a sense of achievement and self-fulfilment at work is related to an increase in the skill content of jobs. The extent to which these initiatives do, in reality, represent a humanisation of production are highly questionable. Autonomy, discretion and flexibility can be argued to be euphemisms for job enlargement and work intensification rather than a shift towards multi-skilling. The approach can also been criticised for its tendency to adopt the management perspective and the emphasis placed on worker motivation.

The relevance of the human relations approach relates directly to the introduction of empowered teamworking at Chemicals UK. This development represents an attempt to apply human relations principles to the firm's production process. It is, furthermore, a partial consequence of the agency of one senior manager who expressed a belief in the human relations approach. I will also demonstrate that the implementation of a human relations strategy, on one production plant in particular, has occurred in conjunction with restrictive forms of technology. The autonomy and discretion that emanates from empowered teamworking on this plant is limited to decisions over the distribution of tasks rather than the manipulation of work. In addition, the adoption of a human relations style approach is intended to increase worker motivation and effort levels rather than a genuine attempt to humanise production. For these reasons, the pseudo human relations approach at Chemicals UK closely resembles a neo-Taylorist system.

Neo-Taylorism

The neo-Taylorist approach adopted at Chemicals UK embodies elements of both Taylorism and human relations strategies. Whilst the setting and measurement of production targets associated with Taylorism remains a feature of the approach, these targets are seen as best achieved through co-operation, functional flexibility and the granting of semi-autonomy to workers. Although a degree of discretion and autonomy over the sharing out of tasks is required of the worker, the result is not necessarily job satisfaction or increased levels of skill. An intensification of effort levels on the part of workers is demanded in order to meet production targets, and to deal with the reduced staffing levels that have occurred in conjunction with the introduction of empowered teamworking. Finally, increased worker flexibility does not necessarily lead to increased skill.

In addition to production plants at Chemicals UK, a broadly neo-Taylorist approach characterises the labour process of craft maintenance workers at GlassCo and Chemicals UK. Maintenance tasks are distributed amongst the men along with clearly defined targets.[2] Once these tasks are allocated, however, craft maintenance workers are responsible for deciding how they should be performed. Thus, as with some production workers at Chemicals UK, worker discretion and autonomy is in tension with constraints built into jobs. Friedman (1990) deals with the issue of worker autonomy in relation to task performance in his theory of responsible autonomy. This theory of does not, howewver, provide an adequate theoretical explanation of the contradictory factors that shape the characteristics of some jobs.

Responsible Autonomy

Friedman (1990) identifies two types of control strategy open to management, each of which represents the extreme end of a continuum of managerial methods, and both of which can be applied within individual firms at any one time. The first, direct control, is closely allied to Taylorism and consists of close supervision of the workforce and minimal worker discretion and responsibility. This form of control is, according to Friedman, generally applied to expendable workers who are peripheral to an organisations core activity. The second, responsible autonomy is applied to skilled core workers who are essential to production. It consists of increased worker discretion, responsibility and status, and involves co-opting workers into company ideologies. It is often linked to job enrichment and increased workforce participation (Thompson 1989). According to Friedman, responsible autonomy is taking on increased importance in the era of monopoly capitalism, and its adoption is influenced by the capacity for workforce resistance and the nature of this resistance. Responsible autonomy is more likely in large production units where labour is well organised. It is also more likely during periods of full employment due to the inability of capitalism to draw on a reserve army of labour, and the resulting increase in the scope for workforce resistance (Friedman 1990).

The view that responsible autonomy represents an alternative to Taylorism can be criticised on the grounds that it is merely a different, and more sophisticated, form of capitalist control aimed at increasing worker motivation and productivity. That is, that reduced levels of supervision and a corresponding increase in worker responsibility signify neo-Taylorist target setting by management, and responsibility for execution left to workers themselves. In addition, the design of jobs remains, fundamentally, in the hands of management. Evidence to be put forward in Chapter Seven also suggests that the dichotomy between direct control and responsible autonomy does not take full account of the tension between the granting of semi-autonomy to workers, and the underlying constraints that characterise some jobs.

Teamworking

A further initiative in the organisation of work is teamworking. Empowered teamworking is an important feature of the labour process at Chemicals UK, and it can be argued that the system is also an example of neo-Taylorism in practice. On a superficial level teamworking appears as an alternative to Taylorism, and refers to a system whereby semi-autonomous groups take collective responsibility for enlarged aspects of production. This contrasts with the Taylorist model where simplified and specialised tasks are the responsibility of individual workers. Teamworking is often put forward as an example of delegative participation in the workplace, and is used to describe a variety of work organisation systems. Geary (1994) identifies three types of teamworking, the first, teamworking in its purest sense, 'refers to the granting of autonomy to workers by management to design and prepare work schedules, to monitor and control their own work tasks and methods and be more or less self managing' (Geary p. 639). A second definition relates to flexibility within skill categories, for example between craft and production workers. On a more basic level teamworking may refer to simple task rotation on a production line. According to Geary, teamworking in its purest sense is limited to a small number of companies (Geary 1994.). In a review of teamworking and autonomy in the Japanese car industry in Europe and Japan, Murakami (1997) identifies four levels of team autonomy. At the lowest level there is no participation by the team in decision making, rather management take the decisions and teams carry them out. The second level involves teams putting forward suggestions which may, or may not, be used by management. Third, co-decision making, refers to shared decision making by managers and workers. Finally, autonomous team decision making refers to teams making decisions totally independent of management. Murakami argues that teamworking in practice rarely embodies high levels of autonomy (Murakami 1997). This conclusion is also drawn by Pollert (1996) who alludes to the possible tension between the granting of semi-autonomy to workers, and the routine and repetitive nature of continuous process and assembly line work. Pollert argues that where work is characterised by technological constraints that limit work to routine and repetitive tasks, and which is designed to meet managerial demands for higher productivity, the introduction of teamworking represents an artificial construct and results in mere task rotation rather than genuine autonomy.

A further dimension concerns the subject matter of decisions. Evidence from the three factories indicates that a distinction should be made between decisions concerning task performance and manipulation of work, and decisions relating to the organisation of tasks. It will be shown that for those workers who have scope for decisions of the former variety, the concepts of discretion and autonomy are perceived as skill, whilst those whose jobs entail the latter type of discretion and autonomy do not perceive these attributes as skills. The shift away from hierarchical direct supervision associated with teamworking appears to signify a relaxation of managerial control over workers. However, such an assumption ignores the forms of control built into the teamwork system. Analysis of the links between Taylorist divisions of labour and teamworking is given in Chapter Seven when teamworking at Chemicals UK is discussed. I will show that the exact forms of control that occur alongside empowered teamworking differ between different types of production plant. I shall also demonstrate that the nature of the system, for example as described by Geary and Murakami, varies between plants.

Management Strategies and Perceptions of Skill

The influence of management strategies on workforce perceptions of skill relates to the various methods of control in the form of management structures and styles, and divisions of labour. With respect to production workers, the classical Taylorist hierarchical management and supervisory structures that characterise GlassCo and Electronics UK generate hierarchically structured perceptions of skill. The flat, non-hierarchical structure at Chemicals UK, on the other hand, generates factory wide vertically structured perceptions of skill. In terms of management styles, close supervision tends to produce perceptions of skill that are articulated in the form of observable and measurable actions. At Chemicals UK the strategy of responsible autonomy generates perceptions of skill that are initially articulated as non-observable or measurable abstract concepts. However, when analysed in more detail it appears that these perceptions do, in reality, reflect underlying constraints that characterise various jobs in the firm. Moving on to the effects of divisions of labour at each firm, these are complex and cannot be properly understood without reference to the articulation of management strategies with technology. Specific combinations between machinery and workers largely generate perceptions of skill.

Finally, it is difficult to identify the exact source of subjective perceptions of skill amongst craft workers at GlassCo and Chemicals UK. It appears that these are generated primarily by apprenticeship qualifications and experience of the apprenticeship system. However, it also appears likely that management strategies have some influence on perceptions. In both organisations management control of craft workers is achieved through a strategy of responsible autonomy over the performance of tasks. Work is performed on an individual rather than team basis and is distributed by a supervisor. Craft workers have complete control over the way in which tasks are performed and are responsible for the finished product. This level of control over the manipulation of raw material is an important factor in the generation of a perception of discretion and autonomy as skill.

Technology

Sociological Approaches to Technology

Analysis of the effects of technology in shaping subjective perceptions of skill cannot be made without brief reference to various sociological approaches to technology. Theories range from technological determinism to those that deny the effects of technology in shaping workplace behaviour and attitudes. From the technological determinist position, technology is awarded the status of an independent variable that determines other aspects of the organisation. The properties of technology are neutral and given, and the approach is rooted in enlightenment models of scientific rationality. An often-cited example of technological determinism is Blauner's 'Alienation and Freedom' (for example Brown 1992, Grint and Woolgar 1997). Blauner argued that the degree of alienation experienced by workers is a direct outcome of the levels of automation found in specific industrial sectors (Blauner 1964). At the opposite end of the spectrum is social determinism. From this perspective, workplace relationships and other worker attitudes are the result of wider social and cultural factors.

Most accounts of the effects of technology in the workplace fall between these deterministic and oppositional theories. The broad socio-technical approach emphasises the links between the technological aspects of production and the social organisation, and/or wider social and cultural influences. Blackburn, Coombs and Green (1985) argue, for example, that advancements in mechanisation do not merely involve the replacement of one machine by another more automated machine. Rather, advancement involves the replacement of one human machine combination by another (Blackburn, Coombs and Green 1985). Similarly, Everts (1998) states that technology is not simply an artefact, it is a total package of the artefact plus the organisational context in which it is embedded. A substantial amount of literature exploring the relationship between technology and other variables such as skill, workplace attitudes and workplace behaviour have been carried out within this broad framework (for example, Cotgrove and Vamplew 1972, Wedderburn and Crompton 1972, Francis 1986, Patrickson 1986, Rolfe 1986 1990, Jones 1988, Kelley 1989, Scarbrough and Corbett 1992).

From the social shaping perspective, the properties of technology, and the effects generated by these properties, are shaped by the political circumstances surrounding their production and implementation (Grint and Woolgar 1997). Hendry, for example, argues that certain social processes influence both the adoption and effects of new technology. These include managerial objectives (for example, increasing productivity and product quality, reducing manning levels and increasing managerial control over the workforce), product market factors, existing skill structures and internal labour markets, and individual, organisational and social relations (Hendry 1990). With the exception of social determinism, these theories commonly assume that, to varying degrees, technology embodies essential core characteristics that are produced by and have effects in interaction with social, economic and political factors.

In contrast to the broad socio-technical approach, Grint and Woolgar (1997) argue in favour of an anti-essentialist theory in which technology is understood as a text that is both embedded in and constitutive of its interpretative context. Seen through this framework, the meaning of technology is a consequence of interpretative readings of the text rather than the result of essential technological properties (Grint and Woolgar 1997). In criticism of this position, it can be argued that even this supposedly anti-essentialist approach incorporates notions of essentialism. If technology as a text is constitutive of its interpretative meaning, an explanation of the origins of the text is necessary.

I am suggesting here that the effects of technology cannot be understood in isolation from the social, economic and political circumstances of its design and implementation, or the social relations that characterise its use. Thus, the approach to technology taken in this book adopts a broad socio-technical perspective. Technology does embody properties which are the outcomes of the agency of past actors, themselves acting within social, economic and political structures, for example, with respect to design and introduction into firms. Nevertheless, once introduced technology is experienced by workers as a structural facilitator or constraint, and is therefore capable of generating causal processes. These processes are however contextual, and the effects of technology on workforce attitudes and behaviour depend on the configuration of other structural factors in each firm. Thus, the differences and similarities with respect to perceptions of skill in each case study are generated by both technology and its relationship to other, firm specific, organisational structural features.

Technology and Skill

Three broad trajectories relating to technology and skill have been outlined earlier. First, the deskilling thesis suggests that increased mechanisation will inevitably lead to deskilling amongst a large majority of the workforce. Second, the upskilling thesis, as associated with some post-Fordist theorists such as Piore and Sabel (1884), suggests that the shift towards flexible manufacturing technology will result in an upskilling or multi-skilling of the workforce. Third, the compensatory theory of skill put forward by Penn suggests that skill trajectories will be uneven due to the diverse nature of modern technologies. Penn also suggests that production workers are likely to be deskilled as a result of new technologies, whilst the maintenance, installation and programming of new automated machinery will result in an upskilling of workers (Penn 1990, 1994).

A particularly optimistic assessment of the effects of automated continuous process production technology in the chemicals industry was put forward by Blauner (1964). He argued that this technology differs from assembly line mass production because jobs in an automated chemical plant cannot be subdivided in the same way as assembly line work, thus reducing the number of standardised jobs and increasing task variety. Work becomes more visual and mental than physical, and chemical operatives are given increased responsibility for product quality, more choice over task performance and more control over the machinery. With respect to skill, continuous process production technology is argued to increase the breadth of knowledge held by the worker, but not necessarily the depth of his understanding. Chemical plant operatives do not, according to Blauner, require an in-depth knowledge of chemistry.

More recent studies that have attempted to provide empirical evidence for and against the deskilling and upskilling theses have tended to focus not on the specific application and capabilities of technology, but on the social organisation of work that accompanies particular technologies. Much of this work has emphasised the split between conception and execution. That is, the way in which the social organisation of work around particular technologies results in the separation of planning and programming functions on one hand, and operation on the other. In direct contrast to Blauner, Nichols and Beynon (1977) show that the division of labour at the ChemCo chemical plant results in the separation of the theoretical and practical aspects of production, and that theoretical knowledge is concentrated in the hands of management. Jobs associated with execution are divided into the 'donkey work' of labourers and the monotonous monitoring of equipment in the control room. The skill required for labouring is physical strength, whilst control room monitors require tacit knowledge gained over a number of years. Nichols and Beynon argue that the division between 'scientific' and 'donkey' work has resulted in the debasement of the practical skills associated with execution.

The advent, in recent years, of computer numerically controlled (CNC) production technology has, according to Jones (1988), resulted in two possible skill trajectories. The first involves the monopolisation of programming and planning tasks in the hands of managers and white collar workers, whilst the second involves programming by blue collar shop floor workers. Jones suggests that in general, the implicit strategy of management is to reduce worker control, and that this tips the balance in favour of task specialisation and deskilling of the workforce (Jones 1988). Hendry (1990), also discussing the impact of CNC machinery, suggests that where operating and programming functions are combined, and blue collar workers are given the opportunity and knowledge to program, and where direct supervision is reduced, the result is a tendency towards upskilling. This outcome is more likely in small factories producing smaller batches, and which require more frequent planning and setting operations. It is argued by Hendry to contrast with the skill trajectories associated with automated flow lines that shift skills away from production and planning towards job planning and maintenance. Patrickson (1986) gives a contrasting example of the impact of new technology in relation to the organisation of work and subsequent deskilling. She provides evidence to show how compositors in the printing industry express attitudes of having been deskilled through the introduction of new technology. In the past compositors had some input into format design and the layout of displays. This function has, however, been taken over by new computerised technology which serves to reduce the role of compositors to one of machine minding.

The basic two-fold division between planning and operation in relation to programmable automation is extended to three by Kelley (1989). She suggests three possible approaches to the application of programmable automation in relation to blue-collar workers. The first, a strict separation between programming and operation, results in strict Taylorist work patterns and a tendency towards deskilling. The second, worker centred control, occurs when planning and programming are delegated to shop-floor workers, and results in the upskilling of these workers. The third possibility, shared control, refers to a system under which programming functions are performed by blue-collar workers whilst programs are written by managers or engineers. The outcome of this system in terms of skill is uneven, and depends upon the balance of tasks between management and workforce.

In an assessment of the extent of upskilling that has accompanied the introduction of flexible automated technology in Germany and the UK, Lane (1988) found that the implementation of such technology in the UK, unlike Germany, has not resulted in a systematic upskilling of production workers. This is largely due to the continued separation of conception and execution in UK industry. In the German car industry, workers are given a good deal of autonomy and responsibility for diagnostic activity, which corresponds with a decrease in repetitive detail work. In the German machine tool industry, workers' conceptual skills are utilised with workers needing both practical expertise and abstract knowledge. This blurring of conception and execution amongst German workers is not repeated in the UK. Here, flexible manufacturing technologies are often combined with a Taylorist organisation of work, and technology is used in way that minimises firms' reliance on skilled labour. The reasons for the partial adoption of flexibility in the UK relates, in part, to the shortage of skilled workers resulting from the decline in the apprenticeship system, and firms unwillingness to invest in long term training. It also relates to management and union struggles, particularly those concerning the retention of craft demarcation lines.

Scarbrough and Corbett (1992) reject the view that workforce skills, in relation to technology, are the result of the social organisation of work that divides conception and execution. They argue that task specialisation does not necessarily imply lower levels of skill, especially with respect to computerised technology which requires abstract knowledge on the part of the user. With regard to perceptions of skill, Scarbrough and Corbett argue that these are not influenced by technology alone. Management attempts to impose meanings on work, such as cosmetic changes in the organisation of work, can also influence workforce perceptions of skill. The case study evidence to be advanced here does not support this latter assertion. Changes in the organisation of work at Chemicals UK, namely responsible autonomy and teamworking, are largely superficial in nature and have a limited effect on subjective perceptions of skill. Rather, underlying job characteristics associated with particular technologies, and the fundamentally neo-Taylorist nature of management strategies primarily shape perceptions.

It is explicit in this discussion that the relationship between technology and skill relates not simply to machinery, but to the way in which the organisation of tasks accord with that machinery. Specifically, the distinctions between conception and execution, and programming and operations. Particular forms of work organisation are not natural or given, and the articulation of technology with the organisation of work is the result of political factors rather than core characteristics of technology. Work is, as Nichols and Beynon argue, organised around technology in a way that suits capital, that is, in a way which best facilitates the creation of profit (Nichols and Beynon 1977). Thus, the perceptions of skill that are generated by interaction between particular technologies and divisions of labour can be argued to be a direct outcome of the capitalist drive for increasing profitability.

Technology and Perceptions of Skill

The generative effects of technology in shaping perceptions of skill at the three case study factories occur in conjunction with other aspects of the labour process. First, the social organisation of work in terms of the division between work associated with conception and work associated with execution. Chapters Five, Six and Seven show that the extent to which functions associated with the design of programs, the performance of programming actions, and the ways in which subsequent machine monitoring are combined or divided produces particular forms of machine-human interaction. This machine-human interaction is closely associated with particular perceptions of skill. Thus, the patterning of perceptions of skill around technology relates not to the specific type of machinery, but to the way in which technology is articulated with human labour.

A second issue in relation to the generative effects of technology is that of its relationship with the managerial strategies discussed earlier. I have argued that there are no necessary combinations between technology and other organisational features. Thus, similar technologies can exist alongside a multitude of organisational forms, for example, with respect to the level of supervision to which workers are subject, and the organisation of workers into teams or as individuals. This dimension of technology in the organisation is, it should be clearly stated, distinguishable from the social organisation of work in terms of the division between conception and execution discussed above. Workers involved in execution only can, for example, be closely supervised or left to work autonomously. Similarly, the organisation of workers into teams, or as individuals, is unrelated to the degree to which their work involves conception and planning. It is the precise nature of the interrelationship between these various factors that generates specific perceptions of skill.

Gender and Skill

The salience of gender as an explanatory concept in relation to work is the subject of recent debate (for example, Siltanen 1994, Alvesson and Due Billing 1997). Before outlining the ways in which gender is a useful explanatory concept in terms of management and workforce perceptions of skill at GlassCo and Electronics UK, three theoretical frameworks concerning gender and employment will be discussed. These are the gendered division of labour, the social construction of skill, and women's attitudes to work.

The horizontal and vertical gendered division of labour is well documented (Dex 1985, Walby 1989, Crompton 1997). Horizontal segregation refers to women's concentration in particular types of occupation such as caring or clerical work. Vertical segregation refers to women's tendency to occupy jobs at the lower levels of the occupational hierarchy. The structural divisions that typify men's and women's employment patterns are argued to have intensified with the shift towards the core and periphery employment patterns identified in Chapter Two. Women make up the overwhelming majority of the part-time peripheral workforce, which itself consists of largely unskilled occupations (Gallie 1996). One particular piece of research that examined the relationship between the structural division of labour and skill was carried out by Horrell, Rubery and Burchell (1994). This study aimed to discover whether women's general low pay was the result of their concentration into low skilled employment sectors, or whether it could be explained by the tendency towards a low valuation of women's skills as indicated by the social constructivist model. Using a sample of 365 men and 333 women drawn from a number of employment sectors, the study developed a number of dimensions on which to base a measurement of skill. These included education and training, degree of discretion, job content (i.e. various social and technical attributes), length of time needed to learn the job, responsibilities and degree of supervision required. The main finding of the study was that 'there is a relatively systematic tendency for men to occupy more skilled jobs than women' (Op. Cit. P. 211). This finding suggests that the low skill status that is often accorded to women results from the nature of the division of labour. This difference was found to decline, however, if only full-time jobs are compared. The results thus indicate that skill differences between men and women correlate with the full-time, part-time split between the sexes in terms of employment patterns at the macro-level.

The second theoretical framework relevant to this research relates to the social construction of skill. Much of the work on gender and skill is carried out within the neo-Weberian framework, and begins with the argument that there is a tendency for women's work to be devalued in terms of skill content. This is, it is argued, the result of wider social ideologies that emphasise women's domestic roles. It is the inferior status of the domestic role that determines the status of women's work. The view that the skills associated with women's work are socially constructed as inferior to men's is advanced by a numerous authors (for example, Coyle 1982, Dex 1988, Bradley 1989, Steinberg 1990, Wajcman 1991, England 1992). Steinberg, for example, argues that the skills associated with women's work are not accorded as high a value as men's skill by employers, and suggests that 'the evaluation of skill is shaped by and confounded with a workers sex' (Steinberg p. 452). She also suggests that job characteristics taken to indicate skill when applied to men are ignored in relation to women's jobs (Ibid). Even where women's skills are taken into consideration for the purposes of job evaluation, they tend to be valued at a lower level than those associated with male jobs.

Wajcman (1991), who also argues that the collective struggles of working class men to retain skilled status have served to exclude female workers, supports this view. Wajcman also recognises, however, that women often lack access to technological skill training, and therefore to the power to achieve skilled status. In a study of women sewing machinists working for Ford during the 1960s, Fraser (1999) shows that women's lack of access to industrial training was instrumental in denying them skilled status. The exclusion of women from training and their lack of access to technology results in the identification of technological competence as a masculine attribute. To understand this identification of technology with masculinity, reference can be made to the division of labour within the household. Many female occupations are a reflection of women's domestic roles, for example, catering, cleaning and the caring professions, whilst men work with tools and machines. Even where women do engage with technology in their work, this aspect of their job is often devalued. Wajcman cites the nursing profession as an example of how women's relationship with technology is ignored in the social construction of skill. Whilst nurses display high levels of technical competence, the job is generally defined in terms of its caring and interpersonal aspects (Wajcman 1991). Even in manufacturing occupations that do not reflect the female domestic role, women's occupations can still be shaped by ideas of domesticity. In her study of 'Stitchco', Westwood (1984) found that men worked as mechanics whilst women worked with sewing machines and irons. That is, women worked with tools they used in the domestic sphere whilst men were responsible for maintenance and repair.

In summary, the way in which skill is conceptualised serves to devalue the skills held by many female workers, and women have tended to lose out in the struggles over skilled status between capitalism and male craft workers. The impact of the identification of technology as masculine, and domesticity as feminine has been to reinforce the gender bias in the social construction of skill.

A third body of literature pertinent to an exploration of gender and perceptions of skill is that of mens' and women's work values. It is argued by Dex (1988) that early studies in industrial sociology either ignored women's experiences, or emphasised differences between men and women. She also argues that past research has been inconsistent in its approach to men and women. Men's attitudes are analysed in terms of the 'job model' which focuses on the importance of work in shaping attitudes, whilst women's attitudes are analysed in terms of the 'gender model' which emphasises the importance of family and personal characteristics. Drawing on a variety of studies, Dex demonstrates that male and female attitudes to work display more similarities than differences. This argument is supported by Siltanen (1994) whose own research suggests that little gender differentiation exists in terms of the emphasis placed on the importance of family life and employment by men and women.

A further study aimed to discover whether women's work values are best understood in terms of the gender socialisation model, which states that women's attitudes are explicable in terms of their prior socialisation, or the social structural model which states that women's attitudes are explicable in terms of structural job related factors. This study by Rowe and Snizek (1995) shows that there are few differences between men and women with respect to work values. Rather, differences are unrelated to gender, and are largely determined by age, education and occupational prestige. It should be noted, however, that the research sample used by Rowe and Snizek were all full-time workers, and the authors suggest that women located in peripheral employment may display different work attitudes. A longitudinal study by Tolbert and Moen (1998) examined the impact of gender and age on men's and women's work values. This study adopted a job model rather than a 'gender model' towards women's attitudes. Interviewees were asked to list their preferences in relation to five job attributes: hours, income, meaningful work, promotion and security. The evidence suggested that gender differences in relation to preferences for particular job attributes had remained relatively small, or non-existent, for the past twenty years. Although some differences between younger male and female workers have emerged over recent years, these remain small (Tolbert and Moen 1998).

Finally, in a survey of 8,000 bank employees and 2,884 white collar university employees, Emslie, Hunt and Macintyre (1999) found that occupational position rather than gender is the stronger predictor of perceptions of lack of job stimulation amongst men and women. They argue that job characteristics are important factors for both men's and women's perception of their working environment. It can be concluded from the above evidence, that the attitudes of women in relation to work are best understood in terms of the structural features of jobs rather than gender socialisation models. This book is concerned with a questioning of whether the same argument can be applied to women's perceptions of skill. It is argued by Emslie, Hunt and Macintyre that attempts to compare men's and women's attitudes to work are hindered by the gendered labour market structure. The emphasis on causal processes taken in this book overcomes this problem to some extent, and I shall argue later that the job model provides the most useful framework for understanding the perceptions of skill held by both men and women.

The relevance of the above theoretical frameworks relate to four particular issues. First, female workers at GlassCo and Electronics UK are subject to a gendered horizontal and vertical division of labour. Women at Electronics UK are, for example, largely concentrated on the assembly line. These jobs require less training, and are characterised by a high level of close supervision. They also contain little technical skill in comparison to jobs that are performed mainly by men. At GlassCo women are again concentrated in the lower levels of the occupational hierarchy. Although both men and women at both factories occupy these jobs, few women achieve promotion into higher-grade jobs. In addition to this, the low skilled part-time workforce at GlassCo consists only of women. This evidence suggests that women are concentrated in lower skilled work regardless of whether they are employed full-time or part-time. It does not, however, contradict the findings of Horrell, Rubery and Burchell, that the differences between men and women correspond to the full-time, part-time split. Their evidence is taken from a large sample employed in a variety of occupations, whereas this research concentrates on a small number of women employed in low skill occupations in two case study factories. It is therefore impossible to make generalisations on the basis of my evidence. The main question in relation to the issue is whether the perceptions of skill held by women will reflect the gendered division of labour in the two factories. The case study evidence from all three factories suggests that divisions of labour have a substantial influence on perceptions of skill amongst *all* workers regardless of gender. The evidence also demonstrates that at GlassCo and Electronics UK, strong similarities exist amongst men and women situated in similar, and in a small number of cases the same, occupational groups.

Second, management perceptions of female workers' skills at GlassCo and Electronics UK are best understood in terms of the social constructivist model. At both firms managers accord less value to the skills held by women than those held by men. In addition, at both firms women are excluded from jobs that require high levels of technological training and competence. Where women do work with technology at Electronics UK, they are concentrated in lower status jobs. They are, furthermore, denied access to training that would open up opportunities to work in more complex technological occupations. The identification of technological competence as a masculine attribute appears strong at both firms and managers, at Electronics UK in particular, express highly gendered perceptions of skill. Third, with respect to male and female work values, and the gender socialisation and structural job models, evidence from this research suggests that the structural job model is the most useful for understanding both men's and women's perceptions of skill.

Conclusion

This chapter has discussed four key theoretical issues: sociological definitions of skill, management strategies, technology and skill, and gender and skill. The objective is to provide a theoretical context through which to interpret the evidence to be advanced in the three case study chapters. The chapter began with a discussion of the concept of skill itself. This paves the way for an analysis of the differences and similarities between sociological definitions of skill, and the perceptions held by managers and workers. The discussion also presented an explanation of why the positivist, neo-Weberian and ethnomethodological paradigms do not facilitate research aimed at uncovering subjective perceptions of skill, and the causal processes that shape them.

The chapter then moved on to discusses managerial strategies, and to outline the strategies employed in the three case study firms. All three display strong evidence of Taylorist and/or neo-Taylorist approaches, and even where human relations strategies are adopted, there is, in reality, little difference in practice between this and Taylorism. Initiatives such as responsible autonomy and teamworking were argued not to signify a shift towards the humanisation of work, rather they are examples of neo-Taylorism in practice. These issues will be developed fully in Chapter Seven during the discussion of Chemicals UK. For now it is merely pointed out that management strategies are important factors in shaping subjective perceptions of skill.

This chapter then discussed technology and its possible effects on perceptions of skill. I argued that a socio-technical approach provides the most useful framework for understanding the causal processes that shape subjective perceptions of skill. The effects of technology relate to the configuration of it and human labour, particularly with respect to the division between planning, programming and operation. That is, between the conception and execution of work. Finally, this chapter has explored some theoretical issues of gender and work. At both case study factories where women are employed there is a marked gendered division of labour. The division of labour plays an important role in influencing subjective perceptions of skill, regardless of the gender of job incumbents. Finally, it was argued that women's attitudes to work are best understood in the context of structural job models rather than gender socialisation models. It was also suggested that, as is the case for men, the job model is most likely to provide the most useful framework for understanding women's perceptions of skill and the causal processes that shape them.

The second half of the book is concerned with examining subjective perceptions of skill, core and periphery in relation to the theoretical debates given in this and the previous chapter. Before moving directly on to the three case studies, Chapter Four will provide an outline of the general model to explain subjective perceptions of skill.

Notes

[1] Interviewees in this study were also questioned directly about their views on discretion and autonomy as skills. The reason for this is that the concepts of discretion and autonomy are often put forward as important elements of skill (for example, Spenner 1990, Burchell, Elliot, Rubery and Wilkinson1994, Horrell, Rubery and Burchell 1994). I conclude, therefore, that the perceptions and definitions of these concepts as skill held by workers is an important area of investigation.

[2] At GlassCo for example, moulds for containers must be made to precise measurements whilst at Chemicals UK work performed by craftsmen must meet specified safety targests.

4 The Model

Construction of the Realist Model

This chapter presents a model of the processes shaping subjective perceptions of skill that is grounded in realist theory. It begins by outlining some of the basic principles of realism that have informed the data collection and construction of the model. This entails a brief digression to describe some principles of realism and an explanation of why specific causal powers have been defined as either structural or agency mechanisms. Finally, the chapter presents the model to explain subjective perceptions of skill, and the causal processes that shape them.

Realist Social Theory

The first principle of Realism is that the social world can only be fully understood through the identification of causal mechanisms that link social objects. This involves a rejection of the positivist assumption that the social world can only be understood through the identification of observed regularities between phenomena. For researchers working in a positivist tradition, social reality is explained by the identification of constant conjunctions between variables which are then assessed for their predictive power using statistical techniques of analysis. Statistical significance between regularities is taken as evidence that these regularities can be generalised from the survey sample to the whole of the population under investigation. This form of positivist research is designed to approximate the experimental methods of the physical sciences. From the positivist perspective explanation of social events is reduced to the identification of the conditions necessary for an event to occur. Whilst this enables predictions relating to observable social phenomena, the realist would object that it does not allow for an explanation of why these phenomena occur. In terms of the proposed model, the searching out of constant conjunctions relating to perceptions of skill would show what factors are associated with particular perceptions of skill. It could not however explain why these relationships occur. For realists, the knowledge gained from identifying regularities is incomplete. According to Bhaskar (1979), theories in social science should concern themselves with explanation rather than prediction. In order to make this explanation possible, the underlying generative mechanisms that link phenomena must be identified and described (for example, Keat and Urry 1982, Pawson 1989, May 1993, Archer 1995, Reed 1997). Only by describing the complex processes through which one factor or variable generates a specific outcome can a true theory of causation be formulated. Thus, the object of Realist inquiry is to discover the emergent properties of structures, cultures and agents, and to then uncover and describe the ways in which these properties interact to create the social world.

A further principle that underpins the proposed general model relates to the stratified nature of society, and discussion of this issue draws heavily on the work of Archer (1995). The starting point for Archer's conceptualisation of the social world is that it is stratified consisting of both people and parts. People and parts are not aspects of the same thing, rather they are entirely separate entities which produce their own emergent properties. They must, therefore, be analysed independently of one another in order that the interplay between each can be uncovered and explained. This entails an analytical dualism that is at odds with competing theories which attempt to conflate structure and agency. Archer identifies three types of conflation which prevent a clear understanding of social reality. A brief digression to describe these conflationary theories will be made in order to highlight the dualistic principle that underpins this model. First is the notion of downwards conflation which is associated with strong structuralist versions of society. From this ontological position the parts, that is the structures, are viewed as determining the actions of people. Individuals are merely agents of structure who are never acknowledged as having the ability to engender social change. Such a reification of the social structure can be argued to marginalise the capabilities of human beings to act and think in an autonomous manner. It results in what Archer terms an over socialised or over determined view of wo/man. One particular problem with this approach is that it fails to provide a satisfactory explanation of social change. Change must take place at the level of structure, for example, through the systematic adaptation of features that are already present in the structure to impersonal forces or factors.

The second form of conflation criticised by Archer is the upwards conflation associated with neo-phenomenology and methodological individualism. From this ontological framework, structure is seen to be the outcome of the actions and beliefs of current agents. The correct area of study for sociology is everyday life, and the ways in which individuals construct their own social reality through interaction with others. Structure, from a phenomenological perspective, is reduced to the effects of the actions of other agents. A major problem with this ontology is the assumption that it is the actions of contemporary agents that shape contemporary society. Social change is deemed to be possible if enough people desire it and are in possession of enough knowledge to bring it about. This assumption is criticised by Archer who argues that there are some structures that cannot be changed immediately, regardless of how many people want change and have the resources to bring it about. Thus, whilst structuralism marginalises agency, neo-phenomenology and methodological individualism marginalise structure. Both ontological frameworks are partial in that they deal with only one strata of social reality (Ibid.).

The third and final type of conflation referred to by Archer is central conflation. This form of conflation is associated with theories such as Giddens structuration theory, and what Reed terms 'Foucauldian inspired post structuralism' (Reed 1997 p.23). The main argument of structuration theory is that structure and agency are mutually constituted, that is that they form two sides of the same coin. Structure is generative of action but at the same time is itself constituted by action. According to Archer, structuration theory puts forward the notion of duality of structure, and which is in direct opposition to the analytical dualism advocated here. Two particular criticisms of this position are put forward by Archer. First, she argues that the interplay between structure and agency over time is not adequately dealt with. Second, structure and agency cannot be examined independently of one another except by using some sort of artificial exercise in methodological bracketing (Archer 1995). A further criticism of structuration theory is advanced by Mouzelis (1991) and relates to Giddens conceptualisation of structure. According to Giddens structure refers to rules and resources. He argues that "…social systems, as reproduced social practices, do not have "structures" but rather exhibit "structural properties…" (Giddens 1994 p. 80). Structure, as a set of rules and resources, is both a medium and outcome of the conduct that organises it (Mouzelis 1991 p. 26). Mouzelis argues that the problem with Giddens duality of structure is that the agency-structure relationship it implies, with respect to rules and resources, is not the only possible relationship. He argues that different types of actor have different orientations to rules and resources. He distinguishes between actors drawing on rules and resources in daily conduct, and actors who use rules not as a resource, but as a topic of inquiry. Mouzelis gives, as an example, the difference between husbands and wives who draw on rules and resources that surround marriage in everyday life, and who therefore reproduce it, and feminists who study the rules of marriage in order to change them. The first example can be explained by duality of structure, whilst the second can only be explained as a subject - object dualism (Mouzelis 1991).

In terms of Foucauldian social theory, this is argued to stem from Foucault's hostility to all forms of realist and structuralist analysis (Reed 1997). Reed suggests that from this post-structuralist ontology social reality is viewed as being chaotic and fragmented, and is in a constant state of change. It cannot be understood through static mechanistic conceptual frameworks which fail to capture the complex and processual nature of social reality. According to Reed, this hostility towards dualism leads to a 'process dominated social ontology and its inherent analytical tendency to collapse agency and structure into localised or micro-level social practices' (Op-Cit.).[1] In criticism of this perspective, Reed argues that by collapsing structure and agency into a flat undifferentiated strata, structure is disconnected from the agency that originally engendered it, for example, from the agency of previous generations. Additionally, the role played by structure in constraining or enabling agency is concealed or ignored (Reed 1997).

In contrast to the above conflationary theories, Archer proposes a dualistic approach in which equal weight is given to the separate strata of structure and agency. Her model places strong emphasis on the notions of emergence, interplay and temporality. She argues that whilst the properties that emerge from structures and cultures do not determine the actions of agents, they constrain the possibilities and opportunities open to them. An example of this is the types of conversation possible in a primitive society. Although conversations my be complex they will not include discussions of atomic physics (Archer 1995). Agency is thus constrained by structures and cultures that pre-exist present day agents.

Realists do not argue, however, that structures are formed independently of agency. The structural and cultural systems that exist at any one time are the outcome of action by previous generations of agents, who were themselves subject to the constraints of earlier structures. Agency does not have the power to build new structures independently of the structures that already exist. What it does have is the power to transform or recreate existing structural and cultural formations. The processes of transformation and recreation are termed by Archer morphogenisis and morphostasis. It is as a result of the interplay between the parts and the people at any one time that society is transformed or recreated.[2] Archer argues that in order to gain an understanding of a particular area of the social world it is necessary to carry out historical research. This enables an analysis of how the interplay between the emergent properties, or generative mechanisms, of each strata in society lead to change or stability. In terms of this research, however, a historical approach was not feasible. Case study research only allows for a snapshot view of reality at any one point in time. Thus, whilst the model draws upon the broad framework set out by Archer it is adapted to the requirements of this type of case study research. What is under investigation here is the identification of emergent properties, and the resulting causal processes that shape subjective perceptions of skill, core and periphery. This entails a discrete analysis of generative mechanisms that originate at the level of structures and people, and a description of the interactive processes that occur between these mechanisms to shape subjective perceptions of skill, and core and periphery at one particular point in time.

It can, on the other hand, be suggested that the research does identify some changes occurring over time. I shall show how changes in product markets have led to changes in senior management personnel, and the organisation of work at Chemicals UK. At GlassCo, changes in the product market and in ownership have led to the introduction of new, flexible technology. Finally, at Electronics UK the utilisation of a JIT production system is an example of changes in the articulation between supply and demand associated with post-Fordist theory.

Generative Mechanisms: Structure and Agency

Before providing an outline of the introductory model, reference needs to be made to the rationale behind the labelling of particular mechanisms as structural or as resulting from human agency. Beginning with the decision to define organisational features as structural mechanisms, it will be suggested in the model that these features are, in part, a result of strategic choice on the part of powerful individuals and groups rather than simply being determined by sectoral and product market factors. It will be proposed later in this chapter, and in the forthcoming case study chapters, that management structures and styles, and the organisation of work, are the possible result of both strategic choice on the part of powerful corporate actors and a response to uncertain product markets. If these organisational features are influenced by strategic choice the question of whether they can be correctly described as structural mechanisms should be asked. Would it not be more accurate to describe them as resulting from the agency of powerful individuals and groups within the firm? In response to this question it can be argued that whilst management strategies are shaped to some extent by strategic choice and therefore the agency of the powerful, once in place they become structural features which embody causal powers. This argument draws on the work of both Mouzelis (1991, 1993) and Archer (1995). Mouzelis questions the traditional sociological tendency to equate macro level phenomena with structure and micro level phenomena with agency. He argues that (micro) encounters between two or three powerful individuals can have (macro) structural consequences. What gives a phenomena a macro character is not the number of individuals involved, rather it is the type of actor and the consequences of interactional situations. He gives, as an example of a macro encounter between three individuals, the meetings between Stalin, Roosevelt and Churchill at Yalta in 1944 (Mouzelis 1991). Thus, the consequences of decisions taken by two or three actors may constrain or enable the actions and perceptions available to less powerful individuals and groups, and are therefore experienced as structural factors.

The arguments put forward by Mouzelis bear strong similarities to those put forward by Archer. Drawing on the work of these authors, it can be argued that structures can be the result of agency, both past and present. In the context of this model to explain perceptions of skill, all the organisational structural features identified could be viewed as the outcome of agency. Technology, for example, is designed and purchased by agents acting now or in the past. However, once designed, purchased and implemented, technology takes on the characteristics of a structural property which embodies causal powers that can constrain or enable the agency of some individuals. It is therefore conceptualised as a structural emergent property of the organisation.

In terms of individual and agency mechanisms, two issues require clarification prior to the delineation of the model. The first concerns the extent to which the causal processes inherent in individuals' emergent properties can be described as agency mechanisms, whilst the second relates to the role of agency in general. The salience of the first question relates to the implications of particular definitions with respect to the stratified and dualistic approach taken. The two individual level mechanisms identified as generating subjective perceptions of skill are prior qualifications and the direction of individuals' employment trajectories. It could be suggested that these causal mechanisms are more accurately described as individual expressions of structural processes. It is the wider economic, labour market and social structure that produces and distributes education, training and employment opportunities. However once these opportunities are distributed and consumed by individuals the experience gained from them becomes the property of the individual. Workers take their qualifications with them as they move between jobs, and these qualifications become the property of the individual as well as properties of the economic and social structure. They represent a resource on which individuals can draw in relation to their current and future actions. Thus, opportunities for education and training that originate at the level of the capitalist system are, over time, transformed into properties of individual agency. This is not to argue, however, that qualifications as an attribute of agency are independent of structure. It is argued by Savage, Barlow, Dickens and Fielding (1992) that qualifications are the property of individuals, but their value cannot be realised independently of organisational structures. This argument supports Archer's view that agency is constrained by structures that pre-exist individuals.

With respect to individuals' employment trajectories, these are the result of people taking up available employment opportunities. Whilst the availability of employment opportunities are determined by the structures of capitalism, it can be suggested that an individual's decision to take up available opportunities is the result of conscious human agency. This not to deny that a workers choice in accepting or rejecting employment is not constrained by labour market structures, rather it is argued that such choice is also shaped by human agency. Both prior qualifications and employment trajectories can, therefore, be accurately described as agency mechanisms.

The second issue in relation to structure and agency concerns the general significance of agency in the proposed explanatory model. It could be argued that the proposed model puts forward an overly structural and deterministic account of the generation of subjective perceptions of skill, core and periphery. Mechanisms originating at the level of firm specific structural features generate worker definitions of skill that are passively consumed and internalised by individuals. Such an interpretation of the evidence would, however, deny the human activity involved in the construction of knowledge. Subjective perceptions of skill, core and periphery are inseparable from interviewees own knowledge of their social world, knowledge that is itself constructed through activity in the world. Writing in relation to the activity of human labour Sayer argues that:

> The process of knowing in this context derives a certain kind of check through feedback from the results of work - not just through observing the world passively as if it were external to us, in order to see if our knowledge 'mirrors' it successfully - but from the results of material

activity, as one of natures forces, operating within nature (Sayer, 1992, p. 18).

By adopting this agency view of the acquisition of knowledge, it can be argued that the act of perceiving skill, core and periphery constitutes human agency. When individuals draw on their own personal salient reference point from which to consider skill, they are drawing on a personal knowledge that is itself partially constructed through their own agency.

The Model

Evidence from the three case study factories indicates that perceptions of skill and their causal processes are highly contextual. They occur in relation to particular organisational structures, and the emergent properties of individuals employed in organisations. The proposed model of the processes that shape workforce perceptions of skill is given in figure 6.1, and takes the form of a loose framework through which to explain the complex causal processes and perceptions of skill found in particular firms. Whilst the model will attempt to move beyond the specificity's of individual firms, evidence to be advanced in Chapters Five, Six and Seven will be referred to in order to illustrate the general arguments put forward. It will be suggested in the model that the capitalist system of production serves to generate emergent properties which contain causal powers. The specific nature of these emergent properties and causal powers vary in relation to particular contexts. These variations are inevitable given the openness of social systems: that is of the organisations under consideration. This openness relates to the changeable nature of firms' product markets and financial performance, and the transfer of personnel in and out of organisations. Of particular importance is the influx of new senior management personnel who have the power to change organisational structures. It will also be argued in the model that the emergent properties of capitalism are stratified in that they exist on a number of levels: at the levels of the capitalist system and particular product markets, and at the levels of the organisation and the individual.

Diagram 6.1: The Causal Processes That Shape Workforce Perceptions of Skill

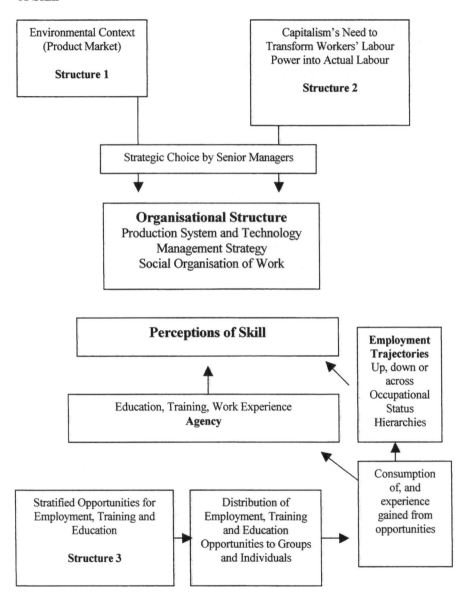

Workers' Perceptions of Skill

The subjective perceptions of skill held by workers develop through active and conscious engagement of individuals in the labour process. This conscious activity facilitates the construction of work related knowledge that forms a reference point through which individuals consider the subject of skill. Perceptions of skill occur at the point at which the causal powers of firm specific emergent properties intersect with the causal powers of peoples' emergent properties. That is, at the point of contact between structure and agency. In order to provide a generalised account of the complex set of mechanisms that are described in Chapters Five, Six and Seven, and which ultimately shape subjective perceptions of skill, it is necessary to explain the processes that shape these mechanisms. Description of the model begins, therefore, with three emergent properties of capitalism that are the original source of the network of processes that generate subjective perceptions of skill. Each property will be described and its causal processes delineated. It will be demonstrated, however, that there is considerable interaction between the causal powers of various properties, and that this interaction generates effects that are unique to specific organisations. Three types of property to emerge at the level of the capitalist system contain causal powers that give rise to the processes that eventually shape subjective perceptions of skill. These are the instability of particular product markets, the necessity for capitalism to transform the labour power of workers into productive labour, and the stratified employment market structure.

It is a major theme of the post-Fordist theories described in Chapter Two that changeable consumer demand patterns have led to a shift away from production geared towards standardised mass markets, towards production geared to niche speciality markets. The relationship between product markets and organisational structures is given in box 1 of diagram 6.1. In order to cope with changing demand patterns, firms are attempting to introduce flexibility into production systems. The case study firms are all operating in conditions of product market uncertainty, and all have introduced flexibility into the production process. The extent and type of flexibility adopted by organisations and the inherent causal processes are dependent on a variety of other factors, for example, strategic choice by senior managers and the types of technology available. With respect to the causal powers of these different types of flexible production system in terms of subjective perceptions of skill, again there is no direct cause and effect linear relationship. The powers of different forms of technology are not inherent in the machinery, rather they operate in relation to their articulation with the social organisation of work in particular factories. This leads to a consideration of the second emergent property of capitalism, the need for capitalism to transform the labour power of employees into actual labour. The relationship between this property of capitalism and organisational structures in given in box 2, diagram 6.1. It was suggested, in chapters Two and Three, that capitalism is able to employ a range of managerial strategies in its attempt to control the labour power of workers, and to facilitate the production and appropriation of surplus profits. These various strategies possess causal powers that shape subjective perceptions of skill. The causal powers of managerial strategies relate to the structure of management, the style of managerial supervision and the social organisation of work. At the two case study firms, GlassCo and Electronics UK, that are characterised by a hierarchical management structure, direct supervision and a traditional Taylorist division of labour, perceptions of skill are also hierarchically structured and task specific. In contrast to this, the management structure at Chemicals UK is less hierarchical, and the style of management supervision approximates the responsible autonomy model. Work is organised around teams rather than individuals. The effects in terms of subjective perceptions of skill are perceptions that occur horizontally across plants, and that are initially expressed as abstract personal competencies of knowledge, training and experience. These concepts were broken down into task related competencies only when interviewees were asked to elaborate upon their responses

A particularly important issue concerning the social organisation of work relates to its articulation with production system and technology, specifically the extent of the separation between planning, programming and operating functions. The causal powers inherent in production systems and technology interact with those of the social organisation of work to generate contextualised perceptions of skill. Previous research discussed in Chapter Three suggests that the effects on skill of technology are dependent on the extent to which operators have responsibility for planning and programming. The case study evidence to be advanced later supports this argument. When putting forward this case study evidence, I shall draw out patterns relating to the combined effects of technology and the social organisation of work. These patterns do not concern the type of technology, rather they concern the causal powers of technology in terms of subjective perceptions of skill. The first combination of technology and social organisation of work is characterised by a high level of integration between planning, programming and operation. This combination is confined to a small number of workers employed at Chemicals UK, and generates perceptions of skill that are categorised as theoretical knowledge. The second combination of technology and social organisation of work is one in which operators have no responsibility for planning, but do have responsibility for programming. This programming responsibility is, however, limited due to a variety of constraints built into particular jobs. This combination applies to various groups of workers in all three factories, and generates perceptions of skill that are articulated in terms of the practical competencies needed to operate machinery. The third combination of technology and social organisation of work occurs where the roles of workers are completely controlled by technology. This combination relates to assembly line operators at GlassCo and Electronics UK. The relationship between this group and machinery is, for example, limited to switching machines on and off when told to do so by others, and to machine minding the automated sorting machines. It shall be demonstrated in Chapter Five that interviewees from this group at GlassCo express no perceptions of skill whatsoever. I will argue that this is explicable, in part, by the simplistic and unskilled nature of the tasks performed. For assembly line operators at Electronics UK, the relationship with technology is limited to performing tasks brought to them by the flowline, and it will be argued in Chapter Six that perceptions of skill amongst this group are articulated in terms of discrete assembly line tasks.

A key assertion to be advanced in the next three chapters is that workers will only perceive discretion and autonomy to be skills where there is *real* scope for the manipulation of work. Artificial attempts to introduce discretion and autonomy into the labour process, such as team working at Chemicals UK and an attempt by GlassCo to impart notions of discretion and autonomy as skill through NVQ training, are in tension with the technological and managerial constraints built into jobs. These constraints limit the scope for discretion and autonomy within work, and thus constrain the generation of these concepts as skill amongst the majority of workers.

A final issue concerning production systems, technology and managerial strategies is that of the impact of JIT production at Electronics UK. It will be demonstrated that this JIT strategy is closely integrated with technology and the Taylorist management structure and style. The impact of JIT production is to generate firm specific perceptions of skill, which focus on the ability to cope with pressure amongst supervisory and managerial staff, and notions of speed and accuracy as skill amongst workers.

The above model suggests that management strategies, in conjunction with production systems and technology, are influential in shaping workers' perceptions of skill. They are furthermore, a response to firms need to control the labour force in order to secure the production and appropriation of surplus value. The variable nature of the strategies adopted, both between firms and within individual firms, suggests that the particular strategies utilised are contingent on other factors, and that the effects of management strategies on perceptions of skill need to be placed in the specific context of their occurrence. Two particular factors are each firm's product market and the strategic choices made by senior managers. The significance of the agency of senior managers in shaping organisational structures is explicit in the work of Child (1997). He puts forward a model of strategic choice in which managers evaluate information that is both internal and external to the organisation, and use this information to make strategic choices. It can also be argued that personal experience and preference influence the actions of managers. The relationship between product markets and the historic need for capitalism to transform the labour power of workers into actual labour, strategic choice by managers, and organisational structures is given at the top of diagram 6.1.

With respect to the impact of strategic choice on management strategies at the three case study firms, evidence to be put forward in Chapter Five suggests that the introduction of new flexible technology at GlassCo is the result of strategic choice on the part of the new senior management team. Namely, to shift production into new niche market areas in response to the environmental conditions. The decision to adopt a hierarchical management structure and close direct supervisory style appears to be an outcome of middle managers evaluation of the industrial relations situation at the firm, and the perceived lack of abilities amongst the workforce. It will be shown in Chapter Five that managers at the firm explicitly reject human relations style strategies. This is due to their belief that the workforce would fail to perform if allowed any level of responsibility or autonomy. It will be demonstrated in Chapter Seven that the decision to adopt the human relations style teamwork system at Chemicals UK was a partial outcome of decreasing profitability in the early 1990s, and the ensuing need to cut staffing levels. That is by management's evaluation of the external and internal circumstances facing the firm. It will also be shown that this decision results, in part, from the beliefs and actions of one particular manager. Finally, in the case of Electronics UK it is impossible to draw any conclusions on this issue due to the refusal of senior Japanese managers to take part in the research.[3] In conclusion, it is suggested that the management strategies adopted by firms are highly contextual, and are shaped by factors that are both internal and external to the firm.

Running parallel to these structural properties and their causal powers, and to the strategic choices made by managers, are the causal processes inherent in the emergent properties of individual workers. These individual level properties can be traced back to the third emergent property of capitalism: the stratified employment structure. At any one time the capitalist system will contain a range of opportunities for education, training and employment. Individuals take up, or are directed into, these structural positions within the capitalist labour process, and their active labour and interaction with these structural positions results in the construction of a personal work related knowledge. This knowledge then becomes an emergent property of the individual. This process is depicted at the bottom of diagram 6.1, and begins with the stratified employment, education and training market that characterises capitalism, and which is shown in box 3. An illustration of how this structural property of capitalism influences perceptions of skill is evident in relation to the craft apprenticeship system.

Evidence from two of the three case study firms indicates, not surprisingly, that a particularly important factor in shaping perceptions of skill amongst skilled craftsmen is the craft apprenticeship system. The reasons for this relate to both the strong skilled occupational identities generated by the apprenticeship system, and the concrete aspects of the craftsman's role. It is argued by Liepmann (1960) that the strength of the apprenticeship system relates to its long history, and its position with respect to the control of entrants into skilled occupations. She suggests that there is no clear distinction between apprenticeship training and other forms of learning other than the long educational servitude of the system. It is this educational servitude that supports the craftsman's claim to the exclusive right to particular occupations and status. Penn repeats this view in a more recent account of the impact of the apprenticeship system on skilled occupational identities (Penn 1990). He puts forward a number of arguments to explain the strong skilled identities of British craftsmen. First is the suggestion that certain occupations are 'actively structured around skilled identities' (Penn 1990 p. 124). Second, young apprentices are socialised into skilled identities by older craftsmen, both in terms of the technical aspects of work and the behavioural aspects. He argues, however, that the principal ingredients of socialisation into craft identity relate not to technical aspects, but to the norms, values and appropriate forms of behaviour, for example, how to relate to members of other craft skilled occupations, unskilled workers and managers.

The neo-Weberian arguments put forward by these authors appear to suggest that the skilled identities and perceptions of skill held by craftsmen are an outcome of socialisation rather than the actual skill training that takes place during the apprenticeship period. In contrast to this assertion, it is argued here that whilst the social aspect of training may well be a partial explanation of the skilled identities of craftsmen, it is not a complete account. The post-apprenticeship work experience of craftsmen is also influential in the generation of their skilled identities. Unlike the majority of production workers in the three case study factories, craftsmen have a high level of control over the manipulation of their work. They are responsible for both the planning and execution of their tasks, and their work entails high levels of discretion and autonomy. It is, therefore, a combination of these features of craftsmen's labour that generate their particular perceptions of skill.

Returning to the assertion that the knowledge held by all workers is a result of their activity in the labour process, this is not static or fixed. As workers move between various roles and structural positions within the capitalist labour process their active interaction with new roles can result in a change in their constructed knowledge, and therefore in the salient reference point from which they consider the subject of skill. Evidence from the case study factories indicates that an important dynamic leading to change in work related knowledge is the direction of an individual's employment trajectory, which is depicted on the right of diagram 6.1. For those without qualifications, and whose previous jobs were of a similar or lower occupational status, that is who have horizontal or upwards employment trajectories, the most salient reference point from which to consider skill is their *current* work related knowledge. Thus, the causal powers that generate perceptions of skill amongst this group stem from the structural emergent properties pertaining to their current job. For those without qualifications, and who have employment trajectories that have taken them down the occupational status hierarchy, the most salient reference point from which to consider skill is the constructed knowledge relating to *previous* employment. For those with trade apprenticeship qualifications[4] employed at Chemicals UK only, it will be suggested, in Chapter Seven, that this groups tendency to perceive skill in relation to knowledge constructed through activity in their current occupation is a possible result of the totality of the break with their previous trade. For craft apprentice qualified individuals who are currently employed in the craftsman's role, or who have moved down the occupational status hierarchy into semi-skilled manual occupations, knowledge constructed through activity in a craft skilled occupation remains the most salient reference point from which to consider skill. In contrast to this, apprentice qualified men who have moved up into higher status jobs tend to draw on the knowledge gained from their *current* occupation when considering the subject of skill. Finally, in the case of those with academic qualifications, it is not possible to put forward firm arguments with respect to employment trajectories. All interviewees in possession of academic qualifications are performing jobs commensurate with those qualifications and it is difficult to separate out the generative effects of job related structural emergent properties, and the emergent properties of qualifications.

Management Perceptions of Workers' Skill

The above model has described the network of processes involved in the generation of subjective workforce perceptions of skill. This outline of the model now turns to the question of how far it applies to management perceptions of workforce skill, and the causal processes that shape them. I want to suggest that management perceptions of skill are shaped by an interplay between structure and agency mechanisms, both of which originate from the second emergent property of capitalism outlined earlier. That is, the need for capitalism to transform the labour power of workers into productive labour. It was argued in Chapter Two that the position of junior and middle managers is contradictory. The occupational status of this group is dependent on their position in the organisation; that is on their organisational assets. These organisational assets have, according to Savage, Barlow, Dickens and Fielding, been devalued in comparison to the professional assets of other middle class groups (Savage et al 1992). The structural position of middle and junior managers can therefore be compared to that of workers. However, a fundamental aspect of the managerial role is the exercising of agency on behalf of the firm. Managers exercise agency on behalf of both the organisation and in order to secure their own organisational assets. I shall also show that management perceptions of skill focus on workers' attitude, commitment and motivation, and on specific task competence. These perceptions are shaped by the historic managerial problem of eliciting the co-operation and consent of workers, which is necessary to the production of surplus profit and to managers' own performance at work. Thus, management perceptions of skill are ultimately shaped by their role in securing valorisation for the firm and in order to secure their own position in the firm.

Conclusion

This chapter has provided an outline of the causal processes that shape subjective perceptions of skill. It has been suggested that the capitalist system of production contains emergent properties, three of which are relevant to the generation of perceptions of skill. These are product markets, the need for capital to control the labour of workers, and the stratified employment structure. The causal powers that stem from the first two of these emergent properties with respect to the generation of organisational structures vary between specific contexts. A further influential factor in shaping the emergent properties of organisations is that of the strategic choices of powerful corporate agents. These emergent properties of organisations contain causal powers that influence the construction of knowledge held by workers. This knowledge is also shaped by an individual's emergent properties of qualifications and prior work experience. The salient reference points through which individuals consider skill are the structural features of the jobs they perform, or have performed in the past, and their qualifications. Whether workers draw on current or previous employment when considering skill depends on the direction of their own personal employment trajectory. That is, whether they have moved up into higher status occupations, remained in a similar status (or the same) occupation, or fallen down into lower status jobs.

The above model highlights the stratified and context dependent nature of the causal processes that shape subjective perceptions of skill. Whilst there are strong similarities between firms in terms of the factors that shape perceptions of skill, the specific form they take depends on other factors that characterise individual organisations. The model also shows how perceptions are inextricably linked to developments in the wider capitalist system. Finally, the open nature of social systems, and the possibility for change in the constructed knowledge held by workers allows for an explanatory model that takes account of the possibility for change in an individual's perceptions of skill. The book now moves on to consider the empirical evidence that led to the construction of this model. The next three chapters will describe the case study factories in detail, and the perceptions of skill, core and periphery held by workers and managers who are employed in them.

Notes

[1] In contrast to the argument put forward by Reed, it can be suggested that Foucault's analysis of localised social practices does not imply an anti-structuralist position. Rather, what Foucault argued against was a search for universal truths or laws which apply regardless of space or time. An example of this relates to Foucault's work on disciplinary control. Although he explores the ways in which various types of discipline have been applied in specific historical circumstances (for example, from the site of the body to the site of the psyche), he draws a link between specific forms of discipline and social structures. Foucault argues that "…the industrial system requires a free market in labor and, in the nineteenth century, the role of forced labor in the mechanisms of punishment diminishes accordingly and "corrective" detention takes its place (Foucault in Rabinow p. 172). Thus, Foucault is arguing that the increase in corrective detention is linked to industrialisation. Such an argument does not, it can be suggested, imply hostility to structuralism.

[2] It should be noted here that the origins of this model lie in Marx's generational model of agency, structure and social change. Marx argued that whilst society is the product of men's reciprocal action, they are not free to choose the form society takes. At any point in the development of productive forces, there will be a corresponding form of commerce, consumption and civil society. Marx goes on to argue that "It is superfluous to add that men are not free to choose their productive forces - which are the basis of all their history - for every productive force is an acquired force, the product of former activity. The productive forces are therefore the result of practical human energy: but this energy is itself conditioned by the circumstances in which men find themselves, by the productive forces already acquired, by the social form which exists before they do, which they do not create, which is the product of the preceding generation" (Marx, quoted in Caute, 1967, p. 46-47).

[3] Explanation for this refusal is given in Chapter Six.

[4] Craft apprenticeship qualifications refers to those such as electrician, welder and fitter, whilst trade apprenticeship qualifications refers to joinery, catering and vehicle maintenance. The decision to employ this categorisation relates to the differential impact of these types of training qualification on subjective perceptions of skill.

5 GlassCo

Background

GlassCo was established in the latter years of the 19th century and is located in a geographical area with a long tradition of glass container production. The firm manufactures clear glass containers for the cheaper end of the mass consumption market, and currently employs around 370 people, the large majority of whom are members of the General Municipal and Boilermakers Union (Works Manager). A number of developments in the European glass container manufacturing sector have occurred in recent years which have implications for GlassCo with respect to the firm's organisational structural features.

First, the product market for glass containers cannot be discussed in isolation from the market for packaging in general. In Europe, glass containers have 7% of the total market share. Its major rivals are plastics (38%), paper and cardboard (33%) and metal and cans (22%). Glass manufacturers are competing not only with each other but also with other cheaper and less fragile materials. A second issue relates to over capacity in the industry (Davies 1993). In the UK this over capacity is set to intensify due to a decision by the last conservative government to award a grant of 13.1 million for the creation of a new glass manufacturing plant in Northern Ireland (Financial Times 23/12/97). This plant is expected to double the capacity of the UK industry and the impact on other UK container manufacturers will be negative and serious: job losses are expected to occur in South Yorkshire and Scotland (Glass Technology Ltd. Information Pack 1998).

The outcome of competition from other materials, and over capacity of production, is a European wide tendency towards rationalisation and the concentration of production in bigger plants. Throughout Europe the number of firms is reducing, whilst individual plants are increasing in size (Cornaz 1992, Davies 1993). In terms of the impact on jobs, it is not possible to predict what the effects will be. However, over the past twenty years the numbers employed in the sector have fallen from around 10,500 to 6,800 (Glass Technology Ltd. Information Pack 1998).

Occurring parallel to this concentration of production is a tendency for smaller firms to search out speciality niche market areas in order to protect themselves from the increased economies of scale open to larger manufacturers (Burrows 1989, Davies 1993). According to Burrows however, this strategy is not without risks. He argues that in order for the industry to survive competition from other materials it must, on aggregate, increase its share of the volume packaging market. A final development occurring in the industry is that it is becoming increasingly capital intensive. Davies (1993) argues that labour costs in the glass container sector are higher than in the general packaging sector. Thus, the shift towards increased automation could be seen as a strategy for replacing labour with machinery.

The effects of the above trends on the organisational features of GlassCo relate to the firm's production process and technology, in particular the strategy of shifting production towards niche market areas. At present GlassCo are located in the cheaper end of the market and their products are sold to 'fillers' who service supermarkets own brands. However, the scope for profitability in this market area is limited. Profit margins on products aimed at the cheaper end of the market are low, and GlassCo cannot compete with the larger firms with respect to economies of scale (Works Manager). According to Davies, for example, the energy costs that occur with higher volume production are much lower than when a smaller number of units are produced (Davies 1993). As a result of these factors, GlassCo are attempting to break into the prestige speciality markets, for example products made for fillers who service upmarket retail chains such as Marks and Spencer. This has led to the utilisation of flexible production machinery which can produce a range of products by changing the glass container moulds. It has also led to the introduction of flexible automated palletising machinery which automatically sorts out faulty products. This particular technological development appears to have been generated by two factors. First, the need to improve the quality of the product in order to compete with other materials and glass manufacturers. Second, it represents the firm's attempts to catch up with developments in the wider industry. GlassCo was, at the time fieldwork took place, one of only two firms in the UK still using manual methods of Sorting.

The significance of these developments in terms of perceptions of skill relates to the impact of new technology on workforce perceptions of skill, an issue that was discussed in Chapter Three. It was suggested that the impact of technology on user's skill relates to both the constraints built into various types of technology, and the social organisation of work around technology, specifically with respect to the separation of programming and operating functions. In terms of the flexible production machinery used to manufacture glass containers, it will be sown that the separation of programming and operating functions results in perceptions of skill that focus on task performance. It will also be shown that the introduction of automated palletising machinery removes what little control workers have over the execution of their work. Not only does this machine identify faulty containers, it also controls the pace of work. The result of this, along with the rigid Taylorist division of labour and close supervisory system, appears to be to constrain the development of perceptions of skill amongst workers employed in this area.

It is apparent that the production process and technology at GlassCo are, in part, related to developments in the wider industrial sector. The social organisation of work and management structure and style cannot, however, be explained without reference to processes that originate at the level of the firm. The organisation of work is characterised by a rigid Taylorist vertical and horizontal division of labour, and a hierarchical and direct supervisory style. Relations between managers and workers are also characterised by some hostility and mistrust. The firm's personnel manager was asked, for example, if the firm had ever considered adopting human relations style approach, or allowing workers a higher level of autonomy. He replied that both human relations and teamwork approaches were of no use to GlassCo due to the 'low quality of the workforce.' This view was also expressed by a second manager who, in answer to this question, replied: "It would be no good here because if they were left to get on with it themselves no work would ever get done" (Hot Area Manager). The Taylorist management strategy and division of labour at GlassCo seem to be shaped, in part, by management mistrust of the workforce.

Structural Features

Production System and Technology

The production of glass containers takes place in the Hot Area (HA) and Cold Area (CA). The process begins with the mixing of raw materials and the production of molten glass. This is then transferred to the HA where bottles and containers are shaped against a mould. This process is carried out using eight automated mould machines which are run simultaneously, and which use different moulds for different products. The moulds are interchangeable and thus allow for flexibility of production. Once the bottles and containers are produced they are sent to the CA which consists of sorting and re-sorting. The Sorting Department is where finished products are checked for faults, loaded onto pallets and re-checked. If a pallet is found to contain a defective product it is broken down and checked again by re-sorters. Sorting is divided into automated and manual sections. The automated section contains the automated palletising machines, which examine the containers and remove any defective products.

Manual sorting consists of single line conveyor belts down which containers are passed. Sorters take the containers from the belt and check for defects manually. The re-sorting process entails the manual breaking down of pallets found to contain faulty containers, and the manual re-sorting of these into those that are defective and those that can be repackaged. There are no machines in this section. In addition to these production areas are a number of maintenance departments, each dealing with its own narrow area of maintenance. Research took place in one maintenance department, the Mould Maintenance Workshop. This is the engineering workshop in which the moulds for the automated HA machines are made and repaired. Machinery in this department consists of a variety of manually operated lathes and machine tools.

The Management Structure and Style

The managerial structure at GlassCo is hierarchical and Taylorist. Each management layer has a clearly defined set of responsibilities and provides line management for the layer below. At the head of production is the overall Manufacturing Manager. Below him are the managers of individual departments. The HA is controlled by the HA Manager. His role entails calculating statistical control settings, and ensuring these are maintained throughout the process. He is ultimately responsible for the process and any training that takes place in the department. The next layer in the hierarchical structure are shift foremen who oversee production and provide line management for charge hands.   There are two charge hands per shift, each providing line support for four individual machine operators. One operator runs each of the eight machines.

The Sorting and Re-sorting Departments are headed by the CA Manager. His job is to oversee all aspects of sorting and re-sorting. He is also responsible for recruitment, training, and for the promotion of sorters to charge hands. Below this man is a foreman for each shift, and who is responsible for organising the rotation of tasks between groups of sorters. He also provides line management for the part-time re-sorters who work the evening shift (5pm to 9pm). The lowest supervisory layer in the department are the charge hands who provide line support for groups of ten sorters. Finally, the Foreman heads the managerial structure in the Mould Maintenance Workshop. His job includes prioritising tasks and the deployment of men to tasks. He is also responsible for the training of apprentices. Below him is the charge hand who provides line support to the apprentice qualified men who work in the department. The managerial style in the three research areas differs between the two production areas and the Mould Maintenance Workshop. In production areas the managerial style closely resembles the direct supervision model. Both HA machinists and CA sorters complained, during interviews, that foremen and charge hands rarely allow them the space to deal with any problems that may occur. Workers are allowed little or no opportunity to use their own judgement or manipulate the work process. In contrast, the craftsmen employed in the Mould Maintenance Workshop are left to work largely unsupervised.

The explanation of why the managerial and supervisory style over production workers adheres closely to the direct supervision model possibly relates to the poor industrial relations that exist at the firm. A particular feature of the firm is a high level of mistrust between management and workers. The origins of this mistrust are unclear, although it possibly relates to wider cultural attitudes in the immediate geographical locality.[1] Poor industrial relations at the firm are illustrated by quotes from both management and workers. During an untaped interview, the Personnel Manager expressed the view that there is a 'strange' culture in the town and the surrounding area. This culture, according to the Personnel Manager, consists of strong anti-work attitudes amongst local people, heavy drinking, wife beating and people having "multiple partners and kids all over the place." This opinion is, however, mild in comparison to that of the CA Production Manager. The following extract is an amalgamation of quotes from this man. They have been included in their entirety because they highlight the high level of mistrust of workforce motives, and the hostility towards workers felt by this man. He is responsible for around a 100 of the total workforce:

The people round here, the drink comes first, work is a secondary thing. I mean the works got to be the first thing because it pays for everything else, but here they just don't realise it. A lot of them here, they think that GlassCo is a terrible place where they have been downtrodden and treated very badly. But what they have to realise is that everything comes from here[…].

When I was first a foreman at a firm down the road, if somebody came for a job and were unskilled or semi-skilled, it didn't matter if they got the job or not. We used to set people on a Monday and they were off by the Wednesday, go somewhere else. They just were not bothered. But that has all changed now to some extent, Thatcher saw to that. Anyway when I came here I was not happy with the people I inherited. You'd got people who had been here since the 1970s and they thought they were cast iron, nobody could touch them they knew all the dodges. So I was careful who I set on, tried to get some nicer people. I mean there is one particular guy here and he is a scouser, a typical scouser. If that's what they're like in Liverpool it's no wonder they've got no work. Liverpool like, they do not want work most of them, that's why everyone has pulled out. So anyway, I am careful now about who I set on. We have talked about it me and A (Personnel Manager) because we are in agreement on this, we said that we want people who really want to work, who are not going to go on the sick all the time or go out and get pissed every night and not be fit for work the next day. So if someone comes here for a job I try to get to know what they're like. I mean I like a drink myself but you cannot be getting pissed every night before you come to work. Another thing that puts me off is when people say that their hobby is watching Utd....it causes trouble if some people support one team and some support another...I don't like football myself[…].

Well in this town and the surrounding area you get a lot of mining or ex-mining families, and the attitude of some of them people, they have a terrible attitude to work, they just do not want to work, nothing really matters to them. I think the climate has probably changed because of

Thatcher and McGregor, because they know that they can't get away with it any more. And the women, they're just as bad you know. When I was down the road at AB Ltd where I worked before I came to GlassCo, I had a strike three Septembers in a row. Walk off, walk out, at least ten days. It was nothing to do with work, you get to September after the 2 week August shut down and get back to work. Well after September till Christmas there is no holiday and they get browned off. The women have probably got a lot of washing and ironing to catch up with so bang, they're gone, out. They're out for a week and they get all their washing and ironing done[...].

We use this room we are sat in now for interviewing. I will come in sometimes, and the women I am interviewing will be sat there smoking. So you sit down with some of them and they're all bleached blond hair with dark roots showing, and a ring on every finger. Usually all these cheap, tacky rings, and it just makes me go yuk. This is what it's like round here, it's a strange area.

The hostility and mistrust expressed by this manager towards workers is matched by the attitudes towards management expressed by some of the GlassCo workforce. Their hostility towards management is neatly summed up in the following quote:

It's them, it boils down to management, how they treat us. The only time we see management is if they come down to give us a bollocking. We never get a pat on the back for doing a good job so if we see a manager coming on to the shop floor we just think, hey-up, we're in for a bollocking here....They like to give a good impression, like with these team briefings where they tell you how the firm is doing an all that, but they're just telling you what they want you to know. When pay talks come round it's funny how they're always doing badly, but then other times we're doing OK (HA Machinist).

The mistrust between managers and workers described above is not uniform throughout the factory. One group of workers, the part-time re-sorting team, are highly valued. This team consists of six women working the evening shift. These women appear to form a typical peripheral and flexible workforce as described in the post-Fordist literature. This definition of the group is not however reflected in management or worker attitudes, and the issue will be returned to later when perceptions of core and periphery at GlassCo are discussed.

Division of Labour and Nature of Work

Work in the two production areas is characterised by a Taylorist division of labour, and each person has his or her own set of tasks to perform. Flexibility is confined to a few workers being trained to perform the jobs of others. The organisation of work between groups and individuals is carried out by foremen and charge hands. The division of labour is also highly gendered. There are no women employed in the HA, whilst in the CA women are confined to the lowest sorting and re-sorting grades. Although a sizeable minority of the sorting and re-sorting workforce are women, there are no female foremen, and only a small number of female charge hands. The production process and technology, the managerial structure and style, and the Taylorist division of labour heavily influence the nature of work in the production departments. Jobs in both departments are characterised by repetition, little scope for autonomy or decision making and, in the case of the sorting and re-sorting departments, a good deal of monotony.

Hot Area

Each machine in the HA is run by one individual on each shift. The work consists of setting the automated machines in accordance with pre-calculated statistical production control methods, and monitoring the automated process. If problems occur during production it is, in theory, the job of the operator to adjust the settings, or to call a charge hand for assistance if the problem is beyond their capabilities. However, when problems do arise charge hands tend to take control immediately and deal with the problems themselves.

In terms of personal characteristics, the operators are all men with no formal educational or training qualifications. When the production supervisor was asked if the firm ever employed apprentice trained labour, he replied that such highly qualified men would not do this job. Machinists are men who have worked in the Sorting Department before being promoted to machine operators jobs. According to the HA Manager, this does not mean that the men are unskilled. Whilst the job is generally viewed by managers and workers as semi-skilled, it is argued by this manager that "it takes a long time to train somebody up for this job from scratch."

Cold Area

Workers in the CA Sorting Department are organised into groups of ten, with each group being supervised by one charge hand. Groups are deployed to specific jobs, such as manual or automated sorting, by the foreman, and the charge hand distributes particular tasks within the group. Work on the automated area consists of operating the palletising machines that automatically examine containers for defects, and removing any that are found. The role of the sorter is to press the buttons that switch the machine on and off, and to watch over the process. The work in manual sorting entails sorters standing alongside a belt and picking up four bottles at a time. They roll the bottles in their hands looking for defects at the necks, bodies and bases. In theory sorters are responsible for deciding which bottles to pass and which to fail. However, many sorters said that it is the charge hand who makes the majority of these decisions.

Six women working the part-time evening shift work in the Re-sorting Department. The women work in pairs and carry out the tasks by hand. This involves opening a pallet containing defective containers and re-sorting them into a 'good' pile and a 'bad' pile. The women are supervised by the Sorting Department Foreman, although they are usually left to perform the job with little interference. The rationale for the contrast in supervisory styles between sorters and re-sorters given by the CA Manager is that re-sorters, unlike sorters, can be left to 'get on with the job'. Despite being employed as re-sorters they are often pulled off this job and sent to other areas, for example loading and unloading pallets. According to the CA Manager they provide a 'flexible service team' who can be moved from job to job. In terms of personal characteristics, sorters and re-sorters are unqualified people whose work histories have been in a variety of unskilled labouring occupations.

The Mould Maintenance Workshop

Work in the Mould Maintenance Workshop consists of making and repairing the moulds for the automated HA machines. This involves a variety of separate tasks such as lathe turning, welding, fitting, mould checking and polishing. The workforce are apprentice trained engineers and craftsmen, and work is organised on an individual basis with men having responsibility for their own particular tasks. These apprentice-qualified men are, however, expected to be flexible and carry out whatever jobs need to be done. Workers in the Mould Maintenance Workshop have no discretion over the organisation of work tasks. They do, on the other hand, work autonomously and decide themselves how to approach, plan and perform tasks.

GlassCo, Fordism and Post-Fordism

The question of how far theories of post-Fordism are applicable to GlassCo can be examined on three levels. First, the firm's position in relation to the wider sector product market. Second, the extent and nature of flexibility within the production process, and third, the organisation of work within the factory. It was argued at the start of this chapter that the glass container manufacturing sector has entered a period of contraction and instability due to competition from other packaging materials. The outcome in terms of the concentration and size of organisations are two parallel tendencies. On the one hand is a shift towards increased economies of scale through a reduction in the number of firms' operating in Europe, and a corresponding increase in the size of organisations. This tendency appears to signify an intensification of Fordism rather than a shift towards post-Fordism. On the other hand, there is, amongst smaller firms, a tendency towards economies of scope, and a shift into consumer demand led niche market areas; a tendency that is generally associated with the alleged shift towards post-Fordism. A further characteristic of post-Fordism is a trend for multi-nationals to achieve flexibility through subsidiaries that manufacture goods for niche market areas. The take over of GlassCo in 1994 can be argued to represent the parent company's attempt to shift into the niche glass production market. These shifts in production and marketing do not, however, signify an attempt at constant innovation and a continuous search for new markets. Rather, the strategy is to search out and retain a new stable customer base in specific market sectors. Despite these contradictions, however, GlassCo's relationship to trends in the wider glass industry and product market can, to some extent, be understood in the context of post-Fordism.

Moving on to flexibility at GlassCo, this relates to technological flexibility in both the HA and CA. In the HA area of the factory, flexible automated production machines can switch production between various products by switching moulds. In the CA area, palletising inspection machinery is pre-set to deal with variations in product specifications. Changeovers between product lines requires co-ordination between the two departments. Writing in relation to the Vetropack Glass Company, Sweden, Isler estimates that the number of man hours needed for change over is around 120 (Isler 1998). GlassCo production schedules indicate that change overs are planned days in advance (HA Production Manager). This evidence appears to support Tomaney's argument that flexible specialisation theory overestimates the extent of flexibility inherent in new technology (Tomaney 1994). The extent to which the flexible production process at GlassCo can be described as flexible specialisation in the sense put forward by Piore and Sabel (1984), that is that switching between production lines is an easy process using flexible specialisation machinery, is limited. In terms of the organisation of work at GlassCo, this is obviously traditionally Taylorist. The hierarchical management structure, the close supervisory style, the rigid demarcations between jobs and the rigid division of labour, and the predominance of unskilled or semi-skilled work are all characteristics of the traditional Fordist factory. Similarly, the use of automated machinery has intensified the division between conception and execution through the separation of programming and operating functions, an outcome that was predicted by Aglietta in 1979. Nor, it is suggested, can the use of female part-time labour in the Re-sorting Department be seen as a core and periphery strategy on the part of the firm.

It can be concluded then, that the organisational structure at GlassCo does not conform to either Fordist or post-Fordist ideal type organisations, and the firm contains features of both. This evidence underpins the assertion put forward in Chapter Two, that to define organisations as either Fordist or post-Fordist is to ignore the complex and uneven development of firms. It can also be argued nevenrtheless, in the context of this mix of Fordist and post-Fordist features, the organisation of work at GlassCo remains rooted in the Fordist paradigm.

Workers' Perceptions of Skill

Workforce perceptions of skill at GlassCo are patterned around three broad factors:

1. Organisational structural features.
2. Groups and individuals position in relation to structural features.
3. The routes by which individuals come to occupy their position.

Perceptions of skill vary between the HA, the CA and the Mould Maintenance Workshop. Perceptions of skill in the HA are articulated in terms of practical task knowledge. All the men employed in this area have upwards employment trajectories in that they have previously performed jobs of a lower status. The salient reference point from which they consider skill is therefore their current occupation as HA machinists. Moving on to the CA, in contrast to all other interviewees across the three case studies, the majority of sorters and re-sorters do not express any perceptions of skill whatsoever. I will suggest that this is due to the structural features associated with jobs in the department, and the low skilled nature of individuals work histories. There are, however, five sorters who do articulate perceptions of skill. Two of these men have been trained to perform higher status jobs at GlassCo, and three have, in the past, performed higher status jobs elsewhere. The salient reference point from which these men consider skill is not the role of sorter. Rather, it is the higher status roles they are trained to perform, or have occupied previously. Finally, perceptions of skill in the Mould Maintenance Workshop emphasise experience, discretion, and autonomy. These perceptions are associated with the mens' experience of the apprenticeship system and post-apprenticeship experience, and also by the nature of their jobs, namely, the responsible autonomy and discretion these men have over task performance.

The analysis of perceptions of skill at GlassCo will begin with workers employed in the HA, followed by those employed in the CA Sorting and Re-sorting Departments. After this a discussion of perceptions of skill amongst apprentice trained engineering craftworkers in the Mould Maintenance Workshop will be given.

Hot Area

The routes through which HA machinists come to occupy their position all follow the same employment trajectory. None of these men possess qualifications, and all have previously performed manual labouring jobs at GlassCo. The organisational route through which individuals obtain the position of HA machinist is as follows. All GlassCo new recruits are employed as sorters or re-sorters. When machinist jobs in the HA become available, sorters and re-sorters are invited to apply. Thus, all these men have upwards employment trajectories in that they have achieved what is regarded as promotion from sorter to machinist. The perceptions of skill held by HA machinists can be defined as 'practical task knowledge', and none express any perception of discretion and autonomy as skill. These perceptions relate to the structural features associated with the job. The perception of practical task knowledge as skill is shaped by interaction between the flexible automated production machinery, and the social organisation of work, specifically the separation of programming and operating functions. As stated earlier, the machines are programmed using pre-defined statistical control settings. Whilst it is the responsibility of the men to set the machines, the calculation of settings is the responsibility of individuals higher up the organisational hierarchy. There is a complete separation between conception and execution, and the role of the machinist to follow pre-defined programming procedures, mind the machine, and to identify any irregularities in the automated process. These responsibilities are, however, constrained by the close supervisory style of charge hands and foremen described earlier.

The perceptions of practical task knowledge as skill held by HA Machinists consists of a knowledge of how the machine works, the practical tasks necessary to monitor the machine, and the types of irregularity that can occur. These men make no reference to theoretical knowledge of the principles of glass production. The following quotes are, for example, given in response to the question "If I were to ask you to define the term skill, what would you think of?"

> Knowledge of your job, knowing what it is you're doing. With our job it's a bit of thinking, a bit of using your hands. You've got to realise what you're doing and watch what you're making. What the machine is doing and if it should be doing it, you know if the feeder is working right. You need some mechanical skill for this job, you have to know the machine.

> It's not skilled our job...well it's not classed as skilled but it is really, very much so. I have been here eight years and I am still learning. You need a lot of knowledge, remembering the complaints and the different ways of sorting them out. You have to remember what you did before.

> I have never thought of myself as a skilled worker but to be honest this job is skilled in a lot of ways. You have to have a knowledge of the job, remember all the complaints that can go wrong because the complaints, well I guess there can be two hundred ways that can go wrong. But then you will get six hundred ways of curing faults. So you need a good memory of what you did ages ago. The basic skills are what you pick up over the years, it's just knowledge. I cannot see someone coming into the

job who has not done it before and just doing it. Even if they had read everything they would not know what they were doing when they got on the machines.

It is suggested that the perception of practical task knowledge as skill is generated by the experience of working with automated machinery for which programming responsibility lies with others. I will elaborate on this conclusion following the discussion of perceptions of skill at Electronics UK and Chemicals UK. I shall demonstrate that the perception of practical task knowledge as skill is held by workers whose work involves monitoring machinery for which programming and operating functions are separated. I will also show, in chapter Seven, that where machinery involves programming by workers themselves, the perception of knowledge as skill takes the form of theoretical rather than practical knowledge.

It can be seen that the division of labour in the HA, which divides programming and operating functions, generates perceptions of skill that focus narrowly on task complexity and performance dimensions. With respect to the dimensions of discretion and autonomy, none of the men perceive these concepts as skill. It is suggested that the hierarchical management structure and close supervisory style stifle the scope for discretion and autonomy in the job. It has also been argued that the most salient reference point for these workers with respect to perceptions of skill is their current occupation. Thus, perceptions of discretion and autonomy as skill are not formed because these dimensions of skill are not a feature of HA machinists jobs. Indeed, they appear to have no salience whatsoever for these workers. This assertion is supported by the following quotes:

DT: Do you have any opportunity to make decisions for yourself?
A: We are supposed to get on with the job and sort out what problems we can ourselves. But usually when anything goes a bit wrong the foreman or the charge hand jumps in and we just stand about waiting for them to sort it out.
DT: How closely are you supervised?
A: The foreman's always around somewhere, watching what you're doing like. Gets on your nerves sometimes.
DT: Do you think that making decisions for yourself and working unsupervised are skills?
A: Wouldn't know about that.

DT: Do you have much opportunity to make decisions for yourself?

A: Er...depends who's on charge hand. Some leave you to get on with it but most of em watch you all the time.
DT: Would you regard making your own decisions as a skill?
A: Could be I suppose, I'm not sure really.

In summary, the interaction between the flexible automated technology and the social organisation of work, that separates programming and operating functions in the HA, generates perceptions of skill that can be defined as practical task knowledge. Perceptions of discretion and autonomy are not material because these dimensions of skill are not attributes of the job.

Cold Area

The CA workforce divides into two groups with respect to perceptions of skill. The first group comprises of sorters and all the re-sorters, whilst the second comprises of sorters only. The notable difference between the two groups with respect to perceptions of skill are the routes through which individuals came to occupy their current job, and in the case of two individuals, their expectations for the future. The employment trajectories of the first group are horizontal in that all have work histories characterised by unskilled manual occupations,[2] and all are now employed as unskilled sorters or re-sorters. The developing model suggests that the most salient reference point for workers with horizontal employment trajectories is their current job. This group are, however, unique amongst interviewees from each of the three factories in that none of them express any perception of skill whatsoever. I want to suggest that the absence of perceptions of skill amongst this group relate to the combination of two factors. First, the low skilled nature of sorting and re-sorting, and second, the absence of any alternative reference point from which to draw on in relation to the issue of skill. That is, their lack of experience of skilled work.

To reiterate, the work of sorters involves the observation of glass containers as they pass by on the automated palletising machines, or picking up containers and manually searching for faults. Technical job characteristics are confined to switching the palletising machines on and off, although the decision to take this action is the responsibility of charge hands and foremen. The work of re-sorters involves opening pallets containing defective products and separating these from those with no faults. The faults to be found are specified on a worksheet, which is closely followed by the re-sorters. Finally, although sorters and re-sorters are rotated between strictly demarcated tasks, these tasks are routine and repetitive. The result of these job characteristics appears to be to constrain the development of perceptions of skill. When asked to give their own definition of the term skill, this group of interviewees tended to reply that they did not know because they are unskilled and/or their job is unskilled:

DT: If I were to ask you to define the term skill, would you think of?
A: I dunno.
DT: Well could you describe the skills you use in your job?
A: None.
DT: But what about when you are looking for faults, isn't that a skill?
A: No it's easy because they are all the same, the jobs that come on. You know what to expect, like with bottles it's the rings so you just look at the rings. You don't need no skill for this job.
DT: How about the skills you need to operate the palletising machines?
A: No it's not complicated, you only have to press a button (Male Sorter).

DT: If I were to ask you to define the term skill, what would you think of?
A: I don't know what you mean?
DT: Well what kinds of skill do you need for your job?
A: Well just doing it like, looking for faults an that, what to throw away. It's not a right skill in this job, it's just getting on with it (Female Sorter).

DT: If I were to ask you to define the term skill, what would you think of?
A: I really wouldn't know.
DT: What about the skills you need in your own job?
A: None really, as long as you know how to do the re-sorting. It's not a skilled job or a hard job, as long as you find your faults you're OK (Re-sorter).

DT: If I were to ask you to define the term skill, what would you think of?
A: I don't know what you mean.
DT: Well what skills do you use in this job.
A: Well it's just knowing what to do, what we call a cock (reject) and what we call a good bottle. That's all there is to it (Re-sorter).

In terms of discretion and autonomy, as with HA machinists, there is no perception of these attributes as skills amongst this group of sorters and re-sorters. It was argued in relation to HA machinists that the lack of scope for discretion and autonomy in the job, which itself relates to the hierarchical and close supervisory system, stifles the development of perceptions of discretion and autonomy as skill. The hierarchical and close supervisory system that characterises the HA is also a feature of the sorting area, and again this limits the scope for discretion and autonomy in the job, thus constraining perceptions of these attributes as skills. Consider, for example, the following quotes from sorters:

> DT: Do you have an opportunity to make decisions for yourself?
> A: You have charge hands and foreman and basically it's up to them what goes and what stops. (i.e. which containers are passed and which are rejected). Even if you make a decision and it's the right one he comes over and either agrees with you or overrules you. It's up to him when it comes down to it.
> DT: Is the ability to make decisions in your work a skill?
> A: I don't know.
> DT: How closely are you supervised?
> A: Too closely, we're watched all the time.
> DT: Is the ability to work unsupervised a skill?
> A: I don't know.

> DT: Do you have much opportunity to make decisions for yourself?
> A: I don't think so, you just...well if there's something wrong with the bottle you just throw it out or ask a charge hand like. If he's not there and you cannot wait for him to get back you have to throw it out.
> DT: Is the ability to make that decision a skill?
> A: I don't know.

It was stated earlier that the direct supervisory style applied to machinists in the HA and sorters is relaxed for re-sorters. However, it has also been pointed out that re-sorters have little scope for decision making due to the simplistic and strictly prescribed nature of their work. I have also argued that discretion and autonomy are perceived as skills only where there is scope for discretion and autonomy over task performance. Where these dimensions are confined to decisions about the organisation of work rather than the performance of tasks, and where autonomy merely describes being left alone to perform strictly prescribed tasks, these attributes are not perceived as skills. This latter point is supported by the following quotes from re-sorters:

> DT: Do you have much opportunity to make decisions for yourself?

A: No, we have to ask a charge hand if we're not sure about anything.
DT: Do you think that the ability to make decisions is a skill?
A: Like I said before, I don't know anything about skill.
DT: How closely are you supervised?
A: Well there's a foreman in Sorting if we need him, but usually we are left alone. They know that they can trust us.
DT: Is the ability to work unsupervised a skill?
A: I don't know.

DT: Do you have much opportunity to make decisions for yourself?
A: No we just follow our instructions, its dead easy.
DT: Do you think that the ability to make decisions is a skill?
A: I couldn't say, I've never thought about it.
DT: How closely are you supervised?
A: We're not, we just get left to get on with the job.
DT: Is the ability to work unsupervised a skill?
A: Not in this job it's not, anyone could follow the instructions we get.

In summary, the absence of perceptions of skill amongst this group of sorters and re-sorters appears to be associated with the low skilled nature of their current and previous employment. Work in the Sorting and Re-sorting Departments is simplistic, and involves little more than observation of containers. Charge hands and foreman take all decisions, often including which bottles to throw away. With respect to technology, the automated palletising machines are simple to use and are, in any case, controlled by others. The absence of a technological component contrasts markedly with production jobs in the other two case study firms. It was argued in Chapter four, and will become clearer over the course of the next two chapters, that technology is an important generator of perceptions of skill amongst production workers. The absence of a technological component, along with the close and direct supervisory style, and the rigid division of labour acts as a constraint on the development of perceptions of skill amongst sorters and re-sorters. It is not, however, only current job characteristics that are associated with an absence of perceptions of skill amongst this group. Neither past or present employment provides a salient reference point on which to draw in relation to the formation of perceptions of skill.

This analysis is supported by the perceptions of skill held by the second group of interviewees in the CA. This group is made up of five male sorters who differ from the previous group in terms of employment trajectories, or expectations of future employment trajectories. Three of these men previously performed supervisory or managerial jobs in other glass container-manufacturing firms. Their employment trajectories have therefore been downwards, and it is their previous higher status roles that provide a salient reference point from which to consider skill. The following quotes were given in response to the question: "If I were to ask you to define the term skill, what would you think of?"

> Well the most important skill I can think of is knowledge of glass, you need to know about glass, how it is made, what can go wrong. You have to do pressure tests and measuring. Depending on your job you need man management skills. When I was at RP glass I was in a supervisory, managerial position and I needed that. But this job I've got here is not skilled really (Sorter, ex-inspection manager RP Glass).

> Experience is skill, experience in glass. You've got to know what you're dealing with, what a faulty jar is, that's the two main things. You need a bit of maturity as well, especially when you're dealing with people. At my old firm that was a big part of my job was dealing with people (Sorter, ex-quality Auditor WS Glass).

The remaining two individuals, although employed as sorters, have both been trained to perform other jobs including the charge hand role. One is also a trade union shop steward. These men can anticipate upward employment trajectories in that if vacancies for charge hands arise they will be promoted automatically. The perceptions of skill held by these men are a direct reflection of these higher status roles. They also perceive skill as flexibility, a perception that reflects their functional flexibility across a range of roles in the factory. The following quotes are again given in response to the question "If I were to ask you to define the term skill, what would you think of?"

> Personally I think communication skills are very important. Not just because of my union work but because of how the job works here. There are a lot of stages involved in glass production and you have to know how to communicate if something is wrong. You also need punctuality, which's a skill. Obvious skills for any job are a knowledge of the job, you know like being able to identify faulty bottles and knowing the difference between a marginal good or bad. You have to get on with people, it's more than just communication, you have to be able to interrelate closely when you're working with people. As a union man I have to understand peoples problems and try to get on with them...and all that, it just comes

with experience you know. Another important skill today is flexibility. Me, I am employed as a sorter but I also do a bit of forklift driving and charge handing. I am flexible...it's...well to me we have to get away from the old trade union ideas of demarcation lines, that goes for anywhere these days, you need people who are capable of multi-tasking.

Well it's an awareness of the job, what is going on and what needs to be done. I have to be safety conscious as a charge hand and make the job easier for people on the shop floor. Skill is also being flexible, doing different things. As well as being trained up as a charge hand and forklift driver I am also trained up on the HA machines. You've got to be able to help other departments out.

For these five individuals, the most salient reference point in relation to perceptions of skill is either previous occupation or the higher status jobs they are trained to perform, and which they have some expectation of entering in the future. These men put forward a range of attributes as skills, for example, knowledge of glass production, communication skills and flexibility. In terms of discretion and autonomy as skills, whilst the two men whose work histories are with GlassCo express no perception of these attributes as skills, the three who came to GlassCo from higher status jobs elsewhere do perceive discretion and autonomy as skills. Their perceptions appear to have been shaped by prior experience of work that contains scope for autonomy and decision making over task performance:

DT: Do you have much opportunity to make decisions for yourself?
A: Not in this job no, but in my last one I had to use my own judgement a lot, it was definitely part of my job at RP Glass. And it is a skill (Sorter, ex-inspection manager, RP Glass).

DT: Do you have much opportunity to make decisions for yourself?
A: Not here at this firm, people don't seem to want you to do your job right. If you even make a suggestion it's ignored or you get shot down in flames, they just think you're trying to be clever.
DT: But I understood that the firms policy is to encourage discretion and autonomy.
A: They just say that, they don't really mean it.
DT: Do you think that discretion and autonomy are skills?
A: Oh yes (Sorter, ex-quality controller, WS Glass).

In conclusion, structural job features and the routes through which individuals came to their current occupation can explain the absence of perceptions of skill amongst the CA production workforce. For basic grade sorters and re-sorters, neither current nor past occupations generate perceptions of skill. For workers whose previous occupations were of a higher status; that is whose employment trajectories are downwards, perceptions of skill are direct reflections of previous occupations. For the two sorters trained to perform higher status roles than their normal jobs, perceptions of skill reflect the higher status role. Finally, the only interviewees in the CA to perceive discretion and autonomy as skills are the three individuals who came to GlassCo from higher status jobs in other glass-manufacturing firms.

The Mould Maintenance Workshop

The perceptions of skill held by apprentice trained craftsmen employed in the Mould Maintenance Workshop appear to be shaped by two factors. First, their experience of the apprenticeship system, and second, the structural features associated with their jobs at GlassCo: specifically, the organisation of work and division of labour, and the supervisory style in the workshop. These men display strong identities as skilled craftsmen, and their perceptions of skill are articulated in terms of experience. This experience is gained from apprenticeship training and by post apprenticeship on the job learning. Mould Maintenance Workshop interviewees also express skill in terms of functional flexibility, a perception that appears to be generated by the division of labour in this department. Although each individual has a particular job to perform, apprentice qualified men are expected to take on other tasks whenever necessary. Apprentice qualified Maintenance fitters, for example, are required to perform welding jobs whilst lathe turners, whose job is to make new moulds, are expected to carry out maintenance work on old moulds and plant equipment. This entails a degree of task flexibility on the part of the men, and is reflected in their perceptions of flexibility as skill. Unlike the majority of production workers, Mould Maintenance Workshop craftsmen express strong perceptions of discretion and autonomy as skill. These perceptions seem to be generated by the scope for decision making and autonomy over task performance which is itself a result of a neo-Taylorist management strategy. The supervisor distributes work, but craftsmen are responsible for completion and quality, and have complete control over task performance. The perceptions of skill initially articulated by these interviewees reflect their apprenticeship experience, and also the flexible division of labour in the Mould Maintenance Workshop. The following quotes are given in response to the question "If I were to ask you to define the term skill, what would you think of?"

Skill I think comes with experience. Like I haven't been taught anything here, I started and after a couple of hours I'd picked it up. I mean when your talking about going to college the things you learn you never lose or forget them, the skills you learn at college. I mean when I came here the only training I had was from an old chap showing me for half an hour and that were it. And in this shop you've got to be flexible, its only a small place and if somebody's off you have sometimes got to step in and do their job (Mould Repairer).

Skill is experience I think, I mean there are skills you develop as an apprentice and which you develop as you got along. I mean the day you think that you know it all is the day that you lose it, in this line of work anyway. You're learning all the time, skills I developed thirty years ago are irrelevant in many ways now. But then they still form the basis of what I am learning. In this sort of shop you also have to be flexible, that's the new thing, flexibility. [...] That's when we are all able to do jobs besides our own. Like a mould repair man can go on a lathe or a fitter can do a bit of welding, that sort of thing (Lathe Turner).

Skill, well going back to when I first started work, when I finished my first year at college this old guy said to me 'right, now they've learned you all this stuff at college I will show you how to do the job.' I did not even know what a lathe was or a miller machine until I went to college, so in that respect you need an apprenticeship. But if you follow the textbook too close you will never be able to do the job. So it's down to experience, skill is basically experience. Take my job, if I worked exactly to a drawing then nothing would pass, no bottles would ever get made everything would be wrong, I could guarantee that. It's experience that leads you to know what will work and what will not work, and if you're new to a job you should use somebody else's experience (Mould Checker- ensures that finished moulds meet the specifications set out in mould designs).

It can be seen that their experience of apprenticeship training, and years of post-apprenticeship on the job experience shape the perceptions of skill articulated by Mould Workshop Craftsmen. A further issue relates to the way in which perceptions of skill are articulated in more abstract terms than is the case with production workers. The perceptions of skill expressed by production workers tend to emphasise competencies and knowledge specific to a particular bundle of tasks that constitute a job, for example the practical task knowledge of automated machines held by HA machinists, the supervisory and 'man management' skills held by charge hands and former supervisors, and the knowledge of glass production articulated by the former quality controller. The perceptions of experience and flexibility as skills that are held by apprentice trained craftsmen are, in contrast, generalised and non-specific. At no time during interviews was any mention made of particular competencies such as lathe turning or other tasks associated with craft trades.

In further contrast to production workers at the firm, apprentice qualified Mould Maintenance Workshop employees hold strong perceptions of discretion and autonomy as skills. This group of workers has complete discretion over how to approach and carry out tasks. Their job is characterised by autonomous mental and physical manipulation of work, a result of which is the strong perception of discretion and autonomy as skills:

DT: How closely are you supervised in your work?
A: I'm not. There is a supervisor and a charge hand but I have been doing this job for so long now that I just do it. I know in my own mind what will work and what won't work. I am just left to get on with it.
DT: Do you think that ability to make decisions for yourself and work unsupervised is a skill?
A: It certainly is, I mean there are some people who could not make a decision to save their lives. I have to be sure of what I am doing but also I cannot be afraid of making a mistake. Because obviously if I do make a mistake they are down on me like a ton of bricks but if I let that affect me I would never get anywhere. You cannot let it get to you, you cannot be afraid to make a decision (Mould Checker).

DT: How closely are you supervised in your work?
A: Well initially you are told what to do, what jobs there are, by your supervisor and then you are just left alone to get on with it. Once you are given a job you decide how to do it.
DT: Do you think that ability to make decisions for yourself and work unsupervised is a skill?
A: I'm sure that it must be, it's just part of my skill really (Lathe Turner).

DT: How closely are you supervised in your work?

A: Well we're supervised in the sense that we get told what to do, what jobs want doing, but after that you're just left alone to do it. Once you get given a job you decide how to it.
DT: Is the ability to make decisions and work unsupervised a skill?
A: Yes (Apprentice qualified engineer).

The perception of discretion and autonomy as an important component of craft skill can be seen to be forming in the mind of a seventeen-year-old apprentice:

DT: How closely are you supervised in your work?
A: It's good, I am mainly supervised by the charge hand but the others help as well.
DT: How about the freedom to make your own decisions?
A: Some of them do but they have been doing the job a long time, they have more experience. If I am doing something I am not sure about I will think about it myself before I get someone to help, you know, work out what needs to be done and then check if I have got it right.
DT: So are you saying that you are learning to make decisions as part of your apprenticeship?
A: Yes I am, and it's a matter of confidence really, building up your confidence in your abilities (Apprentice, age 17).

The supervisor also shares the view that discretion and autonomy are important aspects of a craftsman's skill:

DT: Are the men in this department expected to make decisions for themselves and work unsupervised?
A: They do make a lot of decisions by themselves. If I am not in at the weekend for example, they will have to make decisions by themselves...and yes it is a skill because there are problems sometimes. You can get a bit stuck with something and you have to decide to go one way or the other, you can't just leave it. And it is a skill you have to learn if you're going to do this job (Supervisor).

In conclusion, the salient reference points on which apprentice trained craftsmen draw when considering skill are as follows. Firstly, the experience of taking an apprenticeship leads to a strong craft skilled identity. Secondly, the structural features associated with their current job, for example the neo-Taylorist supervisory style that allows some scope over the manipulations of work, and the flexible division of labour have led to perceptions of flexibility, discretion and autonomy as skill.

Conclusion to Workers' Perceptions of Skill

It has been demonstrated that workforce perceptions of skill at GlassCo are patterned around a number of factors. For production workers the most salient factors are the structural features associated with their current job and by their employment trajectories. Thus, for HA machinists with horizontal employment trajectories, perceptions of practical task knowledge as skill are related to experience of operating flexible automated production technology for which programming is not their responsibility. In addition, the Taylorist management structure and close supervisory style does not facilitate perceptions of discretion and autonomy as skill.

Amongst sorters and re-sorters with horizontal employment trajectories, the low skilled nature of previous and current work provides no salient reference point from which to consider the subject of skill. For this group again, the hierarchical management structure and close supervisory style provides no scope for discretion and autonomy. As a result of these factors, this group of sorters and re-sorters express no perceptions of skill whatsoever. For the three sorters who have downwards employment trajectories, that is who came to GlassCo from higher status jobs elsewhere in the glass industry, the most salient reference point from which to consider skill is their previous occupation. Perceptions of skill focus on knowledge of glass production and managerial skills. These men also have strong perceptions of discretion and autonomy as skills which, it is suggested, relate to the characteristics of their previous jobs. For the two sorters who have trained for higher status jobs, and who have expectations of moving into these jobs at some point in the future, perceptions of skill are associated with them, for example man management skills and flexibility. Finally, for craftsmen, perceptions of skill are associated with experience of the apprenticeship system, and the division of labour and management style in the Mould Maintenance workshop. Skill is articulated by this group in terms of experience, flexibility, and discretion and autonomy.

A final issue to consider at this point is the lack of any difference between the perceptions of skill held by men and women performing similar jobs, and the lack of difference between the causal processes that shape the perceptions of men and women. The lack of any salient reference point from which to consider skill applies equally to both males and females employed in the CA. There was no attempt by women in this area to draw on their domestic and family life in order to consider skill. Thus, it can be argued that the job model rather than the gender socialisation model described by Dex (1988), and discussed in Chapter Two, provides the most useful framework through which to understand women's and men's perceptions of skill.

Management Perceptions of Workforce Skill

Managers' perceptions of workforce skills at GlassCo need to be considered in the context of the poor industrial relations discussed earlier in the chapter. They should also be considered in the context of managers exercising agency on behalf of both the firm and in their own interests. With the exception of craft supervisors in the Mould Maintenance Workshop, all the junior and middle managers interviewed at GlassCo are unqualified individuals. They have either worked their way up the GlassCo hierarchy, or moved to GlassCo from a similar post elsewhere. In the context of the model set out by Savage, Barlow, Dickens and Fielding (1992) in Chapter Two, the assets belonging to this group are organisational. In order to secure their position in the firm they must exercise agency to ensure valorisation, a process that is facilitated if workers display the correct attitudes and commitment to the firm.

Management perceptions of workforce skill divide between production workers and craft workers. With respect to production workers, the skills deemed to be important by managers are the correct attitude towards work and the ability to take decisions and work unsupervised. Given the evidence presented earlier in the chapter, this latter perception appears to contradict the close and direct supervision practised at the firm. However, the firm's new owners have attempted to introduce an NVQ in glass production. The purported aim of this is to develop discretion and autonomy amongst workers. These issues are encapsulated in the following quotes from the four managers interviewed:

DT: What types of skill do production workers need ?
A: As regards the actual jobs, the skills required are not particularly difficult. Its just knowing how to do the job and most of them do have those skills. The main problem we have, and something we are trying to develop is to get them to take decisions for themselves, and that's

something they do not do. This is why we have introduced NVQs, to try to get people used to learning and thinking for themselves.

DT: What attributes would you be looking for when you are recruiting new staff?

A: Well there hasn't been much in recent years but if we were it would be attitude, whether they are willing to learn (General Works Manager).

DT: What types of skill do production workers need?

A: A good attitude to work, whether they're willing to work.

DT: What attributes would you be looking for when you are recruiting?

A: Again it comes down to attitude, they would have to show they have the right attitude. I remember we had this student once, in personnel and she said that we might be loosing out on good people by focusing on attitude. But I said that didn't matter as long as we're weeding out the bad ones.

DT: How skilled are the workforce in general?

A: Some are OK but we have some bad ones who can't be bothered to make an effort (Personnel Manager).

DT: What types of skill do production workers need?

A: Well to work on the HA machines they need to be aware of safety or it could be dangerous.

DT: What attributes would you be looking for when you are recruiting new staff?

A: I don't do it, they do it upstairs in personnel and to be honest I don't get much say, I just get landed with them and that's it.

DT: How skilled are the workforce in general?

A: To tell you the truth we have one or two bad ones, they're not very good, they have a poor attitude.

DT: What do you mean by that?

A: They just don't want to do the work (HA Production Manager).

DT: What types of skill do production workers need?

A: Knowing a good bottle from a bad and showing the right attitude, to get on with it without me having to be on their backs, being able to decide whether or not to reject a bottle. In a lot of cases they will try not to do that. In a fault situation there is an element of …well a bad fault and good bottle are easy. Its the ones in the middle that are difficult so they need to make decisions themselves but they're not comfortable with that a lot of them (CA Production Manager).

It seems apparent that a number of related but contradictory processes are underway at GlassCo, and that managers are unaware of the effects of their actions and beliefs with respect to workers. Managers state that they wish to encourage discretion and autonomy amongst workers, and develop positive workforce attitudes. However, they also harbour a good deal of mistrust of the workforce due to what they perceive as poor attitudes. This mistrust results in a belief that workers will not perform their jobs if left unsupervised, and the close supervisory style of management appears to be a result of this mistrust. The outcome of the close supervisory style is to limit scope for discretion and autonomy on the shop floor, which in turn constrains perceptions of discretion and autonomy as skill amongst the workforce. In summary the perceptions of workforce skill articulated by managers contradict the effects of their strategy towards workers, and it can be argued that until they learn to trust the workforce and relax the close supervisory management style, workers will not develop perceptions of discretion and autonomy as skill.

The differences in perceptions of skill between managers and workers in production departments are not repeated in the Mould Maintenance Workshop. The perceptions of workforce skills held by the Foreman in this department correlates closely with the perceptions of craftsmen. This is possibly due to his own background as an apprentice trained craftsman who has worked up into his present position. His perceptions appear to be shaped by the same factors as those of the craftsmen working under him that is by his experience of the apprenticeship system and his post-apprenticeship experience:

> DT: What types of skill do craftsmen need?
> A: Depends what you want him for. In here they are all skilled in the jobs that they do, but some are able to do more than others. I cannot, for example, ask all of them to do machining because they are not skilled to do it. Multi-skilling, knowing a range of skills, what your looking at there is a broad based apprenticeship. Now not all the people in here have done that apprenticeship and they are just trained to do mould repair. Now mould repair is a skill in itself but it's not....skilled...they would not have the ability to move around the shop doing a broad range of tasks like an apprenticeship would. The skills they have are narrow, only cover one area.
> DT: What attributes would you be looking for when you are recruiting new staff?
> A: An apprenticeship. There are some lads out there who do not have one but they are good at their job. But I could not ask them to do anything other than what they're trained for. Well I suppose they could but it would

take them an awful long time to learn. You learn all the different aspects of a trade in the apprenticeship stage, safety and all that. To go back to that with a forty year old man, it's going to be hard. What we want really are people who we can give a job to and just say go and get on with it. Really what you're looking at in this day and age is not just a one skill person, your looking for someone who has got a wide variety of skills. We really need a new centre lathe turner. Now the bloke who is retiring, all he can do really is turn. Now when I advertise I am going to be asking for a machinist and that is somebody who can do milling, turning and do anything else I ask of him. I am trying to get as broader skill base down here as I can for the future. We have just got two apprenticeships going...and I know that some firms do actually take young people and give them an apprenticeship training, give them apprenticeship skills (Mould Shop Supervisor).

One conclusion drawn from the evidence collected from all three case study firms is that, in general, those who have an upwards employment trajectory tend to perceive skill in terms of their current occupations. In some instances this involves rejecting the skills associated with their past occupations and defining these past occupations as unskilled. This tendency does not, however, apply to apprentice trained craftsmen who become supervisors of other craftsmen. It can be argued that this is further evidence of the strong craft skilled identity amongst this section of the labour force.

The significance of the above evidence relating to management perceptions of skill is not apparent from analysis of one case study only. It is important to note, however, that in the remaining case study factories management perceptions of skill also focus on workers' attitudes, commitment and motivation. I want to suggest that these perceptions are shaped by the need for managers to secure worker co-operation and consent. This co-operation and consent is vital if managers are to perform their own jobs efficiently and thus secure their position in the organisation, and if they are to secure the valorisation process on behalf of the firm.

Perceptions of Core and Periphery

The employment of part-time workers in the Re-sorting Department appears to indicate a core and periphery strategy on the part of the firm. Re-sorting is peripheral to the firm's core activities. The bulk of this work is not carried out at GlassCo itself, rather it is sub-contracted out to other organisations. Work in the department is unskilled, and the value of the re-sorting team appears to relate to the flexible service provided by the six women who make up the group. However, the views expressed by managers indicate that these women are a highly valued group within the firm. Rather than viewing them as peripheral, managers agreed to alter the hours they work in order to ensure they remained in the job. It would be difficult to argue that this is due to them having skills that are hard to replace, due to the low skilled nature of work in the department. It is suggested that the women are highly valued because they display the correct attitudes. This assertion is supported by the following exchange with the CA Production Manager who is ultimately responsible for this group:

DT: Are you responsible for the re-sorting team?

A: Yes they are mine. They have to be reasonable people because, well I have a good relationship with them but we do tend to move them about because there's not that many of them and we just move them from job to job. They're more like a service really than a re-sort team. An important thing about the team is that they need to get on together because they are only a small group, six of them. I have been very careful who I have put in there, I've had lots of women wanting to go on evenings but I have refused. And that is because I have thought I'm not having you go in there disrupting things. Because they do not really have a supervisor I can call in. I sometimes go and see them on a night but that is all.

DT: How important are they to the whole production operation?

A: They're handy to have, although we do not re-sort everything we fail, some of it goes out to contractors. They provide a service, they provide flexibility. I mean I don't have to chase them or check up on them. At the end of the day they do not do me a bad job the re-sort team. There is a fair bit of give and take between them and me. I can do it with them like I cannot do it with the sorters. Like if I do something to help one of them the others would not mind. But I could not do that in Sorting, if I helped one I would have the others saying I want some of that.

DT: Is there a difference in attitude between the sorters and re-sorters?

A: Oh yes, when they first started we set them on for a temporary period of three months and when they came down the yard that night they were really happy and cheerful because, well having small children at home. It's not just the money they come for, it's, well, you get away from having small children running round all day. So they would come here and have a bit of fun and I am flexible with them. Like on bonfire night I always let them have time off and make up their hours later or if they are having a special night out I might let them finish at eight o'clock instead of nine. It would be nice to have the same sort of relationship with the sorters but I can't. The evening team are a good team, they're a right team they are. When they first came I think they were in a bit of a rut, you know stuck at home with small children, and when they came it was all "did I do enough last night, was it OK what I did." So it started off for three months and then we gave it another month and then we made it permanent. So they do a really good job and we have a good relationship. It would be nice to have the same with the sorters. One of the reasons people don't want to be helpful in there (sorting) is because of what somebody else might say. They're very strong on them and us (CA Production Manager).

It would appear that the post-Fordist conceptualisation of part-time workers as part of a peripheral group on the edges of an organisation is, in this case, inaccurate. These women are seen as important to the factory, and managers are prepared to make small concessions to ensure they stay with the firm. The original hours of work for these women were 6 p.m. until 10 p.m. but this was changed to 5 p.m. to 9 p.m. at their request. It was suggested earlier that it is not due to their practical skills that they are valued, rather it is their attitudes and commitment to work. It could also be suggested, on the other hand, that the firm's decision to change the working hours of the women is possibly designed to ensure they remain pliable rather than the result of altruism.

The value placed on the re-sorting team by the CA production manager is reflected in these women's' perceptions of their position in, and value to the firm. They do not see themselves as part of a peripheral employment sector, rather they feel themselves to be a highly valued section of the GlassCo workforce. The re-sorters' perceptions of their position in the firm were elicited from their responses to three questions. The first concerned their view of what the firm is like to work for, the second, how valuable the women felt their work to be in relation to the firm's overall production process, and the third asked if they fell themselves to be in any way different from full-time staff. The following quotes combine responses to these two questions:

This is a decent firm to work for and it's got better since the new owners took over. They're more interested in the workforce and they've made the place better, like the new rest area they've created. [...] Well I do think they value what we do, I mean they wouldn't have changed our hours for us if they didn't would they [...] No, we're just the same.

Its good here, the pays good, I like it [...] I think Re-sorting is important, but we do other things as well. Like if they need help in the warehouse we get sent there.

Its OK, its not bad at all, I used to work as a sorter before I had my little girl and I came back so it must be OK [...] They value us because we get on with the job [...] I don't think we're any different to the full-timers.

The company is good and I like working here, and the pay is not bad at all really compared to some other jobs [...] And they trust us to do the job, it's nice to be trusted [...] I don't feel any different now than when I was full-time.

I have worked here 15 years and I have always liked it, I like factory work and I like it here[...] We do a good job and I think they do value us [...] No, like I say they value us.

It is evident that these women do not perceive themselves as forming part of a peripheral sector, and that they are not defined as such by the firm. Although they do provide flexibility in that they are easily moved around the factory, they are valued by managers. It can be suggested that this group do not perceive themselves as peripheral because they are *not* peripheral. It was argued in Chapter Two that the core and periphery model ignores important differences between various types of worker. Part-time employees with access to occupational benefits and secure contracts, and who are valued by employers, are closer to the core that the periphery. Such workers do not, therefore, perceive themselves as forming part of a peripheral workforce.

Conclusion

The evidence put forward in this chapter, along with evidence to be outlined in the next two chapters, provides the basis for a number of this book's key claims. With respect to the relationship between product markets and organisational structures advanced by post-Fordist theorists, the organisational structure at GlassCo has developed in response to instability in the firm's product market, and strategic choices made by managers. Overcapacity, uncertainty, and a shift into niche market areas by small firms' has engendered a need for flexible production machinery. In addition to this, poor industrial relations and management mistrust of workers has led to the traditional Taylorist management strategy. Thus, it is suggested that the organisational structure combine features that correspond to both Fordist and post-Fordist definitions. This supports the assertion advanced in Chapter Two: that the so called shift towards post-Fordist organisational structures is uneven, and that to attempt to define firms' in accordance with a Fordist - post-Fordist dichotomy ignores the complex development of industrial organisations.

It has also been argued that the articulation of flexible production technology and the traditional Taylorist management strategy has engendered production jobs that are characterised by a complete separation between conception and execution, task fragmentation, and little scope for worker autonomy and discretion. For the majority of workers, who have upwards or horizontal employment trajectories, the most salient reference point from which to consider skill is the current occupation. Thus, the perceptions of skill held by HA machinists focus on practical task knowledge, whilst for sorters and re-sorters, the combination of a low skilled current occupation and previous experience of low skilled work constrains the development of subjective perceptions of skill. The only group of sorters to express a perception of skill are those who have experience of higher status occupations, or who have expectations of gaining higher status jobs in the future. It seems apparent that the perceptions of skill held by production workers at GlassCo bear no resemblance to the upskilling or multi-skilling trajectories advanced by post-Fordist theorists such as Piore and Sabel, and Atkinson and Meager. Even if multi-skilling is defined in the narrow sense of task enlargement, it has no salience with respect to the GlassCo production workforce.

The most useful theoretical framework through which to understand the processes that shape perceptions of skill amongst this group is the labour process perspective outlined in Chapter Two. The articulation between technology and managerial strategies shape the nature of work in the factory, and therefore, perceptions of skill. In addition, some of the predictions made by Aglietta (1979) with respect to the effects of automation are applicable to the nature of work at GlassCo. For example, the suppression of more complex production tasks by the automated machinery in both departments and the resulting simplification of work, the separation of conception and execution, and the control over the pace of work that is given over to the machinery. The predictions made by Braverman and Aglietta are not, however, applicable to all workers at GlassCo. The conditions described above do not apply to craft maintenance workers. For these men, conception in the form of planning is an integral aspect of the job. In addition, these men have complete control over the execution of tasks, and their work is characterised by autonomy and discretion. Such attributes have been argued to be integral to apprenticeship training, and to post apprenticeship work experience. Thus, the perceptions of experience, discretion and autonomy expressed by craftsmen are argued to result from apprenticeship training and the nature of the craftsman's role. In addition, the perception of flexibility as skill amongst the GlassCo craftsmen is associated with the task flexibility required in a small workshop. The final issue with respect to subjective perceptions of skill is that the perceptions held by women, and the causal processes that shape them, are no different to the perceptions held by men. This supports the argument that the job model rather than the gender socialisation model most accurately explains both women's and men's perceptions of skill.

In terms of management perceptions of skill, it has been argued that these emphasise attitude and commitment to work rather than specific task related skills. Although the firm is attempting to impart notions of discretion and autonomy as skill amongst production workers, it has been predicted in the chapter that this is unlikely to prove successful while work remains rigidly Taylorist. The tendency of management to equate worker skills with attitude and commitment relates to the hostility and mistrust that exists between managers and workers. However, I also intend to show that this perception of workforce skill is found amongst managers at Electronics UK and Chemicals UK. The issue will therefore be discussed again in Chapter Eight where evidence from all three factories will be compared. Finally, the chapter discussed perceptions of core and periphery amongst the part-time female workforce. It was found that these women have no perceptions of themselves forming a peripheral workforce. Nor does management perceive these women as such. I have argued that these women do not see themselves as peripheral workers because they are not peripheral.

Notes

---

[1] The firm is located in a former mining town, which was the scene of clashes between police and miners during the 1984/5 miners' strike.

[2] Examples of previous occupations are cleaning, shopwork, manual labourer, confectionery packer and foundry worker).

6 Electronics UK

Background

Electronics UK is a Japanese owned firm that was established in the UK in the early 1990s and which manufactures home audio and video equipment. It is a subsidiary of a large Japan based electronics company that was originally founded in Tokyo in the 1930s. The establishment of Electronics UK represents the parent company's policy of setting up production facilities in Europe. The rationale behind this decision reflects patterns of Japanese inward investment identified by McCalman (1985). He identifies a number of factors that underpin this pattern of investment. The first of these is the need for firms based outside the European Community to establish a base within in order to circumvent EC import tariffs and barriers. McCalman argues that such a strategy is the cheapest option for outside companies. Second, with specific respect to the UK, is the relative absence of employment protection laws in comparison with the rest of Europe. This was said by a British manager to be an important contributory factor behind the firms decision to locate here. A final point relates to the firm's decision to establish an electronics production facility in a locality with no history of this type of enterprise. According to British managers, the decline of the local coal and textile industries has led to the availability of a cheap pool of labour, both male and female. This strategy has not, however, been unproblematic for the company.

From the outset Electronics UK encountered problems. Unstable market conditions resulted in a decrease in demand for the firm's products in the mid 1990s. This problem was exacerbated by the firm's failure to meet production deadlines for orders around this time. This failure was, according to managers, caused by too rapid an expansion and the related problem of having to recruit large numbers of workers in a short space of time. Between August 1994 and February 1995, 400 extra temporary staff were recruited which led to the firm employing large numbers of unsuitable people. Rather than choosing people on the basis of their skills, the procedure involved recruiting on mass and then, in the words of the Training Manager, "working on what we had got." Following the rapid expansion of 1995 and the subsequent failure to meet production targets, the firm retrenched its position and many of those employed at this time were discarded. At the time of research (June/July 1996) the number of employees was 822 in comparison with the 1088 employed in August 1995.

A major external influence on the production system and technology utilised by Electronics UK is the sectoral division between hi-tech research and development, and low-tech assembly operations. Electronics production in UK regions outside the South East is concentrated in low-tech assembly plants (Morgan and Sayer 1988). In the case of Electronics UK, research and development is carried out by the parent company in Japan (Personnel Manager). Electronics UK itself is an assembly operation which is geared towards the European market, and the circumvention of European import tariffs. The autoinsertion and assembly line technology used at Electronics UK to assemble parts from Japan and East Asia reflects the plant's position in the wider corporate production process.

An important feature of the production processes at Electronics UK is the JIT production strategy, which is geared towards flexible production in the context of uncertain product market conditions. Two particular features of the consumer electronics market engender a need for flexible production at the firm. First is the specific market in which it operates: that is, the middle range mass market for home and car audio equipment. Demand in this sector is determined by wider economic conditions. Electronics UK began production in 1990, just prior to the early 1990's recession which, according to the production manager, kept down demand for the firm's products (Production Manager). Second is Electronics UK's position as a sub-contractor for larger Japanese electronics transplants. At the time of research the firm was producing a line of products for another major producer of consumer electronics. The instability of the product market and Electronics UK's position as a sub-contractor engenders a need for flexibility, both in terms of the quantity of production and in terms of the variety of goods produced. This flexibility is provided by the JIT production strategy. In addition to flexibility, the JIT system can also be argued to keep labour costs to a minimal level. It will be demonstrated shortly that JIT production facilitates intensification of effort amongst the workforce. It also allows for a decrease in wastage in terms of a reduction in stocks waiting to be delivered, and in terms of ensuring that high quality standards are met.

Just as the utilisation of a JIT production system at Electronics UK is typical of Japanese production methods elsewhere, the absence of a JIT delivery system is typical of the Japanese consumer electronics sector. It was argued in Chapter Two that JIT delivery and stock control systems are largely absent from electronics production, both in Japan itself and in overseas subsidiaries. This absence is the result of conditions specific to the consumer electronics industry, for example the need to keep buffer stocks which enable firms to quickly switch production from one batch to another in order to meet changeable customer demands. A further issue for Japanese overseas transplants, and of which Electronics UK is a prime example relates to the utilisation of suppliers in Japan and East Asia. Electronics UK is located on a green field site in an area with no electronics industry. As a result there are no ready made suppliers on whom the firm can rely to deliver on a JIT basis. Although the firm aims to build up a network of UK suppliers in the future (Production Manager), at the time of research all stocks were imported from Japan and East Asia.

Structural Features

Production System and Technology

Production at Electronics UK is dominated by the JIT production strategy. This strategy is influential in shaping other structural features of the firm and, therefore, workforce perceptions of skill. It is stated above that Electronics UK does not operate a JIT delivery system. Production does, on the other hand, closely resemble the JIT model. The result with respect to the labour process is similar to that described elsewhere (for example, Delbridge, Turnbull and Wilkinson 1992). There are two related aspects to JIT production at Electronics UK. First, although stocks are not delivered from suppliers on a JIT basis, they are brought to production areas only when required. Responsibility for bringing stocks to the assembly lines is held by a few people, one of whom was interviewed. This woman is the only person on her shift with access to the stock area she controls. She keeps a daily record of all stocks requested and is responsible for collating information regarding requests from particular staff members, and for passing this information on to managers on a daily basis. The second aspect of the JIT system is the articulation of production and demand. No buffer stocks of finished products are held resulting in tight production schedules and a constant pressure to get batches of goods out on time. The culmination of the JIT strategy is a relentless concern with daily productivity targets.

The effects of JIT production are felt by workers at all levels of the occupational hierarchy. Middle managers and supervisors are under constant pressure to increase the productivity of subordinates, whilst shop floor workers are under intense pressure to work at speed and to a high quality standard. Because the firm does not keep buffer stocks it is vital that the goods produced meet the quality standards of customers. To ensure workers meet these demands the firm utilises a number of surveillance methods. The performance of shop floor workers is closely observed by managers and supervisors, and VDU screens detailing daily production targets and totals are placed above assembly lines. In addition to this the close monitoring of stocks enables the firm to control waste and makes visible any mistakes made. Requests from workers for stocks above their set allocation illuminate any mistakes they may have made.

Production is divided into four areas, the Autoinsertion Department and three assembly line areas. Research was conducted in Autoinsertion, and on one assembly line. Autoinsertion is described by managers as the key to the whole Electronics UK operation (Production Manager, Training Manager, Personnel Manager). This department contains specialist hi-tec automated autoinsertion machinery which produces the printed circuit boards (PCBs) used in audio and video equipment. It is the first stage in the production process, and involves operators setting the machines and feeding through the basic component called a surface mount. Different settings are required for the production of the different types of PCB used in various products. Once surface mounts are fed into the machine the process becomes fully automated. Any problem or error will be diagnosed by the machine which will, as a result, close itself down.

Following completion, PCBs are transferred to one of three assembly line areas. Research was conducted on the assembly line which manufactures midi CD systems. At the time of research four types of midi CD were in production, each being made on one assembly line sub-area. Within each sub-area production is carried out on two or three individual flow lines. The production process involves building up from the basic PCB, and each stage entails the addition of components until the finished product is complete. In summary, production at Electronics UK is organised around automated technology and traditional Fordist assembly lines. These technologies coalesce with the JIT production strategy to form a highly integrated production system which is very influential in generating workforce perceptions of skill.

Management Structure and Style

The managerial structure at Electronics UK follows a traditional hierarchical Taylorist pattern. The senior levels are filled by Japanese managers who, according to lower level British managers, view themselves as an elite to whom inferior British staff must defer. The four production areas are controlled by the overall Electronics UK General Production Manager, and three assistant general managers, all of whom are Japanese. Individual production areas are the responsibility of area production managers, all of whom are British. The managerial chain in Autoinsertion begins with the Area Production Manager and below him is the Assistant Manager. At this point the managerial chain divides into production operations and technical (maintenance) operations. In production operations, the senior supervisory level below the Assistant Manager is the Senior Shift Leader. He is line manager to fourteen operators on his shift. His role is to ensure that all machines are running to capacity, and that there are enough operators to guarantee this. Any operator not performing to the expected standard or who has a record of unauthorised absences is put through a disciplinary procedure and it is the responsibility of the shift leader to initiate this procedure. A final aspect of this role is to organise and oversee any training that needs to be carried out. Below the Senior Shift Leader are the shift leaders. These men provide line support for four or five operators. Their role is to oversee the work of operators and to ensure they perform to the expected standard. In technical operations the supervisory level below the Assistant Manager is the Senior Technician. The role of this man is to prioritise and organise maintenance work, to deploy technicians to jobs and to oversee the work of trainee technicians. He is also responsible for ensuring the autoinsertion machines are properly serviced and repaired.

The managerial and supervisory chain in the assembly line area is again hierarchical and Taylorist. The Area Production Manager is ultimately responsible for all aspects of production on the area. His role includes dealing with technological problems and staff problems. Below him are production supervisors who supervise the production process throughout the area. Next in the supervisory chain are the line supervisors who are responsible for the two or three individual flow lines. Their role is to oversee production and organise training. The lowest supervisory role is the line leader. These people are responsible for monitoring the performance of operators on one flow line.

It is evident that the managerial structure at Electronics UK is highly hierarchical. Each managerial and supervisory layer has a clearly defined set of responsibilities, and each is responsible to an immediate line manager. The management style at the firm is best described as overt monitoring and surveillance. The performance of basic grade operatives in both Autoinsertion and the assembly lines is closely monitored by immediate line supervisors whose own performance is similarly monitored from above:

> Operators on the line are closely supervised, that is if the line leader is doing her job properly. They should all be working in close proximity to the line. The line leader is watching their progress all the time and checking on how the line is doing as a whole, looking for problems and jumping in to sort them out if there are any (Area Production Manager).

The performance of operators is not only monitored by immediate line leaders and supervisors, senior Japanese managers are also engaged in surveillance activities. Production on both research areas was observed during fieldwork. In the Autoinsertion Department, four Japanese managers were seen walking around the area closely watching people at work. This pattern was also observed in the assembly line area. The line leader walks up and down the line constantly watching operators work. In addition to this, a Japanese manager walks in the opposite direction, also constantly monitoring the performance of operators. The result is continual and conspicuous surveillance of operatives which, when combined with the VDU screens detailing daily performance targets, leads to a highly pressurised and oppressive atmosphere:

> The Japanese, they're always walking around the department, making sure you're doing it properly. Where I worked before they let you get on with it, trusted you like. But here it has to be spot on or they're down on you (Female autoinsertion operator).

> I hate them watching me (Japanese managers), and then you've got the screens telling you how much work you've done...we all call it Tenko here you know (Female assembly line operator).

It is not only techniques of surveillance that engender an oppressive atmosphere, it is also the consequences of surveillance. The sanction applied to staff who fail to meet expected speed and quality performance levels is accurately described as public humiliation. Anyone failing to meet expected standards is publicly pulled off the line and sent for 'corrective training' (Assembly line operatives, Production Supervisor). This feature of the Electronics UK labour process is disliked by some British managers whose responsibilities include applying sanctions:

> The one thing I really do not like about this job is having to discipline people for not performing well. I don't mind too much for other things like absenteeism or graffiti on the walls, but performance, that's difficult (Production supervisor).

Total Quality Management

Total Quality Management (TQM) involves a firm wide emphasis on quality and a devolving of responsibility for quality down the hierarchy. It is, according to managers, an integral aspect of the production process at Electronics UK. The implementation of TQM techniques results in increased monitoring and surveillance and an increase of pressure on shop floor workers (see also Delbridge, Turnbull and Wilkinson 1992). The system also contributes to the pressurised atmosphere found at the firm. Pulling workers off the line if they fail to meet required standards is viewed as a public humiliation and avoided at all costs.

Division of Labour and Nature of Work

The organisation of work is characterised by a rigid Taylorist and a highly gendered division of labour. Work tasks are broken down into their smallest constituent parts and there is little crossover between occupational categories. Female workers, whilst forming the large majority of the labour force, are concentrated in the lower levels of the occupational hierarchy. The nature of work reflects the JIT production system and the corresponding management structure and style.

The Autoinsertion Department

Autoinsertion is the most hi-tec area in the factory. Sixty people are employed here, 60% of who are female. The workforce is divided into three groups, the first of which are operators and senior operators. Whilst 60% of this group are female, none are senior operators. The second group are the shift leaders whose role is to supervise the operators. Although it is the stated policy of the firm to promote autoinsertion operators up through the hierarchy on the basis of ability (Staff Handbook), all shift leaders are male. Third are the technicians who maintain the autoinsertion machinery. In line with the firms policy of training and promoting from within, a number of autoinsertion operators have been chosen to train as technicians. Again, however, whilst females have applied for these posts none have been successful. The nature of work in the department is heavily influenced by JIT production, technology and the rigid hierarchical management structure.

Operators   All autoinsertion operators have been transferred in from the assembly lines. In order to gain promotion into autoinsertion, as it is regarded throughout the firm, workers sit a test which measures their technical and numerical ability, and also their manual dexterity. They are then given three months on the job training from experienced operatives. The reasons for the test and the relatively longer training period are twofold. First, the autoinsertion machines are expensive and easily damaged (Autoinsertion Production Manager). It is important, therefore, that operators are competent to work them. Second, autoinsertion is the first stage in the production process and errors made by operators would jeopardise product quality. Although operators have responsibility for programming machines, all machine settings are displayed in charts positioned above them. These charts consist of step by step instructions and pictures that detail the whole process. In the past a qualified technician dealt with any machine shut downs. This led, however, to lost production and wasted time if none were immediately available. Now, operators deal with minor problems. In terms of supervision, once the Shift Leader has given out the daily jobs, operators are responsible for the completion of the jobs. Direct supervision is given only to trainees. This autonomy needs to be considered, however, in the context of the close monitoring mentioned earlier.

Whilst the labour of autoinsertion operators is controlled by technology, the job does involve limited proactive and reactive skills. Basic numerical skills are needed to set the machines for production, and operators need a basic understanding of the machines themselves. This demand is ameliorated, however, by the step by step instruction charts which describe the process in detail. A level of manual dexterity is also needed to physically manipulate the machine and the basic components to be fed through. Reactive skills relate to the procedures to be followed if the machine shuts down. Although the machine diagnoses the problem, the operator must decide if she is competent to deal with it herself or whether she should call a technician.

Shift Leaders   Shift leaders have a high level of responsibly for ensuring production runs smoothly and for dealing with subordinates. They are also subject to some degree of pressure. The shift leader occupies a lower middle management position, and part of the job is to mediate between higher Japanese managers and the workforce. A culture clash between the two groups renders this role problematic at times. According to one Shift Leader, Japanese managers have unrealistic expectations of workers that are based on the Japanese workplace:

> Over in Japan, they (managers) will tell someone to do something and they expect that it will be done. If they say to an operator "you will stay here until that job is done and I do not care how long it takes", the operator will stay and do it. But here...well, I mean they (the workforce) will just not do it, they will not put up with that. In the end everything does get sorted out

and the Japanese realise that they are in a different country with different rules....but it makes my job difficult sometimes (Shift leader, Autoinsertion).

Technicians Technicians are responsible for dealing with breakdowns and regular servicing of autoinsertion machines. The job of the basic grade technician is to perform these tasks following deployment by the senior technician. Diagnosis of any problem is made by the technician, along with the decision as to how to proceed. For this group a high level of responsibility is an integral feature of the job. The importance of the autoinsertion machines to the whole production process makes these men the most vital group in the factory (Production Manager). As with all other groups at the firm, these men are subject to high levels of monitoring by a supervisory figure, in this case the senior technician. Additionally, the strong ideology of the 'one best way' ensures that the performance of any task is subject to rigid procedures. This serves to limit the amount of discretion and autonomy in the job.

Jobs in the Autoinsertion Department are diverse and varied. They do however, have some features in common. Each job is subject to strict demarcation lines with little or no crossover between occupational boundaries. Whilst operators now perform tasks formerly the preserve of technicians, these are minor and limited in scope. In addition, each job has a fixed and unambiguous position within the firms hierarchical structure. Each layer from production manager down is directly answerable to a supervisory figure, and discretion and autonomy amongst workers are, as a result, limited.

The Assembly Line

Assembly line work is organised around short, strictly demarcated tasks performed at various stages in the production process. The division of labour is also highly gendered. The majority of assembly line staff are female, although no females occupy a position above line leader. Work in this area is broken down into rigidly prescribed, short, repetitive actions. Operators repeat the same 50 second task continuously over an eight hour day. These tasks are described on a work instruction sheet positioned above every work station, and must be followed exactly. The sole form of discretion operators are allowed to exercise is whether to position their box of parts and screwdriver to the left or to the right. In addition to this is the constant monitoring mentioned earlier, an objective of which is to ensure operators perform tasks in accordance with the Electronics UK 'one best way', and to ensure that they work at the required speed (Area Production Manager, Production Supervisor, Line Leader, Operators).

It is evident that work on the assembly line is traditionally Fordist. There is a long and hierarchical managerial chain and a strict division of labour. Each job has its place within the hierarchical structure and is subject to strict demarcation lines. The work performed by assembly line operatives is repetitive and boring. Workers are constantly observed, and are under intense pressure to perform to the speed of the line in order to meet daily production targets. Levels of discretion and autonomy amongst operators are negligible. This is also the case, however, for those further up the hierarchical structure, although to a lesser extent. Whilst line leaders and line supervisors have direct control over subordinates, they perform their own job in accordance with strict procedures (Personnel Manager). Additionally, the degree of discretion and autonomy given to supervisors is, in reality, limited by the sole objective of meeting daily production targets. This sole concern with short term targets can lead to pressures on supervisory staff. Each of the management interviewees below the Production Manager mentioned pressure as a feature of his or her job.

Electronics UK, Fordism and Post-Fordism

The Just-In-Time (JIT) production strategy is the dominant structural feature at Electronics UK. Other structural features, such as TQM, and the high levels of managerial and supervisory surveillance over the labour of workers, integrate closely with the JIT strategy. This analysis of how far Electronics UK exemplifies a post-Fordist organisational structure will therefore begin by discussing the articulation of JIT with the wider product market, and the firm's labour process. It will then present a brief discussion of technology and flexibility.

The introduction of JIT/TQM is often put forward as an example of a shift from Fordist to post-Fordist organisational structures (for example, Delbridge, Turnbull and Wilkinson 1992). The association between these practices and post-Fordism centres on the integration of supply and demand. Production in the post-Fordist firm is geared towards changeable consumer demand. This uncertain demand results in flexible manufacturing systems in which short run batch production is made possible through flexible technology and flexible working practices. JIT is an example of this process, for example, changing consumer demands are met by producing goods on a JIT basis that eliminates waste. The system thus eradicates the stockpiling of goods and wasted worker time associated with Fordist production.

The argument that JIT/TQM systems represent an alternative to Fordism is advanced by Delbridge, Turnbull and Wilkinson (1992). They highlight a number of ways in which the two systems differ. First, Fordism would attempt to increase efficiency through technological change; JIT\TQM does this by intensifying the labour process and by pushing back the frontiers of management control. Under traditional Fordist system it is possible for workers to establish their own production norms and working practices (for example Nichols and Beynon 1977, Thompson 1989), that is, it was possible for them to resist. However, the close monitoring of work renders this virtually impossible under the JIT\TQM system. Second, whilst both Fordist and JIT systems integrate supply and demand, the nature of this integration differs. Whereas under Fordism supply pushes products through the system, under JIT, production is pulled by demand. Fourth, under Fordism defective goods cannot be traced back to individuals due to the stockpiling of products. This is, however, possible under the no stockpiling JIT\TQM system. Finally, with respect to the possibility of disruption, a particular feature of the Fordist era was the opportunity for industrial action caused by the concentration of large groups of workers under one roof. Such opportunities are reduced in Japanese post-Fordist organisations which have no strike, one union agreements.

The above arguments are applicable to Electronics UK. The intense nature of the labour process and the close monitoring of workers serves to constrain the possibility of resistance. Demand and supply are closely integrated, with demand pulling production rather than supply pushing production. Mistakes by operatives are made visible through the recording of all requests for parts, and a factory wide system for tracing defective goods back to individual operators (Personnel Manager). Finally, establishment of the Electronics UK factory in the UK was made conditional on the negotiation of a no strike, one union deal (District Council Informant).

The view that JIT\TQM systems are a manifestation of post-Fordism is not universally accepted. Discussing the concept of Toyotaism outlined in Chapter One, Dohse, Jurgens and Malsch argue that:

> Toyotaism is simply the practice of the organisational principles of Fordism under conditions in which management prerogatives are largely unlimited (Dohse, Jurgens and Malsch 1985).

Dohse and his colleagues argue that Taylorism is integral to Japanese industry, and that the Japanese "out Taylor us all." They also point out that the system was introduced to Japan from the USA. The suggestion that JIT is a manifestation of Fordism appears to be based on the rationalisation that is common to both systems. JIT, rather than signifying a break with Fordist rationalisation, is viewed as an intensification of Fordism. They also argue that the intensification of control associated with the JIT system serves to overcome the forms of workforce resistance associated with Fordism rather than consistuting a complete break (Op-Cit.).

It is concluded here however, that the introduction of the JIT system does represent a qualitative shift in the labour process. This conclusion draws on Delbridge and Turnbull's view that Japanese management systems push back the frontiers of control. Studies of the labour process in traditional electronics firms, such as that carried out by Cavendish (1982), show that whilst the work performed by female assembly line workers is intense and difficult, there remains a small space for resistance. Whilst these opportunities for resistance are largely symbolic and limited to trivial issues, they do nonetheless exist (Cavendish 1982). The opportunity for any form of workforce resistance at Electronics UK appears, from the evidence collected, to be virtually non-existent. It is this process of pushing back the frontier of control that distinguishes the labour process at the firm from the more traditionally Fordist labour process at GlassCo. The outcomes in terms of generating perceptions of skill are, furthermore, a reflection of both Fordist and post-Fordist elements. For example, the hierarchically structured and fragmented nature of perceptions throughout the factory compare with the hierarchical and fragmented nature of work under Fordism. The emphasis on speed and accuracy, however, can be argued to reflect the close monitoring and surveillance that exists at the factory.

Moving on to technology, it can be suggested that the firm contains a mix of post-Fordist and Fordist machinery, and that these different types of machinery are closely articulated with each other. The assembly flowlines, for example, typify Fordism, whilst the autoinsertion machinery can be defined as post-Fordist in the sense that it is easily programmed to flexibly produce a variety of PCBs for a variety of products. This technology does not however generate an upskilling or multi-skilling of the workforce as predicted by Piore and Sabel. The division between conception and execution has not been rescinded, and the use of technology has not resulted in de-layering of the management hierarchy. Rather, flexible technology is allied to a rigid Taylorist management system. It can be suggested that the impact of the limited automation at Electronics UK corresponds most closely to the predictions of Aglietta (1979), for example, the autoinsertion machinery performs the more complex production tasks, and responsibility for designing and planning programmes is given over to skilled technicians. Thus, automation has stripped machine operating functions of all qualitative content.

Workers' Perceptions of Skill

Workers' perceptions of skill at Electronics UK are patterned around the production system and technology, and an individuals position in relation to the horizontal and vertical division of labour. Perceptions of skill are also heavily influenced by the overt surveillance techniques which are themselves closely related to the JIT production strategy. It will be shown that in the Autoinsertion Department, skill is defined as technological or mechanical competence, whilst on the assembly line skills are defined in terms of the discrete tasks performed on the line. In both departments, skill amongst basic grade operatives is defined as speed and accuracy, whilst moving up the occupational hierarchy perceptions widen to include communication and managerial skills, and the ability to cope with pressure.

Autoinsertion

It was stated earlier that this department is the most technologically advanced in the Electronics UK factory. It was also pointed out that, although autoinsertion operators program the machines, responsibility for designing the programs lies with senior technicians in a separate department. Thus, whilst the sophisticated autoinsertion machinery generates perceptions of skill that focus on concepts of technical and mechanical competence, these relate to task complexity and execution rather than proactive planning functions. Emphasis is also given to notions of speed, accuracy and the ability to cope with stress. This reflects the JIT and TQM systems in operation at the factory. For those workers located in the higher levels of the occupational hierarchy, the perception of technological competence as skill is supplemented by perceptions of interpersonal, communication and 'man management' skills. Thus, from the basic grade operator:

> DT: If I were to ask you to define the term skill, what would you think of ?
> A: To be skilled you have to be on the ball, you have to be switched on to whatever it is that you're doing no matter what the job is. You also have to be mechanically minded. With this job there are so many things really, things to learn and processes you have to go through. It is very important that we get things right straight off. I mean if we mess up then the whole product is messed up...We are dealing with big machines and we have a lot of responsibility. We even do some of the technicians job now...When I first came here there were no women in autoinsertion but sex discrimination law says no discrimination so they had to relent and let us in. Then they realised what women can do, that they're just as

mechanically minded as men and just as competent (Female Autoinsertion Operator).

This woman's perceptions of skill emphasis the mechanical and technical nature of her work. She is also keen to overcome what she perceives to be gender stereotyping of women as technologically incompetent. When the tape recorder was switched off this woman began to complain about the highly gendered attitudes of both Japanese and British managers. She said that although she is as technically competent as the men, she is continually passed over for promotion simply because she is a woman. She also complained that although she carries out tasks that were previously done by technicians, she is given no recognition for this.

The view that technical competence is an important aspect of skill is also held by individuals higher up the supervisory chain In addition, perceptions of skill amongst these interviewees widen to include interpersonal and communication abilities. The following quotes are again in response to the question: "If I were to ask you to define the term skill, what would you think of?"

> Well...machinery skills, some understanding of technology, how to operate and deal with this sort of machinery. The job is complicated, it's technical and it takes a long time to learn it. It's the most highly skilled department in the whole factory. Another type of skill I think is being able to get stuff out on time and not make a mistake when we're programming it. If we do the PCBs will be wrong and that costs money. A third sort of skill is the ability to communicate with people... Yes I would say that communication is a skill. Another one is how to prioritise work, what has to be done first and what can be left (Senior Autoinsertion Operator).

> Being able to listen to people and you know, being fair with the operators working under you. Obviously you need to understand machinery. I was a good operator, I know how to operate all the machines in here. If an operator comes to you with a problem you have to know what to do, what you're talking about, how to deal with it. There are checks to be done and the running of the machines and the right parts. You have to have a numerical brain, a mechanical brain. In my job you have to cope with stress and that can be a skill I think. It can get pretty hectic in here. Like today for example, it seems that before you know where you are there is a list of jobs to be done, jobs that you have to get done. It gets pretty awkward sometimes (Shift Leader).

The technicians in the department not surprisingly, share the strongly technological perceptions of skill held by these autoinsertion operators. Two technicians were interviewed, one a trainee technician and the other the Senior Technician:

> Skill I think is a good understanding of mechanical things, having a flair for mechanical things. This job is much more skilled than my previous job (heavy engineering). The types of machines, it's a lot more technical, you need to be much more accurate. The tolerance is a lot tighter and we have to keep on top of the work, keep the machines going. That's important in a place like this (Trainee Technician).

The perceptions of skill held by this interviewee emphasis technical competence and the need to keep up with the workload. This perception is comparable to the views expressed by the basic grade autoinsertion operator quoted earlier. The final interview with the Senior Technician again reveals a broadening of the concept of skill to include interpersonal and organisational abilities:

> Number one is the ability to prioritise, decide what jobs need to be done first and to decide quickly. You have to be able to juggle regular servicing needs with breakdowns. Man management is also a skill, communication that sort of thing. And of course you have to understand the machines, that's very important. Me personally, I have to deal with a lot of pressure in my job and I would say that is also something of a skill (Senior Autoinsertion Technician).

The concepts of discretion and autonomy appear to have little salience amongst the autoinsertion workforce. This is possibly due to the absence of any real opportunity for discretion and autonomy within the context of the direct supervisory system, the rigid division of labour and the imperative to meet daily productivity targets. As in the other two case studies, interviewees were asked if their jobs involved autonomous decision making. Given the obvious and overt surveillance techniques in operation at the firm questions relating to the level of supervision were irrelevant. All interviewees from all levels of the occupational hierarchy said they had little opportunity for decision making and none felt discretion to be a particularly important skill:

> DT: Do you make decisions for yourself in this job?
> A: Well here it's very much like he's answerable to him and he's answerable to someone a bit higher up. You can't really do anything off your own bat, like if I want to make an improvement in the department I have to ask the area production manager, I can't just do it myself.
> DT: Do you consider the ability to take decisions at work to be a skill?

A: Is it a skill? [...]   No I think skill in my job is making sure maintenance jobs are done, knowing how to prioritise and cope with pressure, that sort of thing (Senior Autoinsertion Technician).

To summarise, perceptions of skill in the Autoinsertion Department focus on an aptitude for technology and machinery, and a need for accuracy and speed to keep production moving. Higher up the occupational hierarchy, perceptions of skill widen to include managerial and organisational skills. In short, perceptions of skill closely mirror the demands of the jobs performed by individual interviewees.

The Assembly Line

The patterning of perceptions of skill around job characteristics in Autoinsertion is repeated in the assembly line area. Perceptions of skill articulated by assembly line operatives also emphasise the need for speed and accuracy. These perceptions are again argued to arise from operators' awareness of constantly being watched. The following quotes are again in response to the question: "If I were to ask you to define the term skill, what would you think of?"

To be skilled you have to be up to speed and accurate. You have to ask yourself what you can and cannot do. There are people in this factory who are not really skilled, who are not fast enough or do not have the handling skills so they have to go on prepping, that's preparing components for the operators (Female Operator).

Definitely flat packing because you could not just put anyone on flat packing stage and expect them to be able to do it. somebody would have to be with them and watch them to make sure they were doing it right because it is so important. Another skill on the PCB line would be putting cable in, there seems to be a knack to doing it you have to do it right. It's no good messing about on that job, so putting cables in is a skill, not everyone can do that (Female Operator).

Well first of all skill would be speed. You have to have speed on the line, definitely. You need hand/eye co-ordination and accuracy. You've got to get that up to scratch. On the job I am doing now you have to concentrate on what you're doing. I mean I am soldering and you just can't turn away. I have to watch what I am doing all the time (Female Operator).

Moving up the occupational hierarchy, again perceptions of skill are closely related to the demands of individual jobs. The first quote is from the female stock controller who is responsible for the assembly line stock area. Her job is to record all stocks requested by individual operators, and to pass this information to the production supervisor:

> It's the ability to cope with responsibility, use your own initiative and not sit in a corner doing nothing, someone who can be trusted. I run the stock room like I run my own house. I know where everything is and I don't stand for anything (Stock Controller).

In terms of the two assembly line interviewees employed in supervisory positions, again their perceptions of skill correspond closely to the demands of their own job. As with the supervisory staff in Autoinsertion, perceptions of skill widen to include interpersonal, management and organisational skills. They also refer to the ability to cope with pressure, a perception that is argued to stem from the JIT system and the constant need to complete batches of goods on time:

> Skill is being able to communicate for a start. I think you have to be able to deal with people and problems. Not everyone can do that. You also have to be able to gain respect and handle pressure, you have to be a certain type of person to cope with pressure. When they were promoting people from the line to supervisors jobs it was the best operators and those who can deal with pressure who got promoted (Line Leader).

> Well man management, time management, coping with the people who work under you, and I think that the most important skill you can have is coping with stress. In my own job this is key because it is a very stressful job. The targets for the factory are hard to meet and...well we are under a lot of pressure to meet them. We also need paperwork skills and mathematical skills to cope with studying schedules and that sort of thing....And the way the lines are measured, efficiency, line quality, speed and whether we are meeting production targets, things like that. Any way a line can be measured it is measured so you need to be able to understand your production targets (Production Supervisor Assembly Line).

In summary, the perceptions of skill held by assembly line staff correspond with specific jobs held by interviewees. Assembly line operatives perceive skill in terms of discrete assembly line tasks such as flat packing, inserting cables into PCBs and soldering whilst for supervisors and managers skill is perceived in terms of communication and managerial abilities. When interviewees in the assembly line area were asked if they had scope for discretion and autonomy, lower level staff appeared to have some difficulty understanding the concept. This difficulty needs to be considered in the context of these individuals' employment histories. All have come to Electronics UK from previous jobs that entail repetitive detail work. Thus, they have no salient reference point from which to consider discretion and autonomy as skills.

The above evidence suggests that breaking down tasks into their smallest constituent parts results in breaking down skills into their smallest constituent parts. This in turn generates perceptions of skill that reflect this breakdown. It has been shown that the perceptions of skill held by the workforce are closely linked to the horizontal and vertical division of labour. Divisions are found between the two departments sampled and between the occupational levels. Workers in Autoinsertion view skill in terms of technological competence, whilst workers in the assembly line area emphasise physical actions such as dexterity, speed, and hand/eye co-ordination. At the higher levels of the occupational hierarchy perceptions of skill emphasise interpersonal, communication and managerial skills. This evidence suggests, that the hierarchical structuring of work at the firm generates hierarchically structured perceptions of skill.

Perceptions of skill are also influenced by the intense nature of the JIT system described earlier. This system results in pressure to constantly meet tight output targets, and to continually work at high speeds. TQM results in pressure to maintain a high level of accuracy whilst working at these speeds. For all workers, but especially so for supervisory staff and higher level staff, the ability to cope with pressure and stress is perceived as a skill. The constant monitoring of assembly line workers, and the public humiliation of those not meeting targets, also engenders an atmosphere of fear amongst the workforce. A common pattern during interviews was that workforce interviewees would ask me to turn off the tape before making comments critical of the firm. This pattern was not repeated at the two British owned case study firms.

Employment Trajectories and Perceptions of Skill

The principal argument of this book is that individuals perceive skill in relation to the most salient reference point on which they can draw. For the majority of interviewees the most salient reference point is their current job. Thus perceptions of skill are associated with the firm specific structural features that shape particular jobs. These interviewees all have upwards or horizontal employment trajectories in that they entered their current occupation from occupations of a similar or lower occupational status. Employment trajectories can be either internal or external to the case study firms or external, that is individuals entering their current job from a different employer. An issue that is specific to Electronics UK concerns the tendency amongst those who have moved up the firm's internal occupational hierarchy to dismiss, and in some cases denigrate, the skills associated with their earlier job at Electronics UK. A small number of interviewees, who began working at Electronics UK as assembly line operatives, now say that line operative is an unskilled occupation. These interviewees were all asked to compare the skills used on the assembly line with the skills they need for their current job:

> Oh this job is much more skilled than on the lines, much more technical. The lines not skilled at all, it's just doing the same thing over and over. It's dead repetitive and boring (Female Autoinsertion Operator).

> Dexterity skills are what they need, being able to use their hands. That's about it. Those jobs are so simple you just do it automatically. It's not skilled on the line anyone can do it...I knew when I came here I would not stay on the line, I knew I would be promoted because I am too skilled for the line (Line Leader).

> It's simple on the line, anybody can do it, it's not skilled. I came from heavy engineering and I picked it up easily. But in Autoinsertion it's much more complicated so it's more skilled (Trainee Autoinsertion Technician).

> It's not skilled on the line, not really. It's just routine and repetitive. I mean in my job I've got some control, and it's a case of running things like I do my own home (Stock Controller).

It may be that the experience of having been chosen for promotion has led these people to dismiss the skills used by line operators. On the other hand, it could be that their experience of their new jobs, that is their experience of work that is not routine and repetitive, has led them to downgrade the skills of assembly line workers. The responses given tend to contrast the routine, repetitive and boring nature of work on the line with the skills required for higher level jobs. For example the technical nature of skill in the Autoinsertion Department, the supervisory skills of the line leader and the control over her work enjoyed by the Stock Controller.

A second issue with respect to upward employment trajectories relates to qualifications. It was shown, in Chapter Five, that the apprentice qualified Mould Maintenance Workshop employees at GlassCo have strong identities as skilled craftsmen, and that the experience of undergoing an apprenticeship is a significant factor in shaping their perceptions of skill. These perceptions are not evident, however, amongst two apprentice qualified engineers now employed in the Autoinsertion Department. For these two men the skills acquired through apprenticeship training are viewed as irrelevant to their current jobs. The men were asked how useful their apprenticeship training was to their performance in their current job:

> I think that on the job experience is more important to skill than qualifications. Take me, I have got a City and Guilds in mechanical engineering which is like service and repair. What happens in this firm is that people get trained up as they go along. I basically started at the lower end of the job and got experience as I went along and that is how I acquired my skills, not through having an apprenticeship (Senior Autoinsertion Technician).

> Well speaking personally, I came to this firm as an engineer and I have changed direction really. With my qualifications I would not have been able to come into the company as a supervisor but obviously the Japanese and UK management saw me working as an engineer and felt that I had the right skills for this job. When a supervisor's job came up I applied and I got it. I have been at Electronics UK for five years and I have been doing my job for nearly three. I do not think my qualifications are important for this job except that I know how long repair jobs will take (Production Supervisor).

The dismissal of their craft apprenticeship qualification by these interviewees is a result of their upward employment trajectory. It was pointed out earlier a general pattern across all three case study firms is that those who have moved up the occupational status hierarchy perceive skill in terms of their new occupational status. Thus, the perceptions of this group are commensurate with the developing model.

Conclusion to Workers' Perceptions of Skill

When considering the subject of skill, workers at Electronics UK, like GlassCo and Chemicals UK, draw on their own personal most salient reference point. Unlike the other two case study factories, however, for all workers at Electronics UK the most salient reference point is the current occupation. Whereas at GlassCo and Chemicals UK a number of employees have employment trajectories that have taken them down the occupational status hierarchy, all the Electronics UK interviewees have upwards or horizontal employment trajectories. Their perceptions of skill are patterned around the organisational structural features that characterise jobs at the firm. The impact of employment trajectories relates to the way in which those who have upwards employment trajectories tend to denigrate the skills required for their previous jobs.

To reiterate, perceptions of skill at Electronics UK are patterned around the organisational features that shape individuals' jobs. These are:

1. The hierarchical management structures and close supervisory style.
2. The social organisation of work.
3. The production process and technology.

I have demonstrated that the hierarchical occupational structure, and the rigid division of labour around strictly demarcated tasks generates task specific perceptions of skill. Thus, in the Autoinsertion Department perceptions of skill focus on notions of mechanical competence, whilst in the assembly line area they focus on specific tasks such as soldering, cable insertion and flat packing. In both departments individuals located at higher levels of the occupational hierarchy define skills in terms of the competencies required for their own jobs. Thus, perceptions of skill widen to include communication and managerial skills, and the ability to prioritise work. With respect to the production process at the firm, I have argued that this is dominated by the JIT system. The outcome of this system has been shown to be an overt monitoring and surveillance, and an increase in pressure on shopfloor and supervisory staff. In order to ensure that workers perform at the required levels of speed and accuracy, they are closely observed by managers and supervisors. This, in turn, engenders perceptions of skill that emphasise speed and accuracy. For middle managers and supervisors, the pressures that emanate from the JIT system are reflected in perceptions of the ability to cope with pressure as skill. Finally, the interaction between technology and the social organisation of work has implications for perceptions of skill. In Autoinsertion, workers are, like HEPA machinists at GlassCo, responsible for programming and operating machinery. They are not, however, responsible for planning or designing programs. Thus, the division between conception and execution put forward by Braverman and Aglietta is a feature of work in the department. It is suggested that the task specific perceptions of mechanical competence as skill are, in part, a result of this division. Perceptions of skill amongst Autoinsertion staff do not include any notion of theoretical or conceptual knowledge.

With respect to the technology-social organisation of work combination on the assembly line, it was suggested in Chapter Four that this is comparable to the combination found in the GlassCo Sorting Department. That is, the nature and pace of work is controlled by technology. Machine-human interaction on the flowline is confined to workers carrying out short, repetitive, operations brought to them by the line. This results in perceptions that focus on discrete assembly line operations. It is further argued in the chapter that the features of work serve to constrain all forms of discretion and autonomy open to workers, both with regard to the organisation of tasks and the manipulation of work. This in turn constrains perceptions of these concepts as skill.

In terms of the parallel process of employment trajectories, at Electronics UK the impact relates solely to the views of those who have moved up the occupational hierarchy. I have argued that amongst those who have moved up the internal occupational hierarchy there is a tendency to dismiss the skills required for lower level jobs. Similarly, the two apprentice trained craftsmen, both with upwards employment trajectories, dismiss the importance of apprenticeship training in relation to their current job. The weak identification with their craft skill expressed by these men contrasts with the strong craft identities displayed by craftsmen at GlassCo and Chemicals UK. The reasons for this contrast are unclear, and no assertions can be made on the basis of this evidence. It is however possible to put forward one tentative possiblity, that is that apprenticeship training remains a salient reference point in relation to perceptions of skill only where individuals remian employed in related occupations, or take up lower status occupations. When individuals obtain what they regard as higher status jobs, apprenticeship training may lose its salience.

A final point to make is that, as with GlassCo, there are no differences between the perceptions of skill held by male and female workers who occupy the same or similar jobs. Perceptions of skill amongst all workers at Electronics UK, regardless of gender, relate to the most salient reference point from which individuals can draw in order to consider skill. In the case of the Electronics UK workforce, this is the current occupation. In terms of perceptions of skill held by women, the most useful model through which to understand these is, as with men, the job model. Evidence from Electronics UK, along with that from GlassCo, provides support for the arguments put forward by Dex (1985, 1988) and Siltanen (1994). They argue that women's experiences and attitudes towards work are shaped, like those of men, by features of the job and conditions at work rather than by their gender.

Management Perceptions of Workforce Skill

Before beginning the discussion of managers' perceptions of workforce skills at Electronics UK, a methodological problem that arose during the fieldwork stage should be mentioned. Requests to interview senior Japanese managers were refused, with the reason being that the language barrier would make communication difficult. However, given that many of the Japanese managers at the firm live and work in the UK, it can be suggested that difficulty over language was a pretext for the real reason for refusal. It is possible that this is related to Japanese managers suspicions about the motives for this research, a view that was advanced by one British manager who wished to remain anonymous. Whatever the origins of the refusal, however, the outcome is a lost opportunity to uncover the perceptions of skill held by Japanese personnel who have control over the labour process in a Japanese UK transplant. The management perceptions of skill discussed here are confined to those held by British managers. As at GlassCo, they were uncovered by asking managers what types of skill are required of the workforce, what attributes are sought during recruitment, and what is the general level of skill amongst the workforce. Management perceptions of workforce skill divide with respect to the two research areas, and between supervisory and shop floor staff. It will be demonstrated that, as with workers' perceptions of their own skills, management perceptions of workforce skill reflect the firm's hierarchical occupational structure and the division of labour. The also contain highly gendered attitudes towards skill. For all managers the crucial components of skill are attitude and commitment to the company. This assertion is supported by the following quotes which were given in response to the question: "What are the most important skills you require of your workforce?"

It sounds basic but one important skill is commitment, commitment to making the company a success which I think is almost taken for granted in Japan. Also what we call factory discipline, simple things like knowing you have to get to work on time on a morning (Personnel Manager).

Well what we really want are people with good attitudes, I take the view that as long as people come to work and do their job, that is all that matters (Production Manager).

Attitude. I mean you get some people who have the right practical skills but they lack the ability to attend work, they just do not turn up. Surprisingly the majority of people we have had to let go, it has been for that reason [...] some people here can do the job but they're never here (Production Supervisor, Assembly Line).

The basics, like reliability and making an effort (Autoinsertion Manager).

Moving on to job specific skills, managers, like workers, perceive skill in relation to the set of tasks performed. Thus management perceptions of skill within departments are patterned around the attributes of specific jobs. It appears that management perceptions are also associated with the gender of specific job incumbents. Thus from the Autoinsertion Production Manager:

> DT: What skills do you require from workers in this department?
> A: It depends on the work. In autoinsertion you have three skill areas. You have the people who operate the machines and those people just need the ability for simple mathematics and to know how to operate machines. Really they just need to know how to load the machine, switch it on and off and free jams and things. Then you have shift leaders who look after the shift. They have to know how to organise the shift, if you have people off sick to deleage their responsibilities and make sure the machines are run twenty four hours a day. The third skill area is the technicians who are the most important people in the department, basically because they repair and maintain those very expensive machines. If they break down they have to repair them as quickly as possible because they have to keep running all the time. So they must be very mechanically competent.
> DT: Why is it that 75% of operators are female but there are no female trainee technicians?
> A: (long pause) I don't know ...well...technicians need a high level of technical competence (Autoinsertion Production Manager).

The views of this manager in relation to the technological competencies needed by basic grade operatives appear to differ from those of operators themselves. Operators believe that they need a high level of mechanical competence, whilst this manager believes that they need only to know how to switch the machine on and off, and deal with jams. In addition, whilst this manager does not explicitly suggest that men are more technologically competent than women, this assumption is implicit in his answer. In contrast to this veiled assumption, the view that women are better suited to low level routine detail work is clear in the perceptions of workforce skill held by managers in relation to the assembly line area. As in the Autoinsertion Department, management perceptions are patterned around the competencies required for specific jobs. The following responses were again given in answer to the question: "What skills do you require from workers in this department?"

> Well for operators you are talking about very basic skills. It boils down to simple hand/eye co-ordination, and manual dexterity. It depends as well what you mean by skill, what is the difference between a skill and a personal quality or discipline, which from the point of view of running a successful production operation is equally important. I guess the most important thing we are looking for is attitude of mind, its discipline and an understanding of what manufacturing is about. But skills on the production

line are pretty basic. [...] 75% of assembly line staff are female and there are good reasons for that. Obviously they are better at the manual dexterity we talked about. I find it hard to explain because I don't know why this is, but its certainly a fact that on short cycle repetitive work women are better than men, they just are (Personnel Manager).

On the line all they need is hand/eye co-ordination and manual dexterity. The job entails placing different components on a circuit board. If you imagine a flowline that is turning out 500 identical products, you've got 500 cycles of work. Most people would think, God, how do they cope with that...And I think women are more suited to it than men, they can switch off and do that kind of work quite well, they seem more psychologically capable. Its an old joke, women can talk and work at the same time...I don't know why but they are able to do boring tedious repetitive stuff again and again over weeks and throughout a life time of work (Training Manager).

I suppose you could say that working on the line is a sort of skill, its the ability not to get bored. Some people get bored very quickly and they start making errors. Also someone who is good with their hands, I mean its not about being good with machinery or anything, its about being good with your hands. . [...] women make up the large majority of the assembly line because they are better at this type of repetitive work. They can concentrate better, they're more willing to stay in one place, do the same thing without getting bored (Production Supervisor, Assembly Line).

It can be seen from these quotes that, not surprisingly, managers perceive assembly line skills in terms of manual dexterity, concentration and willingness to accept the discipline of the line. These types of skill do not appear to be held in high regard by these managers. What is more, such skills are defined by managers as women's skills. It is difficult to discern from interview transcripts whether these managers view manual dexterity, hand/eye co-ordination and concentration as 'basic' because they are performed by women, or whether it is a belief that women are less capable than men that keeps women in the lower levels of the occupational hierarchy. According to two female interviewees, one an autoinsertion operator and one an assembly line operator, there is reluctance at the firm to promote women into higher-grade occupations. Both had applied for promotion into jobs in which men predominate, that is as trainee technicians, but both had been repeatedly rejected. It is not possible to establish whether this rejection resulted from gender stereotyping or lack of competence on the part of the women. It can be suggested, however, that the views expressed by managers indicate a degree of gender stereotyping in relation to suitability for particular jobs.

With respect to the higher-grade occupations in the assembly line area, as with job incumbents themselves, management perceptions of employees skills widen to include communication and supervisory skills. The following quotes are in response to the same question as above:

> For line leaders and such we would be looking at things like reliability and willingness to put some effort in. Obviously they have to be good operators so that they know what is being built on the line. We are looking for people with a genuine interest in the job, but what we are really looking for is people who can look after a group of people. It boils down to people skills, the ability to communicate and it does not matter whether you are making hi-fi equipment or packing mushrooms, supervisors need people skills (Production Supervisor, Assembly Line).

> Basically they need some product knowledge but it is mainly about man management. It is about how they handle people. A supervisor for example will have about fifty to a hundred people under him so he has to know how to handle a lot of people (Production Manager, Assembly Line).

It can be seen that management perceptions of skill are, like those of workers, patterned around the horizontal and vertical division of labour. They also reveal a strong association between attitude, commitment and skill. Finally managers perceptions of skill are highly gendered, although no conclusions can be drawn as to whether the skills required by line operators are devalued because they are held mainly by women, or whether women predominate in the lower skilled occupations as a result of their gender.

Moving on to the question of what types of skill are sought out in new recruits, discussions focused on the problems associated with the strategy of recruiting at the lower levels of the occupational hierarchy. The two managers responsible for recruitment stated that this strategy emphasised assembly line skills to the exclusion of other types of skill, and that this led to problems in relation to the promotion of workers from the line:

> DT: What types of skill do you seek out when you are engaged in recruitment?
> A: Good question, I am not really sure to be honest. I mean there are lots of ways of selecting people and we use psychometric testing. The problem with that is that it is good at slotting people into the right shaped hole, put the problem being that what you would want to do ideally is to eventually move them on up to a more senior position in the company. That is the ideal situation and psychometric testing cannot do that for you, its a one off

basis. I think when we are recruiting we look for dexterity but the big thing is personality, how people will fit into the organisation (Training Manager).

DT: What types of skill do you seek out when you are engaged in recruitment?
A: Initially we are looking for people with good assembly line skills, but we also want to employ people who will take on other roles, progress if you like. Now a lot of people who have benefited from this policy have had to take on responsibilities which to be honest they were unprepared for because of their previous experience and the length of time we have been operating. Its easy for the Japanese to talk about doing this kind of thing, they have factories that have been operating for forty years and people who have moved through these roles by natural progression over a long period of time and who have experience. We do not have that (Personnel Manager).

It is suggested that these comments reflect the general perception that skill requirements differ between jobs and occupational levels. The type of person suitable for assembly line work may not necessarily have the skills required for technical or supervisory work.

The final issue to consider in relation to management perceptions of workforce skill relates to the general skill levels of the workforce. Responses to questioning on this issue resonate with the emphasis placed on attitude as an attribute of skill. They also reflect problems with the firm's core and periphery labour strategy. When asked the question: "What are the general levels of skill amongst your workforce?" the personnel manager replied:

In a factory this size we are bound to have some problems with attitude, and it has to be said that these problems arise from giving temporary contracts to new recruits. People employed on permanent contracts elsewhere are reluctant to accept them and that has worked against us.[...] We are now paying the price of offering only temporary contracts. We have had problems with some of the people we have taken on on a temporary basis, things like attitude, attendance and commitment. Many of them have not been of the quality we would have wanted. However we have let most of them go now, the ones with bad attitudes (Personnel Manager).

And from the assembly line production manager in response to the same question:

Some of the people we have taken on in the past have not been competent of fast enough...Maybe the symptoms were that they were incompetent or too slow but the actual cause of the reason that they were not fast enough was that they had the wrong attitude.

In conclusion, management perceptions of workforce skill at Electronics UK focus primarily on attitude and commitment. This is evident from initial responses to questioning about the most important skills required of workers and responses to questioning about the general skill levels amongst the workforce. It was pointed out in the previous chapter that these perceptions are common to the three factories, and that they relate to managers need to exercise agency on behalf of the firm in order to secure their own position in the organisation. None of the junior and middle managers interviewed possess a professional qualification, although a small number do have a craft apprenticeship. It can be argued, therefore, that the assets of this group are organisational.

In terms of practical on the job skills, the perceptions of managers reflect the horizontal and vertical division of labour in the firm. Managers appear, however, to view the skills demanded of basic grade operators as more simplistic than the operators themselves. It has been suggested that this latter tendency may possibly relate to the gender of the majority of basic grade operators. Managers at the firm appear to hold stereotyped images of women in the workplace. A final point, which is dealt with in more detail below, is that managers blame past problems with the skill levels of workers on the deliberate core and periphery strategy utilised by the firm., specifically, the policy of offering temporary contracts to new recruits.

Perceptions of Core and Periphery

Electronics UK operates a deliberate core and periphery strategy (Personnel Manager). This strategy involves the use of numerically flexible labour, and divides the workforce into four categories. The category furthest away from the core are those on temporary short term contracts, which are either for a fixed period or are open ended. The second group are probationary staff. All new recruits to the firm, whether on temporary or permanent contracts, must serve a three month probationary period. Following this period, all those not on temporary contracts will move into the category of permanent staff. This move is dependent, however, on workers displaying 'a satisfactory attitude and commitment' (Staff Handbook), and rests on the decision of the supervisor or manager. The final staff category are established staff who have been employed for more than two years. In practice all new recruits are now employed on a temporary basis, usually on an open ended contract.

Following a two year period of continuous employment all workers automatically receive the same employment rights as other full time permanent employees throughout the UK. Any member of staff not deemed suitable will usually be sacked prior to completion of this two year period (Personnel Manager). A second core and periphery strategy utilised by the firm in the past was the employment of temporary agency labour. This strategy proved unsuccessful due to the low pay and poor conditions received by agency staff. Temporary workers employed directly by the firm are, for example, paid the same rates as established staff and receive the same sickness and holiday pay. Agency staff, on the other hand, received no holiday or sickness benefit and were paid at a lower rate than those directly employed by the firm. This led to discord between individuals and groups, and was felt to be a threat to productivity. For this reason the practice of utilising agency staff was ended. The rationale for using a core and periphery labour force strategy at Electronics UK is twofold. First, to ensure numerical flexibility in response to unstable market conditions, and second, to ensure that workers who do not meet the standards demanded by the firm can be more easily discarded (Personnel Manager). It was shown in the discussion on management perceptions of skill however, that this policy has serious drawbacks in terms of recruiting workers with the skills required by the firm, that is the 'skills' of good attitude and commitment.

Whilst it seems evident that Electronics UK operates a deliberate core and periphery strategy, it has proved difficult to access peripheral workers perceptions in relation to their position in the firm. The reason for this difficulty is that the majority of those who were employed on a temporary basis at the time of the firm's expansion have since been discarded. Electronics UK had also ceased to employ agency staff at the outset of the fieldwork stage. At the time of research only four workers employed on temporary contracts were available for interview. Perceptions of core and periphery are therefore confined to these individuals. Evidence collected from these four interviewees indicates that three of them, although they are aware of their temporary status, do not feel themselves to be particularly exploited or peripheral to the company's core activities. Their main concern appears to be to secure a permanent contract. The fourth individual does however feel exploited, and his perceptions can be argued to reflect the post-Fordist stereotype of the peripheral worker. The following quotes are given in answer to the question: "How do you feel about working on a temporary contract?"

> At the moment I am temporary but I am hoping that when I have been here two years I will become permanent…just hoping because I like it here. A lot of people moan but I don't mind it really (Stock Controller).

> Well I hope to be made permanent when my two years is up, I mean I came here for security so I would like to be permanent. When I worked as a brickie I was always in and out of work, it was very insecure, especially in winter. Obviously I would have preferred to be permanent from the start (Assembly Line Operator, male).

> I gave up a permanent job in tailoring to come here because I felt it would be a good company to work for. I think it will have been worth it if I get on permanent (Assembly Line Operator, female).

In contrast to these views:

> I think its crap being on this sort of contract. It's the same loads of places now. A mate of mine's in engineering and he's always in and out of work (Assembly Line Operator, male).

And later, in response to the question: "Do you feel that your contribution to the firm is valued as highly as those on permanent contracts?"

> It depends if you're prepared to make the effort. I have always tried to make the effort and I think you are valued if you do that (Stock Controller, female).

> I'm not sure that they value anyone that much to be truthful, whether you're temporary or permanent (Assembly Line Operator, male).

> Yes they do, I think so anyway (Assembly Line Operator, female).

> I don't think we're valued at all. When I started here they said there would be opportunities to climb the ladder so to speak. But there's that many here its impossible. If I had my chance again I wouldn't come here, I would try to find something else (Assembly Line Operator, male).

Finally, when asked if they feel themselves to be different in any way to permanent staff, the first three said no whilst the fourth also said no because everyone at the firm is treated badly. The above quotes indicate that of the four interviewees, the first three display a pragmatic acceptance of their temporary status, whilst the fourth appears to view himself as forming part of a peripheral employment sector. Explanation of why the first three individuals hold no perceptions of themselves as peripheral possibly relates to the argument put forward in Chapter Two, that a distinction should be drawn between different types of temporary worker. These interviewees appear to view their temporary status as a step towards permanent employment. All are attempting to secure access to the core. In addition to this, these temporary workers are in a qualitatively different position to the agency workers used by Electronics UK in the recent past. They have, for example, access to certain occupational benefits and are paid the same rates as permanent staff. In conclusion, I want to suggest that these interviewees do not perceive themselves as peripheral because their conditions of employment are closer to the core than the periphery. With respect to the fourth interviewee, his views appear to be influenced by the experiences of others and by the gap between his expectations of the job (opportunities for advancement) and his subsequent experiences.

Conclusion

This chapter began with a description of the organisational structure of Electronics UK, and how this generates the mechanisms that shape the subjective perceptions of skill held by workers. It then outlined the perceptions of workforce skill held by managers. Following this an examination of the perceptions of core and periphery held by workers who occupy a peripheral position in relation to the core - periphery dichotomy proposed by Atkinson (1984) and Atkinson and Meager (1986) was made. The evidence outlined in the chapter provides a basis for the key assertions advanced in the book. First, I have argued that the organisational structural features of Electronics UK are themselves shaped by developments in the wider product market and industrial sector. The firm's position as an assembly operation generates the mix of autoinsertion and assembly line technology, whilst unstable demand and Electronics UK's position as a sub-contractor to larger consumer electronics manufacturers generates a need for flexibility of production. This flexibility is provided by the JIT system, which allows for the close articulation of supply with demand. It has also been suggested that the JIT system of production is a dominant feature of the production process, and has generative effects in terms of the nature of work, in particular the close monitoring and surveillance of shop floor workers. It has been shown that the alignment of flexible JIT production, flexible technology, and rigid Taylorist management structure and style signifies a combination of Fordist and post-Fordist organisational features, thus leading to a further key assertion; that individual firms cannot be defined as either Fordist or post-Fordist, and that to attempt to do so ignores the complex development of organisations. Thus, whilst the organisational structure can be argued to have developed in response to new post-Fordist patterns of demand, the resulting organisational features are a complex mix of Fordist and post-Fordist.

With respect to the effects on the labour process, as with GlassCo, the above combination generates jobs that are characterised by a complete separation between conception and execution, which contain low levels of discretion and autonomy, that are graded in terms of a hierarchical occupational structure, and that that are fragmented and rigidly demarcated. I gave also argued, however, that the labour process at Electronics UK represents a qualitative shift away from traditional Taylorism. This relates to the way in which the JIT/TQM system pushes back the frontier of control in favour of management. These findings correspond closely to the studies of Japanese electronics transplants reviewed in Chapter Two (Taylor, Elger and Fairbrother 1993, Delbridge and Turnbull 1994). Thus, perceptions of speed and accuracy as skill amongst shop floor workers, and the ability to cope with pressure on the part of supervisory and middle management staff are argued to be linked to the intensity of the JIT system, and the resulting levels of surveillance.

A third key assertion is that when considering the subject of skill workers draw on their most salient reference point. For all workers at Electronics UK, the most salient reference point is their current occupation. The result in terms of perceptions of skill are hierarchically structured perceptions that focus on the specific requirements of individuals jobs and tasks. The argument that the most salient reference point for Electronics UK workers is their current occupation does not, however, exclude the relevance of employment trajectories. Rather, none of the workers interviewed at this firm have downwards trajectories, and thus none perceive skill in relation to their previous employment. It has, on the other hand, been argued that those with upwards employment trajectories have a tendency to denigrate the skills demanded of their previous occupation, a tendency not found elsewhere. No firm explanations of this difference between workers at GlassCo and Chemicals UK, and workers at Electronics UK is apparent from the data. Finally, women's perceptions of skill at Electronics UK are the same as those of men, and are shaped by the same causal processes as men's perceptions. Thus providing support for the assertion that women's and men's attitudes to work should be examined in terms of the structural features of employment.

Moving on to the issue of management perceptions of skill, like GlassCo these focus on attitude and commitment to the company. The perceptions held by managers at this firm also focus on the specific tasks performed by workers. However, managers appear to view workers skills as possessing a lower level of complexity than do workers themselves. Finally, management perceptions of skill are highly gendered, and, it can be argued, signify a degree of gender bias against women workers, a bias that is described in the literature reviewed in Chapter Three.

With respect to perceptions of core and periphery at Electronics UK, with one exception individuals do not perceive themselves as forming part of a peripheral workforce. I have argued that temporary workers who are employed on fixed contracts, and whose temporary status may well be a step into permanent employment, should not, necessarily, be regarded as peripheral. Temporary workers at Electronics UK have access to a number of occupational benefits such as sick and holiday pay. Their formal position should not be defined as peripheral in the same way as agency or casual workers. Thus, the notion of periphery has no salience for these workers because they are not members of a peripheral workforce.

7 Chemicals UK

Background

Chemicals UK was established in 1915 and is now a subsidiary of a larger multi-national company. The firm employs around 730 people, 300 less than in 1990. Its traditional products are chemical intermediates that form the raw materials for other chemical manufacturers finished goods. During the mid 1990s the firm suffered a sharp fall in profits which fell by 59% between 1994 and 1995 (FT, Independent). The causes of this fall in profitability were in some ways similar to those facing the wider organic Chemicals sector, whilst others were specific to Chemicals UK. In terms of the former, the chemicals industry in general experienced a slow down in the intermediates market in mid 1990s (Personnel Manager, FT, Independent). Slowdown in the pigments market led to cancelled orders in early 1995, whilst the market for optical brightening agents was hit by a rise in the cost of raw materials alongside a decrease in the price of the end product (Company Newsletter). In addition to these sector wide developments, problems specific to Chemicals UK further contributed to the fall in profitability. Chemicals UK's intermediate products can be so far back in the production chain that the firm does not feel the effects of market change immediately. One example was a global increase in the price of paper that took place in the early 1990s. Prior to this increase, and in expectation of it, a worldwide rise in demand for paper occurred. As a result Chemicals UK stepped up production of the dyes and optical brightening agents used in paper production, and the pigments used in inks. When the worldwide reduction in demand due to the rise in the price of paper fed through to the firm it was left with large amounts of unsold stock (Personnel Manager). A further problem was a marketing war between one of the firm's customers and a competitor, which led to the termination of an important contract (Directors Report 1994).

These adverse market conditions resulted in the adoption of a number of strategies aimed at reversing the decrease in profitability, and which are again partial reflections of wider sectoral trends. Prior to the particular developments of the mid 1990s, the firm had begun to shift production away from high volume, low value added activities towards low volume high value added products. Chemicals UK has moved into the development and manufacture of speciality chemicals made to the specifications of individual customers. This process involves developing custom chemicals through the pilot and scale up stage towards full-scale commercial production where applicable. The firm has also moved into the niche pharmaceuticals market, a development argued to be the key to the company's future (Transport and General Workers Union Convenor, Area Production Manager).

A second development at Chemicals UK arose out of the City of London's concern with the firm's performance on the stock exchange. This led Chemicals UK's international parent company to replace almost all the senior management layer, most of whom had backgrounds in the chemicals manufacturing industry, with accountancy and business trained managers (ex-Pharma-plant Manager). A third strategy is the restructuring of work practices through the introduction, in 1994, of 'empowered teamworking', the stated aim of which is to facilitate responsibility and autonomy amongst the workforce. A detailed account of empowered teamworking is given later in the chapter. One possible objective behind the introduction of these work practices relates to the opportunities it affords for reduced staffing levels and labour costs. The response of the trades union to this development in the labour process is pragmatic. The firm is highly unionised with 100% of shop floor workers belonging to the Transport and General Workers Union (TGWU). The union is aware of the firm's financial difficulties and although they believe empowered teamworking to be a euphemism for effort intensification, increased workloads, job enlargement, and eventually a smaller workforce, they feel that resistance could result in the closure of Chemicals UK (TGWU convenor).

The process through which the product market has shaped Chemicals UK's organisational structure relates primarily to the sharp fall in profitability in the early 1990s. The general slowdown in demand for chemical intermediates, that hit both chemicals UK and its competitors, can possibly be understood in the context of Pettigrew's assessment of the sector. He argues that the market for chemical products mirrors demand for manufactured goods as a whole (Pettigrew 1985). Thus, the fall in demand for chemical intermediates in the early 1990s is a possible reflection of the recession of that period.

The relationship between decreasing profits and the organisational structure concerns the division of labour, and the scope for reduced staffing levels. The number of people employed by Chemicals UK fell from a high of over 1000 in 1990 to 730 in 1996. This reduction in staffing levels was made possible by the introduction of empowered teamworking in 1994. The division of labour into teams rather than around individually defined roles and responsibilities facilitates an intensification of workloads and an increase in productivity from fewer workers (TGWU Convenor). As one process operative observed:

> There seems to be a lot fewer men doing a lot more work since this teamworking business was brought in (Process Operative, Nitro-plant).

In addition to this, any absenteeism can, under the teamwork system, be covered by remaining team members performing more tasks per day. It is suggested then, that the organisation of work at Chemicals UK relates back to developments in the chemicals intermediates market. This relationship is not, however, deterministic and it was not inevitable that this particular structural feature would develop in the way that it did. The introduction of teamworking can be viewed within the context of strategic choice on the part of new senior managers. It has been stated that decreased profits led to the imposition of new accountancy and business trained managers. These new managers appear well versed in the ideology of generic management. One Process Chemist told of a new director saying that 'you do not need a knowledge of chemistry to run a chemical plant, just a knowledge of management techniques.' A further example of managerialist ideology is illustrated by a story from a second process chemist. He explained how Chemicals UK had encountered problems with the quality of scaffolding provided by a sub-contracting firm. As a result of this, Chemicals UK replaced the first scaffolding firm with a second. However, when the new sub-contractor proceeded to employ all the scaffolders previously employed by the old firm, the Area Production Manager did not perceive this to be a problem. He argued that the new sub-contractor would use new management techniques, and the quality of work would automatically improve. The Area Production manager himself subsequently confirmed this story.

The influence of this manager appears to be strong. He has complete authority over production in a large area, and many of the changes in the organisation of work seem to stem from his beliefs. His academic background, although originally in chemical engineering, is more recently rooted in management and business administration. During the interview he made much reference to managerial theory and how the practice of such theory applied to Chemicals UK. One example of this was his enthusiasm for human relations strategies as a means of increasing worker motivation and commitment. Speaking about the introduction of teamworking and flexibility:

> There are two aspects. One is that really, having lines of demarcation is no longer viable in the 1990s. It really does not get the best out of individuals by saying that this is your job and your job only…or by having someone breathing down their neck. My philosophy is that where people have the appropriate skills you let them use them. It allows people to get more job satisfaction in that they progress with the job without waiting to get someone like me to come and sort it out for them. The theory behind it is that everybody has something to contribute in the workplace, no matter what their skill level or what their experience has been. It's based on the premise that the person doing the job is the expert on that job and he should be the one who has the best ideas about how to improve it. It's easy for people to come along and say that they can find a better way of doing that to someone who is doing the job day in and day out…but, that guy (the process operative) really ought to be the one who knows what the shortcuts are (Area Production Manager)

It is suggested that whilst the changes in the organisation of work at the company result, in part, from contingencies caused by market instability, the solutions adopted are not solely determined by this instability. There is a good deal of scope for senior managers to influence the labour process in accordance with their own beliefs. The division of labour at the firm is a result of both environmental factors, and of strategic choices made by influential senior managers. With respect to the development of the production system at Chemicals UK, this is influenced by trends in the wider industrial sector such as over capacity and market saturation. These trends are a partial result of globalisation in the form of competition from developing countries (Personnel Manager), and have led to a general trend away from standardised mass produced chemicals towards speciality and niche market chemicals. This general trend is reflected in Chemicals UK's decision to shift production resources away from mass standardised continuous process production, and towards batch produced speciality chemicals.

With respect to technology, this again reflects wider sectoral trends. A major post-war development in the chemicals industry was the shift from batch production to continuous process production. Although the trend is now towards speciality batch manufactured niche market products, the technology used on batch plants is of the continuous process type. The variations between the technology on batch plants and continuous process plants relate to the manual or computerised control systems, and the time taken to manufacture the product. That is now fourteen hours rather than eight weeks. This difference has substantial implications for workforce perceptions of skill.

Finally, the recruitment and training policies at Chemicals UK again reflect the drive towards reduced manning levels and therefore the fall in profitability caused by unstable market conditions. A long-term aim of the firm is to employ only craft apprentice trained men as process operatives (Personnel Manager). This will, if successful, result in a need for fewer men. If teams are made up of generically skilled process and craft skilled operatives, their jobs will be open to further enlargement to include maintenance of the plant. It will also be possible for the firm to employ fewer craft technicians, as this group will no longer be responsible for maintaining the plant.

Structural Features

Production System and Technology

Research was conducted on three production plants, Nitro-plant, Project-plant and Pharma-plant, and in the Craft Maintenance Workshop. Variations in the production systems and technology between production plants engender differences in workforce perceptions of skill. Nitro-plant is a continuous process production plant which mass manufactures one high volume, low value added, standardised product over an eight week cycle, and involves a continuous feed of chemical feedstocks (raw materials) through the system. This plant is completely computerised, and the role of the process operative is to monitor the computer, which identifies any complication with the process. The computer automatically shuts down the process if either product quality or safety is threatened.

Project and Pharma-plants, on the other hand, are batch process plants on which high value, low volume chemicals made to the specifications of individual customers are manufactured. These plants use manual process technology and a short run batch process that lasts for around fourteen hours. There is no computer to ensure safety or to continuously feed feedstocks through the system, and these tasks are the responsibilities of the workforce. Finally, the Craft Workshop is where all craft maintenance workers are based. Craft technicians are responsible for a variety of individual plants including Nitro, Project and Pharma-plants. A number of maintenance operations are carried out in the workshop, which contains manual lathes and machine tools.

Management Structure and Style

Production at Chemicals UK is the ultimate responsibility of the Production Manager. Below him are four Area Production Managers, each of whom are responsible for a particular geographical area of the factory. Below the Area Production Manager who is responsible for the geographical area on which Nitro-plant is located are shift managers who cover the same geographical area. These men have line responsibility for twenty-four men working on six individual production plants. Unsupervised process operatives organised into empowered teams of four carry out work on each plant. Below the Area Production Manager on Project and Pharma-plants is a Plant Manager who covers both these plants. Below him are the process workers who run them, and who are again organised into empowered teams. As on Nitro-plant, there is no direct supervision of the team. The management style on these three production plants approximates the human relations model, and the flat none-hierarchical structure appears to generate more equitable relationships between managers and workers. This has, as will be shown later, implications in terms of the way in which workforce perceptions of skill are *initially* articulated.

The managerial structure of the Craft Maintenance Workshop consists of the Engineering Supervisor and the Assistant Supervisor. The role of the Supervisor is to prioritise and co-ordinate maintenance work on the plant and in the workshop, and to deploy craft technicians to jobs. One function of the Assistant Supervisor is to provide line support for Craft Technicians if and when needed. As with the GlassCo Mould Maintenance Workshop engineers however, this function is rarely necessary. Craft technicians are highly qualified and seldom need help to perform their tasks (Assistant Supervisor).

Division of Labour and Nature of Work

Nitro-plant Empowered teamworking on Nitro-plant embodies three specific characteristics. First, workers are self-supervised rather than subject to the direction of a supervisory figure. The shift supervisor is contacted only in an emergency. Second, the team is collectively responsible for running the plant, and individuals are not subject to rigid job demarcations. Third, responsibility for deployment of men to tasks falls to the men themselves. It can be argued that the concept of empowered teamworking promotes an impression of worker discretion and autonomy. The extent to which this impression reflects reality must, however, take account of the ways in which production systems and technical constraints on individual plants can limit the scope for discretion and autonomy. On Nitro-plant discretion and autonomy are limited by the computerised continuous process technology. Although managers are called only in an emergency, the computerised control system ensures that emergencies rarely arise   (Shift Manager, Process Operatives.). The result of teamworking is to allow workers to decide who performs which tasks, and simple routine task rotation within the team. Rather than being self managed, these men are managed by the production system and computerised technology.   Teamworking on Nitro-plant accords most closely with Murakami's lowest level of team autonomy (Murakami 1997). It can also be viewed in association with Pollert's assertion that teamworking is an artificial construct in the context of routine, repetitive assembly line production (Pollert 1996).   On this plant, all decisions relating to process and product are taken by managers, whilst the actions of process operatives are controlled by continuous process technology. The sole form of autonomy held by the workforce is the sharing out of work within the team.

In terms of the nature of work, the role of the process operative is to carry out start up, monitor and shut down procedures, and to identify irregularities in the process before the critical shutdown point is reached. This involves long periods of watching a red light switch itself on and off, and performing basic adjustment procedures through the computer. The job entails little or no manipulation of the process, and there is little scope for discretion in relation to task performance.   There is, on this plant, a complete separation between the conception and execution of tasks. The main skill requirement is the ability to react to warning signals given out by the computer. No real understanding of the chemistry or the chemical reactions involved in the process, or of the principles behind the process itself is necessary. Rather, process operatives need to know which tasks need to be performed at particular points in the cycle, and which buttons to press when warnings are given out by the computer.

In summary, the jobs performed by process operatives on Nitro-plant are routine, repetitive and entail little or no manipulation of the process. Discretion is limited to task allocation within the team. The emancipatory effects of teamworking and the human relations management style are outweighed by the controls built into computerised continuous process production. Direct control by a supervisory figure has been exchanged for direct control by the computer and the production process.

Project-plant and Pharma-plant In contrast to Nitro-plant, the short run batch production process and the manual technology on Project and Pharma-plants engender work that is characterised by high levels of discretion, responsibility and autonomy. Work on Project-plant is organised around what are termed by the firm to be empowered 'teams' of two, a graduate process chemist and a process operative. Process Chemists are responsible for organising and mixing raw materials, setting off the chemical reaction needed to ignite the process, and performing analytical testing procedures throughout the process. The role of process operatives is to assist with these tasks and to perform process operations such as starting up, monitoring and closing down. They are also responsible for ordering raw materials. In practice these two men work closely on all aspects of the process (Process Chemists, Process Operatives).

Because of the manual short cycle nature of production both roles demand proactive planning and reactive monitoring skills. Process chemists and operatives must know what raw materials to mix, in what quantities, and with respect to varied products. Process operatives and chemists are also expected to deal with any process problems that occur. Both jobs demand an understanding of the chemistry, chemical reactions and the process itself. Work on Pharma-plant is organised around empowered 'teams' of two process operatives. The labour process is, with one exception, identical to Project-plant. The analytical testing procedures performed by Process Chemists on Project-plant are carried out in the analytical laboratories. Empowered teamworking on the two plants corresponds closely with Murakami's third level of team autonomy, that is autonomy at the level of co-decision making. Product development takes place in the development laboratories, but responsibility for the success of new products during the initial manufacturing stage lies with the teams, the Plant Manager and the Area Production Manager. Decisions on how to proceed are taken by managers in consultation with the two man teams. Thus, the division between conception and execution of tasks on Nitro plant, and at GlassCo and Electronics UK, is, to some extent, rescinded on Project and Pharma-plants.

Craft Workshop Here tasks are organised around individuals rather than teams. Once deployed craft technicians have total responsibility for the performance of tasks, and the work embodies high levels of discretion and autonomy. The jobs performed by craft maintenance workers such as fitters, electricians and welders require manipulation over materials and procedures. In terms of work organisation, tasks are allocated to individuals who have a personal responsibility for carrying them out. Any reference to teamworking in the craft workshop relates to men helping one another out if required. The Engineering Supervisor and an Assistant Supervisor provide line management for craft technicians. This does not mean however, that these workers are subject to hierarchical controls. Supervisors are responsible for allocation of work rather than overseeing job performance. Craft technicians are accorded the status of independent qualified and skilled workers who posses the ability to monitor their own work.   It can be seen that there are strong similarities between craft maintenance workers at Chemicals UK and GlassCo. It will also be shown that these similarities are reflected in comparable perceptions of skill.

It can be seen from the above description that the organisation and nature of work differs between the various research areas. Although empowered teamworking is a feature of each of the three production plants, the nature of work itself is defined by the production process and technology. In short, the computerised continuous process production on Nitro-plant exerts a high level of control over the labour of process operatives. Workers on this plant have little scope for autonomous manipulation of the process. Decision making is limited to task allocation within the team, and low level technical decisions regarding what button to press and when. In contrast to this, the short run, manual, batch production process on Project and Pharma-plants does involve manipulation of the process in addition to decisions over task allocation. For Craft technicians, whilst there is no discretion over task allocation, decisions over the performance of work are left to the men and thus entail manipulation of work itself. It will be demonstrated later in the chapter that these differences in the nature of work, which are themselves generated largely by differences in the production process and technology, have implications for the generation of particular workforce perceptions of skill.

Flexibility

A further aspect of empowered teamworking at Chemicals UK is the introduction of flexibility into the labour process. Flexibility at Chemicals UK takes three forms. First, functional role flexibility within the team. Rather than workers being responsible for one particular job, they are collectively responsible for running the plant. This involves performing a wider range of tasks associated with running the plant. The effect is not vertical upskilling where workers are trained to perform more highly demanding tasks, but rather constitutes horizontal role enlargement. Whilst this is recognised by the men themselves, they are willing to accept the system due to perceived benefits in terms of job variety and productivity. A further feature of this role enlargement relates to the corresponding reduction in staffing levels. In the early 1990s the firm employed around 1200 people (TGWU Shop Steward). Since the introduction of flexible teamworking the workforce has been reduced, through natural wastage, to around 730.

The second form of functional flexibility is flexibility between occupational categories. This involves training process operatives in basic craft skills, thus enabling them to perform basic maintenance on the plant. The objective is that the occupational division between process operatives and craft technicians will eventually be eradicated, and replaced by generically skilled operative/maintenance workers (Training Manager, Personnel Manager). To facilitate this the firm provides two-day training courses in basic craft skills to all process operatives. Additionally, all future recruits will possess a craft apprenticeship qualification. The third form of flexibility refers to process operatives being deployed to a variety of plants rather than to one plant on which they are employed. This is the managerial prerogative definition of flexibility. Whilst no attempt to impose this form of flexibility has yet been made, discussions with managers reveal it to be a future objective:

> We are still not getting the flexibility in what I call my team ... in the six plants that I cover. I mean you could have another plant down the lane that is seriously undermanned and under product pressure and I have no flexibility there yet. I would want to go further and introduce flexibility within the areas and not just the plants (Shift Manager).

Integral to flexibility is the notion of multi-skilling. However, role enlargement involving extra tasks does not constitute genuine multi-skilling. I will show later that the notion that skills can be easily learned through a two-day training course in basic fitting techniques, and that these easily acquired competencies constitute multi-skilling, is not reflected in the perceptions of skill held by the Chemicals UK workforce. Chemicals UK have not attempted to promote flexibility and multi-skilling through force or coercion. The firm is endeavouring to alter the attitudes of the workforce and to induce a collective culture of flexibility. This involves the continual promotion of flexible working practices in the monthly company newsletter given out to employees. There was, for example, a flexibility article in each of the four company newsletters accessed.

Chemicals UK, Fordism and Post-Fordism

The question of whether post-Fordist theories provide an adequate framework through which to understand Chemicals UK's organisational structure is discussed in the context of the theory of the flexible specialisation thesis outlined in Chapter Two, and the managerial strategies outlined in Chapter Three. The following discussion will show that whilst on a superficial level Chemicals UK appears to embody aspects of the alleged shift to post-Fordism, it is, in reality, a Fordist organisation.

Flexible Specialisation

Over capacity and market saturation within the European heavy chemicals sector has resulted in an industry wide shift in production and sales effort towards higher value added speciality products, and away from lower commodity products (Pettigrew 1985). This strategy is reflected in Chemicals UK's attempts to shift production towards short run batch products made to individual customer specifications, and products geared towards new niche markets. The firm are engaging in the former production strategy on Project-plant whilst Pharma-plant aims to exploit demand in the niche pharmaceutical intermediates market. The issue for consideration here is whether this strategy reflects Piore and Sabel's theory of flexible specialisation (Piore and Sabel 1984, Sabel 1996). It was pointed out in Chapter Two that these authors differentiate between small innovative newly established firms engaging in short batch production and large firms that attempt to flexibly shift production away from mass markets towards new niche market areas.

A further characteristic of flexible specialisation is that " competition must be arranged in such a way that flexible specialist firms remain innovative and do not remain fixed in their niche markets" (Bagguley 1994 p. 163). Whilst Chemicals UK is, most obviously, an example of a large firm attempting to shift its product base away from mass standardised goods towards speciality goods for niche areas such as pharmaceuticals, the extent to which this strategy can be described as flexible specialisation is questionable. The rationale behind the shift into low volume, high value products is to gain entry into specialist markets, and once there to secure long term contracts with customers to develop a stable and secure customer base. This strategy has been employed on Project-plant, which produces weed killer intermediates for a large multi-national chemical corporation (Area

Production Manager). The strategy is, however, questioned by some middle management personnel who, during informal discussions, referred to the risks of basing long term strategy solely on contracts with a large and powerful customer. The goal of moving into and remaining in specialist niche markets also dictates the production of pharmaceutical intermediates on Pharma-plant.

A further important difference between the flexible specialisation model and the situation found at Chemicals UK relates to the impact of technology. Flexible specialisation is made possible by the development of new technologies and production techniques able to perform varied dimensions of the whole production process. This allows firms to switch easily between differentiated products (Murray 1988, Wood 1989). In terms of skill, the flexible specialisation thesis unreservedly promotes the idea of upskilling in the form of flexible skills required to operate new technologies. Whilst the production processes on Project-plant does allow for a relatively uncomplicated transfer between specialist production lines, the technology is, as already stated, continuous process technology. In addition, the organisation of work remains similar to that found elsewhere at the factory. The similarities between the production process on the three plants is summed up by the following process operative who has experience of working on all three:

> Making chemicals is like baking a cake. You have the ingredients and the tools and vessels. Once you can bake a cake you can make a big one or a small one in a big bowl or a small bowl, well...it's the same here. The process is the same on Nitro-plant and Project-plant, the same but on a different scale (Process Operative, Pharma-plant).

It is apparent that in terms of the flexible specialisation model of post-Fordism, Chemicals UK remains well within the parameters of Fordism. This assertion supports Matthew's argument that 'the chemicals industry has responded to market saturation with innovation and product specialisation, yet retained Fordist production techniques, work organisation and skill restriction' (Matthews (1989) quoted in Scarbrough and Corbett 1992). The articulation of manual batch production and the empowered teamwork system on Project and Pharma-plants has, however, led to a qualitative difference in terms of work experience. That is, that the responsibility for planning, programming and operation represents a rescinding of the Taylorist or Fordist separation of conception and execution. In addition, of all the production areas sampled, work on these two plant areas most closely resembles the predictions of Piore and Sable. These differences have implications in terms of subjective perceptions of skill. Thus, whilst the shift to niche production on Project and Pharma-plants does not correspond exactly to the flexible specialisation model, it does signify a shift away from classical Fordism, and this shift has generative effects on perceptions of skill.

Division of Labour and Nature of Work

In terms of the organisation and nature of work, the issue here is whether the introduction of empowered teamworking and functional flexibility represent a shift away from the Taylorist work methods associated with Fordism, or whether they remain, in reality, fundamentally Taylorist. Discussion of this issue will focus on two specific points. The first relates to Braverman's assertion that Taylorist methods of control are increasingly built into the capitalist labour process. The second relates to Braverman's view that a strict Taylorist division of labour, and the breaking down of tasks into their smallest constituent parts is an inevitable feature of late capitalism. With respect to the first point, Friedman criticises Braverman for confusing one strategy for exercising managerial authority with management authority itself. He argues that Taylorism is not the only possible means of exercising control (Friedman 1990). It is argued here, however, that methods of control emanating from the introduction of teamworking, whilst giving the superficial appearance of an alternative to Taylorist control are, in both practice and theory, highly similar. This assertion is framed within the context of an alleged link between Weberian and Foucauldian conceptualisations of power and authority (O'Neill 1987).

A connection between modern production systems and Foucault's conception of control and surveillance has been made by a number of authors (Foucault 1977, Knights and Wilmott 1985, 1989, Deetz 1992, Sakolosky 1992, Sewell and Wilkinson 1992, Barker 1993, Clegg 1994, Collinson 1994, Knights and Vurdubakis 1994, McKinlay and Taylor 1996). The essence of the argument put forward by these authors is that the hierarchical nature of strictly Taylorist control systems has given way to horizontal systems, which closely correspond with Foucault's interpretation of Bentham's panopticon. The panopticon is a circular prison overseen by an inner watchtower from where inhabitants of each cell can be continually viewed. Although prisoners may not be watched constantly, they understand the possibility of this and behave accordingly. The disciplinary imperative to conform is thus internalised by the individual. Foucault termed this conformity 'normalisation', and applied the model of the panopticon to a number of institutions including the factory (for example Rabinow 1984, Layder 1994). From this perspective control within the factory is achieved through particular mechanisms that act as the inner watchtower. The discipline imposed on workers through scientific management and direct control strategies have given way to self discipline, and discipline from the peer group. This is illustrated by the functioning of teamworking at Chemicals UK.

Drawing on this model, the characteristics of teamwork at the firm signify an increase in total control rather than a shift towards autonomy, for example, the setting of production targets for the whole team rather than for the individual creates a sense of responsibility towards work mates as well as towards the company. Workers are unlikely to disrupt production unless sanctioned by the whole group. Additionally, anyone not working to the required effort levels is likely to be pressurised into conformity by other members of the team. This argument is supported by the views of two process operatives who complained about the effort and performance levels of certain of their work mates:

> You have to be able to work in a team and that team work as one unit ...and...You do not want someone who is like a dog with three legs. If you are a team you all have to work towards the same goals, you have to move about. If a job wants doing you do not say that is his job and he should do it. You just go and do it yourself. Some people say they like flexibility and teamworking but they have not changed the way they work. Take X...there are some jobs he just does not do. The sooner we get him to do them the more the work will be shared out, but to hear him talk you would think that he knows everything (Process Operative, Nitro-plant).

> Y (one of the team members) is a bit lazy, he will not pull his weight. Why should I work hard all shift while he sits in the office doing nothing (Process Operative, Nitro-plant).

The linkages between Weber's notions of power and authority, and Taylorism stem from the similarities between Weber's classic bureaucracy and certain scientific management principles; for example, the hierarchical structures and the delimiting of duties in line with objective and impersonal criteria (Bendix 1977). For Weber, power derived from the ability to impose ones will on the behaviour of others (Weber 1948). He identified a number of sources of power, one of which is legal authority. This form of authority confers the right to command on some, and the duty to obey on others. It is legitimated by the impersonal nature of the authority structure, that is, authority arising from the position rather than from the person (Weber 1948). According to O'Neill (1987), capital has traditionally preferred to subcontract worker discipline to managers and engineers. Through the utilisation of scientific management techniques, managers were able to establish a high degree of control and surveillance over the worker (O'Neill 1987). However, the abilities of workers to resist these controls are documented in the labour process literature (Beynon 1975, Nichols and Beynon 1977, Thompson and Ackroyd 1995) and control has never been completely seized by capital. It is vital therefore, that the power of capital over labour takes the appearance of a naturalistic order. O'Neill states that:

> It is of course in the interests of bureaucratic management to make worker discipline, punishment and rewards, appear to flow from naturally established rules and procedures. Analytically, there occurs a kind of progression in industrial discipline moving from paternalistic controls to assembly line machine paced routines and, finally, to bureaucratically imposed discipline. What is involved is a shift from heteronomous paternalistic controls to autonomous internalised discipline and identification with corporate goals and values (O'Neill 1987 p. 56).

It is within the context of the naturalisation and internalisation of controls and the resultant self-discipline that Weberian and Foucauldian notions of power can be linked. From the Weberian framework this naturalisation results from the perceived legitimacy of the impersonal bureaucratic system, whilst for Foucault, self discipline is the result of the technologies of discipline and surveillance associated with the social panopticon, and the process of normalisation this creates. In the context of the above theoretical propositions, the control functions built into empowered teamworking at Chemicals UK represent, it can be argued, an intensification of both Weberian and Foucauldian methods.

In terms of Braverman's view that a Taylorist division of tasks and labour is inevitable under monopoly capitalism, evidence from Chemicals UK supports this assertion, for example through a comparison between the alleged multi-skilling associated with teamworking and functional flexibility, and the principles of Taylorism. The abandoning of specific job demarcations associated with teamworking on Nitro, Project and Pharma-plants seem to indicate that the strict divisions of labour, and the breaking down of tasks into constituent parts associated with Taylorism have been largely discarded. This is, however, a simplistic assumption based on an ideal type version of Taylorism. Whilst the labour process at Chemicals UK does not accord with this ideal type, the underlying principles are largely consistent. Although labour is divided into teams rather than on an individual basis, each team member is allocated particular tasks from a predefined assortment. The singular difference between this and the extreme Taylorist model is that of task rotation. These tasks are broken down as far as possible given the nature of the product and production process. Empowered teamworking and flexibility have not led to a vertical upskilling, but to horizontal job enlargement. Whilst it could be suggested that workers on Project and Pharma-plants have, to some extent, acquired new skills in terms of planning, and using their own discretion and working autonomously, this is still within the narrow role of the process operative. It is concluded therefore, that the labour process at chemicals UK is most accurately described as Fordist.

Functional Flexibility

The notion of functional flexibility has been the subject of heated debate and was discussed in depth in Chapter Two. With regard to functional flexibility at Chemicals UK, the neo-Taylorist or neo-Fordist definition provides the most useful model. According to representatives of the Transport and General workers Union, the introduction of functional flexibility at the firm was a direct response to Atkinson and Meager's model described in Chapter Two, and attempts to bring about functional flexibility began in the two years subsequent to the publication of this model. Functional flexibility at Chemicals UK covers three areas. First, task rotation within defined limits, for example between team members. Second, job enlargement to include a wider range of tasks such as process operatives carrying out minor maintenance work. Third, the managerial prerogative to deploy labour in a more dictatorial manner. The evidence suggests that functional flexibility at Chemicals UK does not correspond to post-Fordist notions of a multi-skilled core. In general, empowered teamworking and flexibility have not led to a vertical upskilling but to horizontal job enlargement. Whilst workers on Project and Pharma-plants take responsibility for planning and programming, they represent only a small section of the total workforce. With respect to multi-skilling between occupational categories, one or two days training in basic maintenance work do not transform a process operative into a skilled craftsman. However, the firm's long term policy of increasing the educational and training profile of the workforce adopts a human capital approach to skill and is exemplified by the recruitment of apprentice trained craftsman to process operative posts, and the promotion of the City and Guilds 060 process operative qualification in an attempt to create a multi-skilled workforce.

Workers' Perceptions of Skill

Perceptions of skill at Chemicals UK are, like GlassCo and Electronics UK, patterned around the firm's structural features, the position of individuals in relation to structural features, prior qualifications, and employment trajectories. The patterns that emerge from the Chemicals UK data are, however, more complex than those at the first two firms. This complexity stems from the high levels of heterogeneity amongst workers performing the same or similar jobs. Unlike GlassCo and Electronics UK, where the majority of production workers are unqualified and/or have horizontal or upwards employment trajectories, the Chemicals UK workforce in both production and maintenance departments consists of those with no qualifications, those with craft apprenticeship qualifications and those with trade apprentice qualifications. Trade qualifications are defined as those such as joinery, catering, building and motor maintenance. The distinction between these and craft apprenticeships is made due to the dissimilar effects of each on perceptions of skill. Along with the varied mix of qualification profiles, the Chemicals UK workforce is also characterised by a complex patterning of employment trajectories. The impact of this heterogeneity on the patterning of perceptions of skill will become apparent as the chapter progresses.

A further distinction between Chemicals UK and the first two firms relates to the way in which perceptions of skill are initially articulated. At Chemicals UK, responses to questions asking interviewees to define skill were expressed in terms of generalised competencies of knowledge, experience and training. In contrast perceptions of skill at GlassCo and Electronics UK were, from the outset, articulated in terms of specific concrete job competencies. It is suggested that this difference between the first two case studies and Chemicals UK relate to differences in management structure and style, and the division of labour. GlassCo and Electronics UK are characterised by hierarchical management structures, direct styles of supervision and rigid Taylorist divisions of labour. These features, along with the automated and assembly line technology, and overt surveillance at Electronics UK, combine to produce jobs that are routine and repetitive, and which allow no scope for autonomous decision making. In contrast, the labour process on Nitro-plant is characterised by tension between constraints built into the production system and technology, and the empowered teamwork system. Although empowered teamworking has limited impact on the fundamental nature of process operatives' jobs, it does allow for more equal relationships between managers and workers. It also allows limited discretion and autonomy over the organisation of work within the team. On

Project- and Pharma-plants, work is characterised by the manual batch production system and empowered teamworking. Work on these two plants resembles, to some extent, the predictions of Piore and Sabel, for example with respect to the reconstitution of conception and execution. This reconstitution of conception and execution is reflected in perceptions of skill on this plant.

The following analysis is organised around perceptions of skill rather than departments. The reason for this is that perceptions of skill at Chemicals UK cut across the boundaries of individual plant areas. The analysis is presented in a clearer fashion if individual research sites are subsumed under the headings of knowledge, training and experience as skill. The analysis will begin with a brief outline of the patterning of perceptions of skill before going on to discuss knowledge, training and experience as skill in more detail. Finally, an examination of the notions of discretion and autonomy as skill will be conducted within the context of tension between the constraints of the production system and technology, and the empowered team work system.

Perceptions of skill at Chemicals UK are expressed as knowledge, training and experience. With the exception of craft apprentice trained men, the perception of knowledge as skill is found amongst all workers. This perception divides into 'practical task knowledge' which is held by Nitro-plant operatives, and 'theoretical knowledge' held by Project and Pharma-plant operatives. It will be shown that the difference is the result of the variable generative effects of production systems and technologies on these plants. A perception of training as skill is found amongst Nitro-plant operatives and apprentice qualified craftsmen. For Nitro-plant operatives, training as skill is defined as informal on the job training, whilst for craftsmen it is defined as formal apprenticeship training only. This divergence will be shown to relate to the types of training undertaken by individuals. Finally, the perception of experience as skill is uniform and is expressed by interviewees in all research plants. Running parallel to these patterns and processes are individuals' qualification profiles and employment trajectories. The combination of these parallel processes is a complex model of perceptions of skill at this factory.

Knowledge

The importance of knowledge as a skill amongst chemical plant operatives is identified by previous studies (Blauner 1964, Nichols and Beynon 1977, Halle 1984). None of these studies has analysed the concept in detail however. Halle argues that the knowledge required by different occupational groups within a chemical plant is identical. The only difference is the way in which knowledge is acquired (Halle 1984). In contrast, this research suggests that the notion of knowledge as skill has different meanings in different work contexts, that is between individuals and groups employed on different production plants. The perception of knowledge as skill is held by all workers with the exception of apprentice qualified craftsmen employed either as craft technicians or as process operatives on Nitro-plant, and by the unqualified or trade qualified men working in the Craft Maintenance Workshop.   Interviewees who do perceive knowledge as skill are employed on Nitro, Project and Pharma-plants. This group consists of unqualified and trade qualified people, and those with academic qualifications ranging from GCE 'O'level to chemistry degrees. The perception of knowledge as skill amongst this group is not, however, identical in nature and two distinct varieties of the perception are found.

First is the definition of knowledge as skill as an understanding of the practical tasks and functions necessary to the performance of the job, but with no real understanding of why these tasks are necessary. This perception is comparable to that found amongst HEPA machinists at GlassCo, and can be argued to reflect the separation of conception and execution on these areas. Second is the definition of knowledge as skill as a theoretical understanding of the chemistry, of chemical reactions and of the process. The perception of theoretical knowledge as skill is universal on Project and Pharma-plants, whilst the perception of practical task knowledge is, with the exception of craft apprentice qualified process operatives, universal on Nitro-plant.

This pattern suggests that the differential structural features on each plant generate a particular perception of knowledge as skill. The computerised continuous process production on Nitro-plant generates perceptions of practical task knowledge as skill, and the short run manual batch production on Project and Pharma-plants generates perceptions of theoretical knowledge as skill. The perception of practical task knowledge as skill found on Nitro-plant is explicable by the low levels of theoretical knowledge needed to run the plant. The manufacture of one standardised product over an eight-week cycle demands little knowledge of chemistry, or of the chemical reactions that can occur when certain chemicals are mixed. Computerisation negates the need for any detailed knowledge of the process:

DT: If I were to ask you to define the term skill, what would you think of?

A: Skill is knowledge, knowledge of the job.

DT: What do you mean by that?

A: The kind of knowledge we need is about how to run the plant. If I start that button and press that pump, material goes from A to B. But if I leave a valve open it will go to point C. So I have to remember to shut the valve before it starts. That kind of knowledge is memorising the stages you go through because the process is continuous (Process Operative, Nitro-plant.)

DT: If I were to ask you to define the term skill, what would you think of?

A: I would define skill as a knowledge of the job ...It's knowing how to monitor the plant, making sure it's running properly. But chemical compounds, there is no need for us to know about stuff like that (Process Operative, Nitro-plant, ex joiner).

In contrast, perceptions of knowledge as skill on both Project and Pharma-plants are articulated as theoretical knowledge. This is explicable in terms of manual, short run, batch manufacture of variable products. The manual nature of these two plants renders workers responsible for product quality and safety. The variability of products manufactured dictates that workers must ensure they mix the correct raw materials in accurate quantities each time the process is carried out. These factors combine to produce a perception of theoretical knowledge of the chemistry, chemical reactions and the process as skill:

DT:If I were to ask you to define the term skill, what would you think of?

A: Knowledge is a skill, very much so. You may not consciously think about it but many times a shift you take little decisions. Like whether you should speed the process up or slow it down. So I am taking small decisions frequently which without my chemistry knowledge I would not be able to do (Process Chemist, Project-plant).

DT: If I were to ask you to define the term skill, what kinds of things would you think of?

A: To be a skilled process operative you need to know the process.

DT: Could you explain what you mean by 'know the process.'

A: You're dealing with dangerous chemicals here, so if anything goes wrong you have to know what the properties of the chemicals are, what they will do if they're exposed to air or something else. You need to know exactly what's in a line, what it'll do if you breathe it in (Process Operative, Project-plant).

DT:If I were to ask you to define the term skill, what would you think of?
A: One important skill on this plant is knowledge...I need to know how the process works. I mean if I put the wrong quantities in the mixing or do not mix in the correct order there could be a violent reaction or give off toxic gas. So you have to know about the chemicals you're dealing with (Process Operative, Pharma-plant).

The above evidence suggests that production systems and technology on each plant shape job characteristics, which in turn generate perceptions of knowledge as skill. The association between the perception of practical or theoretical knowledge as skill, and the production system and technology on each plant can be analysed in the context of the division between programming and operation discussed in Chapter Two. On Nitro-plant the programming of the computerised technology is performed by workers, whilst programs themselves are written by managers. This corresponds with the possibility for shared control outlined by Kelley (1989). The result is a perception of knowledge as skill that focuses on the knowledge required for the execution of operating functions. Comparisons relating to the impact of technology and perceptions of skill can be drawn between Nitro-plant, the HEPA at GlassCo, and the Autoinsertion Department at Electronics UK. In all these factory departments the work involves programming and operating machinery, but does not involve any input into the design or planning of programs. In addition, in all these three departments perceptions of skill emphasise task performance and complexity, but exclude an understanding of the theoretical principals associated with programming and planning. In contrast, on Project and Pharma-plants operators have knowledge of the theoretical principals required for planning and programming. They also have an opportunity to use that knowledge and take responsibility for programming functions. Thus, the perception of theoretical knowledge as skill held by operators on this plant is argued to reflect the scope for programming and planning.

This is, however, a partial explanation, and only by reference to prior qualifications and individuals' employment trajectories can the causal processes that shape the perception of knowledge as skill be fully explained. Beginning with unqualified interviewees, it is a general pattern across the three case study factories that the impact of firm specific structural features depends upon individuals' employment trajectories. For unqualified interviewees whose previous work has been in occupations which are of the same or lower status than their current job, the most salient reference point through which individuals consider skill is the current job. For those whose previous work history is in jobs of a higher status, previous occupation provides the most salient reference point. In terms of the unqualified interviewees at chemicals UK, all have been employed in their current job for a lengthy period of time (all recent recruits have a craft apprenticeship qualification), and those who have occupied jobs elsewhere were all previously employed in manual labouring occupations. Employment trajectories are, therefore, horizontal or upward. For these men, the structural features of production system and technology on Nitro-plant generate the perception of practical task knowledge as skill.

Second, for individuals at Chemicals UK with trade apprentice qualifications, the structural features relating to current jobs exert a greater influence than qualifications. The reason for this is unclear and no firm assertions can be made. It is possible to speculate, however, that the answer relates to the employment trajectories of this group. It is a contention of the book that horizontal or vertical employment trajectories are important mechanisms in the generation of workforce perceptions of skill. The employment trajectories of these trade apprentice qualified interviewees are characterised by a shift from trades to technical occupations. The totality of the break with previous work and/or qualification background is a possible explanation of why the most salient reference point for this group is the current occupation.

Third, all those with academic qualifications perceive theoretical knowledge as skill, and all are employed on Project or Pharma-plants. Starting with process operatives, these men posses either GCE 'O' level Chemistry or the City and Guilds 060 process operative qualification. These basic academic qualifications engender a basic knowledge of chemistry and chemical reactions, and which is supplemented by that gained from the job. There is a high level of correspondence between the type of knowledge required to perform the job and the knowledge gained from qualifications This also applies to process chemists, although their degree informed knowledge is patently deeper.

Finally, amongst the craft apprentice qualified there is, with one exception, no perception of knowledge as skill, either amongst those employed as craftsmen or the two men now employed as process operatives on Nitro-plant. The explanation of why their current job does not provide a salient reference point from which they can draw in relation to perceptions of skill concerns their downwards employment trajectory. In accordance with the model outlined in Chapter Four, these two men perceive skill in relation to their previous occupation and qualification profile. Because they have moved down the occupational status hierarchy, their most salient reference point in relation to perceptions of skill is their previous apprenticeship training and post-apprenticeship work experience.

Their perceptions of skill remain rooted in their craft skilled identities. This leads to a questioning of why it is that knowledge is perceived as skill by production workers but not by craft qualified interviewees, either at Chemicals UK or GlassCo. It can be assumed that to perform the role of craftsmen some form of knowledge is necessary, and that this knowledge is acquired during an apprenticeship. One possible explanation of why craftsmen do not perceive skill in terms of their craft knowledge relates to their strong identification with apprenticeship training. The perception of training as skill at Chemicals UK will be discussed shortly. However, the views expressed by the above two interviewees when asked if they believe knowledge to be a skill provide some insight into this issue. For these men, knowledge is merely something that develops from performing a job, any job. Skill, on the other hand, develops from formal apprenticeship training:

> DT: Do you consider knowledge to be a skill?
> A: Knowledge, no, that's not a skill, it's just knowing what you're doing and that's easy. It's not like you have to train (Nitro-plant Process Operative, age 30s, ex-British Coal fitter).

> DT: Do you consider knowledge to be a skill?
> A: Knowledge is easily picked from the job. Craftsmen have to do an apprenticeship and that's skill (Nitro-plant Process Operative, ex-British Coal fitter).

To use this limited evidence to make a general assertion about the absence of a perception of knowledge as skill amongst apprentice trained craftsmen is unfeasible. To put forward any explanations of this issue would require far more empirical evidence. In addition, whilst apprenticeship training is explicitly articulated as skill amongst craftsmen at Chemicals UK, this is not the case at GlassCo. Nevertheless, the GlassCo interviewees do hold strong craft skilled identities and this divergence may be one of emphasis.

A final point to make concerns the one craft apprentice qualified man employed on Pharma-plant who does perceive knowledge as skill. It is suggested that this interviewee's perceptions of skill are explicable in terms of his upward employment trajectory. Whilst this twenty-seven year old man has moved from a craft skilled job elsewhere into a process operative job at chemicals UK, he does not feel this to be a shift down the occupational hierarchy. At the time of research he was preparing for an Open University BSc Chemistry to be paid for by the firm. This man was described by managers as highly intelligent, and appears to be destined for a move up the occupational hierarchy. In the context of the general model, his perceiving of knowledge as skill rather than in terms of his craft is a characteristic of his anticipated upward employment trajectory. In summary, the perception of knowledge as skill is held by the majority of production workers, but is dependent on the direction of an individual's employment trajectory. The specific nature of the perception of knowledge as skill is shaped by the production system and technology on individual plants.

Training

The perception of training as skill, and the form it takes, is associated with prior qualifications, and the firm's training policies. As with knowledge, the perception of training as skill is found amongst certain groups only. It also has two separate meanings for contrasting groups. Workers on Nitro-plant and in the craft workshop hold this perception of skill. These workers have either no qualifications, or a craft or trade apprentice qualification. The first group consists of Nitro-plant employees with trade or no qualifications. For this group, training as skill refers to both formal accredited training and informal on the job training where experienced workers pass on skills to inexperienced operatives. For the second group, training as skill refers to formal apprenticeship training leading to recognised certification such as City and Guilds or HNC. This group consists of all apprentice-trained craftsman, regardless of whether they currently practice their craft or area employed on, and also the unqualified and trade apprentice qualified employed in the Craft Workshop. Given the apprenticeship background of craftsmen it is perhaps not surprising that they should perceive training as skill only in terms of formally accredited external courses. There is a strong sense of craft skilled identity amongst these men, which appears to result from their apprenticeship experience:

> DT: If I were to ask you to define the term skill what would you think of?
> A: Skill is apprenticeships, I mean you cannot pick up a skill without proper training. The YTS, that was abysmal. Its training and schooling, when you're talking about a skilled man you're talking about someone who's been to college, someone who's got his papers (Craft Technician).

> DT: If I were to ask you to define the term skill what would you think of?
> A: I would define skill as training.
> DT: What do you mean when you talk about training?

A: Apprenticeship training... that's very different from on the job training. It gives you a different outlook on life. You learn how to do your job in different situations, how other people work and how to get along with others. It's very important to learn these things (Craft Technician, ex power station).

This craft identity is retained by apprentice qualified men, even where their employment trajectories take them down the occupational status hierarchy. This tendency, to perceive skill in terms of their craft, amongst those who have moved down the occupational hierarchy is illustrated by these men's attitudes to the two different types of training:

DT: How does your current job compare with fitting in terms of the skills you need?
A: Process operatives not a skilled job. How can I put it [...] there's no set training to it. When I first started I just went around with another bloke showing me what to do. That's just picking it up, it's not training, it's now't like an apprenticeship (Nitro-plant Process Operative, ex British Coal fitter).

DT: How does your current job compare with fitting in terms of the skills you need?
A: This jobs nowhere near as skilled as fitting, its something you can do with a bit of training from the other blokes. I would not describe that as skilled, I mean its not like doing 5 years training at college to be a fitter or electrician. There is no comparison (Process Operative, ex-British Coal fitter).

The above evidence suggests that apprentice qualified craftsmen, either working as craftsmen or having moved down the occupational hierarchy, perceive formal apprenticeship training as skill as a result of their experience of working for this qualification.

Moving on to unqualified and trade qualified men, it has been argued that this group's subjective perceptions of skill are associated with the structural features that characterise their previous or current job, depending on the direction of their employment trajectory. It will, for example, be demonstrated shortly that the perceptions of informal training as skill found amongst this group on Nitro-plant correspond closely with training programs on the plant. Closer analysis of the position of unqualified and trade qualified individuals working in the Craft Workshop indicates, however, a lack of correspondence with this patterning. These men's training follows the on the job model rather than the apprenticeship model. Why, therefore, do they perceive training as skill only in terms of the formal apprenticeship ideal? In the context of the general model, it is suggested that this is explicable in terms of these men's upward employment trajectory. Although they do not possess apprenticeship qualifications, they are performing a skilled craft occupation. A general result of such a move up the occupational hierarchy is that people begin to perceive skill in relation to their new occupational status. Thus, trade qualified and unqualified craft technicians perceive training as skill in the same way as their qualified colleagues:

> DT: If I were to ask you to define the term skill what would you think of?
> A: Skill, well it's schooling and college and all that. A skilled man is someone who's done an apprenticeship (Unqualified Craft Technician, ex-manual labourer).

> DT: If I were to ask you to define the term skill what would you think of?
> A: In this job it's having an apprenticeship in fitting or welding or whatever (Craft Technician, ex-painter and decorator).

In contrast to this, the unqualified and trade qualified process operatives on Nitro-plant perceive training as skill both in terms of formal apprenticeship training and informal on the job training:

> DT: What do you mean when you talk about training as skill?
> A: Well…It's like…craft technicians think of themselves as being a lot more skilled than us process operatives, they look down on us as plant pots because all we do is run the plant. But there are lots of different types of skill and whatever you are trained to do, you become skilled at that job. You can get someone who has done a five year apprenticeship, who has a bit of paper to say that he is skilled, and that is the only difference between him and us, the bit of paper. We are trained on the job and it takes time to become a skilled process operative (Process Operative, ex-joiner).

> DT: What do you mean when you talk about training as skill?
> A: Process operative is a skilled job, years ago anyone off the street could come and do it but not now, you have to train for it now. A skilled job is something you have to train for.[…]The type of training we do is… well when I started it was just work of mouth from the other operatives, and it still is really but now we get these manuals as well (Process Operative).

The causal process that shapes this particular perception of training as skill is the firm's training policy Put simply, the training given to all new recruits at Chemicals UK is the informal on the job variety, and thus generates a perception of on the job training as skill. In summary, perceptions of training as skill are patterned around two processes. First, the forms of training individuals have undertaken, that is formal apprenticeship training and on the job informal training. Second, and running parallel, are the routes through which individuals come to occupy their current job, that is by the direction of their employment trajectories. For craft apprentice trained men who are either currently practising their trade, or who have moved to jobs of a lower occupational status, that is who are now employed as process operatives, the most salient reference point from which to consider skill is their apprenticeship experience. Thus, for them, perceptions of training as skill focus on formal apprenticeship training only. For individuals employed on Nitro-plant who have trade apprentice qualifications or no qualifications, perceptions of training as skill are associated with the informal on the job training undertaken for their current job. Thus, perceptions of training as skill amongst this group emphasise on the job training as skill. In contrast to this, the two trade apprentice qualified and one unqualified men employed in the Craft Workshop perceive training as skill as formal apprenticeship training. This appears somewhat surprising given that their own training at Chemicals UK was of the on the job variety. These men can, on the other hand, be suggested to have upward employment trajectories in that although they are not apprentice-trained craftsmen, they are employed as craft technicians. It maybe, therefore, that the most salient reference point from which they consider skill is their role as craft technician rather than their own training background, and that this leads them to perceive skill in relation to the formal training requirements of the job they are now performing.

Experience

The perception of experience as skill is widespread amongst the Chemicals UK interviewees. Unlike perceptions of knowledge and training as skill, the perception of experience as skill is uniform amongst all groups and individuals interviewed. It is defined as a skill that develops over time, and which is acquired through practice and repetition. It is, therefore, specific to particular occupations. Whilst the definition of experience is uniform, two processes that appear to shape it are identified. First, lengthy unbroken experience at a particular job or trade, and second, the breakdown of this lengthy experience. These processes are not mutually exclusive and the second can be seen as a consequence of the first. In terms of the former process, for craft technicians employed in the Craft Workshop, post apprenticeship practice and repetition over time is viewed as vital to the development and maintenance of craft skills. The perceptions of these men can be seen, from the following illustrative quotes, to display strong similarities with those of the GlassCo craftsmen:

> DT: If I were to ask you to define the term skill what would you think of?
> A: What makes someone skilled is qualifications and experience. It's the repetitiveness of doing a job everyday that makes you skilled, it takes time to become really skilled. Time and practice (Craft Technician, employed 34 years).

> DT: If I were to ask you to define the term skill what would you think of?
> A: Skill is experience of doing your job over and over again. Most of the lads in here have apprenticeships and you obviously need that to get the basics, but you need experience as well if you're going to be a fully skilled craftsman (Craft Technician, employed 7 years, ex engineering firm.)

For those who have worked at chemicals UK for a lengthy period of time, experience as skill develops through long term repetition at a specific job. This group comprises of unqualified process operatives and graduate process chemists. The following quotes are given in response to the same question as above:

> We process operatives are skilled, and its a matter of getting the years in, getting the experience. It's that what makes you skilled, to know what you're doing [...] I've been here 14 years now (Process Operative Pharma-plant).

> I think skill is a matter of experience, daft as it sounds. I have been a process chemist for a long time and the broad chemistry knowledge isn't as good as it once was. So I would think that experience is the best skill I've got. Knowing what will work and what won't because I've tried it before (Process Chemist Project-plant, employed 31 years).

This evidence suggests that lengthy unbroken experience at a specific craft or job generates a perception of experience as skill. The employment trajectories of the above two groups follow similar patterns. That is, the acquisition of competencies via education, training or work experience followed by lengthy practice and repetition. For the following group this linear pattern has been broken. These men are all craft or trade apprentices qualified, but are now employed as Nitro-plant process operatives. Unlike the previous two groups, whose employment trajectories have been horizontal in that they now perform the job they were trained for, the following group have employment trajectories that have taken them down the occupational status hierarchy, or which represent a complete break with their past employment. There is a tendency for this group to see themselves as having been deskilled in terms of their previous craft or trade due to their lack of recent experience. It is a general feeling amongst these men that continuous involvement is necessary to the maintenance of specific occupational skills:

> I was a skilled caterer but I could not do it now, just pick up where I left off after three years. When I came out I was very skilled ... experienced like. But when you stop you get out of practice. The job I do now, because I do it day in day out I am skilled at it (Process Operative, Nitro-plant, ex cook).

> I'm not a skilled fitter now, not any more. My papers say I'm skilled but I know I'm not because I've been out of it for so long. I was skilled doing it every day but that experience has gone (Process Operative, Nitro-plant, ex British Coal Fitter).

The view that the maintenance of craft or trade skill requires constant practice and experience indicates that, for these men, experience is an important aspect of skill. Thus, the perception of experience as skill is generated by a process of lengthy, unbroken experience at a craft or occupation. This perception is also reinforced when individuals' employment trajectories involve a break with their previous craft or trade.

Discretion and Autonomy

It was demonstrated in Chapters Five and Six that perceptions of discretion and autonomy as skills are associated with the extent to which opportunities for discretion and autonomy characterise particular jobs. The structural mechanisms of production system, technology, management strategy and the organisation of work shape such opportunities. At GlassCo and Electronics UK, the labour process is characterised by constraints engendered by each of these structural features. At Chemicals UK, however, it has been argued that whilst the production system and technology on Nitro-plant does generate constraints, these are in tension with the, albeit limited, discretion and self-supervision generated by the empowered team work system. Perceptions of discretion and autonomy as skill on Nitro-plant must therefore be analysed in the context of this tension. With respect to Project-plant, Pharma-plant and the Craft Maintenance Workshop, it has been argued that workers have some discretion and autonomy over the manipulation of work, and that this has an influence on subjective perceptions of skill.

The concepts of discretion and autonomy were introduced into interviews rather than freely articulated by interviewees. Individuals were asked whether their job offered opportunities to take decisions without intervention from a supervisory figure, and whether they were supervised closely in their work or left to perform the job independently. They were than asked to describe the types of decisions they were authorised to make, and to describe the activities of supervisors. Finally, interviewees were asked if they believed discretion and autonomy to be skills. Responses to these questions at Chemicals UK culminated in the identification of two categories relating to the definition of discretion and autonomy, and also to the perception of these concepts as skills. Both groups defined autonomy as being left to work unsupervised. The first group defined discretion as control over the organisation of work; that is over allocation of tasks within the team. For these interviewees discretion and autonomy are not perceived as skills. The second group defined discretion as the ability to take decisions about the work itself, that is an independence to manipulate the process. This group does perceive discretion and autonomy as skills.

The way in which groups define the concept of discretion is shaped by structural factors on each plant. It has already been argued that the computerised continuous process rigidly controls process operatives on Nitro-plant, and that any discretionary tendencies emanating from empowered teamworking are counterbalanced by this control. This is again reflected in the responses given by process operatives when asked to describe the nature of discretion on the plant:

DT: Could you describe the types of decision you take at work?
A: All the processes we do now, what with computers and that, they're simplified to such an extent that you can do the job without getting in touch with the shift manager. But the day to day running of the plant, who does what, keeping it running, we decide that (Process Operative, Nitro-plant ex-motor mechanic).

DT: Could you describe the types of decision you take at work?
A: We decide in the team who does what rather than someone telling us what to do...Well everything goes through the computer so you only

have to decide what button to press. I suppose you have to decide which button but that's all. But even then the computer makes it easy, like it will ask you if that is what you want to do and all that (Process Operative,Nitro-plant).

This definition of discretion based on task allocation coincides with the perception that discretion and autonomy are not skills. Rather, they are seen as being merely part of the job:

DT: Do you think that the ability to take decisions for yourself is a type of skill?
A: It's just a part of the job, you know working on our own and sharing the work out between us. If it's a skill its a limited one (Process Operative, Nitro-plant).

DT: Do you think that the ability to take decisions for yourself is a type of skill?

A: I don't think that they're skills, knowing my job, running the plant, that's the skill (Process Operative, Nitro-plant).

In contrast to the above interviewees, those employed on Project and Pharma-plants and in the Craft Workshop all define discretion as the opportunity to manipulate work itself. They also perceive discretion and autonomy as skills, definitions and perceptions which are again related to structural job characteristics on each area. The manual, short run, batch production on Project and Pharma-plants results in high levels of responsibility for workers. Whilst a craft technicians job can be routine and repetitive, autonomous manipulation of work is an integral feature of the occupation. These structural features are, as with Nitro-plant, reflected in responses to questions about the opportunity for, and nature of discretion:

DT: Could you describe the types of decision you take at work?
A: We obviously make decisions frequently. Like for example when we are reacting in vessels, we get a batch sheet telling us what temperature to do it at. Well on this plant we are trying things out, trying to get the best yield. So we have a go at reacting at a different temperature to try and improve the yield (Process Chemist, Project-plant).

DT: Could you describe the types of decision you take at work?
A: It's up to us to start the batch, mix the feed stocks, monitor and close down the process. And all the time we will be making the necessary decisions and adjustments. If something happens unexpected I will need

to think how to get it right and I will have to make a decision to try something (Process Operative, Pharma-plant).

DT: Could you describe the types of decision you take at work?
A: We are loosely supervised. The supervisor tells us what to do but he doesn't break it down and say, you will mend that pipe and you will mend it that or this way. No, he gives you a job then it's up to you to decide how you prepare yourself and how you do it (Craft Technician).

When asked whether they believe discretion and autonomy to be skills, all interviewees from this latter group replied that they are. It appears that perceptions of discretion and autonomy as skills are shaped by structural features associated with their jobs, that is by the scope for manipulation of work itself. For Project and Pharma-plant workers, the scope for such manipulation is the result of the high level of integration between planning, programming and operating functions. For craft technicians it arises, as with GlassCo Mould Maintenance Workshop employees, from the organisation of work and nature of the task. Tasks are distributed by the supervisor, but once distributed craft technicians have complete autonomy over task performance, that is they have a high degree of scope to manipulate work. All interviewees across the three case studies whose jobs require some manipulation over work content, that is craftsmen at GlassCo and Chemicals UK, and Project and Pharma-plant process operatives, perceive these concepts as skill. Process operatives at Chemicals UK whose jobs demand discretion over task allocation only, do not, on the other hand, perceive discretion and autonomy as skills. There are however, two exceptions to these generalities that are explicable in the context of employment trajectories. The two craft apprentice trained process operatives employed on Nitro-plant also define discretion as the opportunity to manipulate work. They also perceive discretion and autonomy as skills, although they do not believe them to be a feature of their current job:

DT: Could you describe the types of decision you take at work?
A: None really, when I was a fitter at the pit I made lots of decisions. I would get a note at the start of a shift telling me what had to be done and I would just go off and do it. It was up to me to decide how, it was part of my craft, and yes it was a skill. There is no call for that kind of thing in this job. Like I said, its dead boring (Process Operative, Nitro-plant, ex British Coal).

The definitions of discretion and the subsequent perceptions of skill, held by these two men are shaped by their previous occupation, and, it is suggested, by their experience of working through an apprenticeship.

Conclusion to Workers' Perceptions of Skill

It was suggested, in Chapters Five and Six that work at GlassCo and Electronics UK is constrained by the structural features that shape the labour process. Production systems, management structure and style, and the organisation of work all combine to engender jobs that are rigidly prescribed, and which allow no discretion and autonomy by workers. This results in perceptions of skill that are expressed, from the outset, as concrete competencies, which closely reflect the demands of individual jobs. In contrast to this, production jobs on Nitro-plant are characterised by tension between constraints built into production systems and technology, and by the limited freedom associated with the empowered team work system. The result of this tension appears to be perceptions of skill that are initially articulated in terms of generalised concepts of knowledge, training and experience. It is only through closer questioning that these perceptions of skill are broken down to reflect the specific task competencies associated with particular occupations. Once broken down, perceptions of knowledge as skill divide into practical task knowledge and theoretical knowledge, whilst training as skill breaks down into formal apprenticeship and on the job varieties. Specific perceptions of knowledge as skill are generated by types of production system and technology on individual plants. In particular, the nature of the division between planning, programming and operating functions; itself a feature of both machinery and the division of labour around machinery. Types of training undertaken generate specific perceptions of training as skill. The perception of experience as skill, on the other hand, is uniform across the factory, and is associated with lengthy unbroken experience at one job, or by a breakdown of this experience.

In terms of craft maintenance workers, perceptions of skill focus on formal apprenticeship training and experience, and are highly similar to those articulated by GlassCo craft workers. Finally, whether individuals hold a perception of discretion and autonomy as skill depends on the way in which these concepts are initially defined. These definitions are themselves dependent on structural features associated with particular jobs. As with both GlassCo and Electronics UK, perceptions of discretion and autonomy as a skill are generated only where there is a real opportunity for manipulation of work. Discretion over task allocation does not result in perceptions of discretion and autonomy as skill. Running parallel to job specific structural features are individuals' employment trajectories, the direction of which influences the way in which he or she experiences job related structural features. Thus for those moving up the occupational status hierarchy the most salient reference point through which to consider skill is the current job, whilst for those moving down the occupational hierarchy, the most salient reference point is previous occupation.

Management Perceptions of Workforce Skill

Management perceptions of skill at Chemicals UK are comparable to those held by managers at the first two case study factories, and also to workforce interviewees at Chemicals UK. On a generalised level, managers' perceptions of skill, like their counterparts at GlassCo and Electronics UK, emphasise workers attitudes. In terms of the job specific skills required of workers on different plants, managers' perceptions display similarities to those held by workers themselves. On Nitro-plant these focuses on a practical understanding of the process and on the ability to follow instructions. On Project and Pharma-plants, management perceptions of workforce skills focus on intelligence and a more in-depth knowledge of the process and the chemistry. These job specific perceptions of skill are, like those of the workforce, associated with and shaped by the nature of the production process, technology and division between planning and operation on each plant.

The general perception of workers' attitudes as an aspect of skill was expressed by seven of the nine managers interviewed, and the following quotes are given in response to the question: "How would you define the term skill in relation to shop floor workers?"

> Well for someone to be skilled they need to be highly motivated and that comes down to their attitude to work in general (Area Production Manager - Project and Pharma plants).

> It's a combination of things but a good attitude is an advantage in any job (Pharma-plant Manager).

> Er...you can have people who are skilled in the practical aspects of a job but who are not good at that job. And its down to attitude, a willingness to deal with the things they're asked to and a willingness to learn (Operations Manager, Nitro-plant).

> I'm into conscientiousness myself (Technical Manager, Nitro-plant).

> Skill starts with attitude to work and whether he wants to work. You can have a guy who is brilliant but if he does not want to work he won't. You can get a guy who is prepared to work and his attitude is right then he will develop the skills (Training Co-ordinator, Nitro, Project and Pharma-plants).

The strong emphasis placed on attitude as an attribute of workforce skill is not exclusive to managers at Chemicals UK. These perceptions have been found amongst managers in all three organisations. It has also been argued that these perceptions are the outcome of capital's need to transform workers' labour power into productive labour, and that this transformation is the responsibility of managers.

Moving on to managers perceptions of the skills required for specific jobs, the division between workers on Nirto-plant and Project and Pharma-plants in relation to the perception of knowledge as skill are comparable with the perceptions held by managers. Managers on Nitro-plant perceive workforce skills in terms of basic practical knowledge, and an ability to follow steps written out in job specification instructions and instructions given out by the computer. The following quotes were given in response to the question: "What types of skill do Nitro-plant process operatives need?"

> Well most of what they do is controlled by PCS units which are like mini-computers and which monitor the stills on an ongoing basis all of the time. If something goes wrong with the still the computer closes the process down automatically. When the stills are running OK there's not really much for the process operatives to do, just take samples periodically. They need to understand what the computer is telling them and they may have to respond by making a few adjustments. It's when there is a problem with the still that skill comes into it, and that's down to a combination of knowing what steps to take and experience of seeing it before and remembering what they did last time (Area Production Manager, Nitro-plant).

> Obviously they need to know how to run the plant, to follow the standing instructions that say how it should be run. A good skilled operator also knows what to do if something happens that does not fit, know where to look to put it right (Assistant Operations Manager Nitro-plant).

> All operations on the plant have been computerised so a lot of the control characteristics have been taken away from operators...its all done on the computer. So basically they have had to learn how to read and operate the computer. So skills...well now they have lost direct supervision the skills they need are more to do with teamworking,

helping their mates out when they're under pressure (Shift Manager, Nitro-plant).

The view that skill on Nitro-plant involves following instructions, and taking practical remedial action if the process goes out of set parameters, is also held by the technical manager. He, however, goes further and argues that intellectual capabilities are a distinct disadvantage for a process operator on Nitro-plant. The views articulated by this man are again in response to the question: "What types of skill do process operatives on Nitro-plant need?"

> The big one is memory, I don't know if you would call that a skill. I mean with all this pipework and the processes to go through, it takes a lot of time to memorise it [...] We have some operators who are a bit more intellectual but it doesn't make them better operators. Someone who is conscientious, who is there when he should be, who helps out when asked to and who knows roughly why he is doing it without necessarily knowing the technical aspects. He is better than someone who knows all the technical aspects but who prefers to sit in the tea-room [...] It's not really a skilled job you see, so people who are more intellectually able tend to use their intellect to get out of work. Also they are more easily bored and they don't do the job as well. I mean, I don't want to be cruel but you could go out of your mind watching red lines go up and down all day long and writing down numbers every two hours. You need to keep your concentration, but that sort of person is not that good at reacting when something does go wrong. Those with a bit more intellect are better at that, but then they get more practice because they have not noticed the problem in the first place   (Technical Manager, Nitro-plant).

The perceptions of workforce skill articulated by the above managers are comparable to the perceptions of practical task knowledge as skill held by process operators themselves. Both focus on the practical tasks necessary to oversee the continuous process, but tend to exclude theoretical knowledge of the process and chemistry. The perception of the ability to follow instructions as skill can, furthermore, be argued to preclude any notion of discretion and autonomy in relation to Nitro-plant employees. In contrast to this, management perceptions of workforce skill on Project and Pharma-plants stress intellectual capabilities, and a theoretical knowledge of the process and the chemistry. They also emphasise the ability to use ones own discretion. The following quotes are again in response to the question: "What types of skill do process operatives on Project-plant/Pharma-plant need?"

Well it's down to capability, when we recruit for Project and Pharma-plants we go for the cream of the other plants. Men who are more intelligent, who think more about what they are doing, who are able to cope with unfamiliar situations and pressure and who can be left alone to get on with it. The jobs on these plants are different to elsewhere in the factory. It's more varied making batch than continuous process. The process operators on Pharma-plant have a high level of discretion within set boundaries and run the plant with little line management. The shift chemists are obviously more skilled than the process operators on Project-plant because of their chemistry degree, their knowledge of chemistry. But process operators also have to have some chemistry knowledge (Plant Manager, Project-plant and Pharma-plant).

Intelligence is a skill they need because it influences how well they pick things up, and experience, that's a skill. Pharma-plant is unique in the factory in that the men have to be highly skilled, they have a lot of responsibility, especially with the team work system and the removal of supervisors (Plant Manager, Pharma-plant).

They need a lot of knowledge on these plants because the chemistry and the process is much more complex than anywhere else on the site (Area Production Manager, Project and Pharma-plants).

It can be argued that the emphasis placed on intelligence and knowledge by these three managers is similar to the theoretical knowledge as skill expressed by shop floor staff. It can also be suggested that the differences in relation to job specific workforce skills articulated by these two sets of managers are associated with, and shaped by, the production process, technology, and the social organisation of work around technology on each plant.

It appears that the processes that shape management perceptions of workforce skill at Chemicals UK follow the same patterns found at GlassCo and Electronics UK. The agency role of managers in securing profit for the firm through the co-ordination and control of workers, and the need for managers to secure their own position in the organisation is expedited if workers display a positive attitude to work and commitment to the company. There is, however, one important difference between the junior and middle managers interviewed at Chemicals UK, and those at GlassCo and Electronics UK. All junior and middle managers at Chemicals UK have a degree in Chemistry or Chemical Engineering. Their position in the organisation does not depend solely on organisational assets, it is also dependent on the credentials they bring into the organisation. Even if these individuals were to lose their job at Chemicals UK, they retain marketable assets in the form of credentials. This does not, however, completely negate the suggestion that junior and middle managers need to exercise agency on behalf of the firm in order to secure their position in the organisation. The argument put forward here is comparable to that advanced by Savage, Barlow, Dickens and Fielding (1992). They suggest that although individuals own educational credentials, they require an organisational context in which their value can be realised. Thus, middle managers at Chemicals UK need to secure organisational assets in order to exploit the value of their educational assets. By exercising agency on behalf of the firm, these managers are securing organisational assets and their position in the firm.

Conclusion

The evidence put forward in this chapter again provides a basis for a number of key assertions put forward in this book. First, the Fordist - post-Fordist dichotomy does not provide a useful framework through which to understand the nature of the organisational structure. Although Chemicals UK has developed in response to uncertain markets, and whilst the firm is attempting to shift into niche market areas, this has not facilitated the transformation to a post-Fordist organisational structure. The salient reference point from which individuals consider the subject of skill results from an interaction between firm specific structural features, and individuals' employment trajectories and qualifications. Evidence from Chemicals UK suggests that for production workers, the organisation of work around technology result in a separation between conception and execution. However, amongst craft workers and a small number of production workers on Project and Pharma-plants, conception and execution in the form of planning, programming and operation has, to a degree, been combined. Amongst craft workers this combining of conception and execution is an integral aspect of the job. For Project and Pharma-plant workers it is a result of the alignment of technology and the social organisation of work. Whilst the continuous process technology on these batch plants has been argued to be Fordist, the organisation of work around the technology and the nature of skill most closely resembles the predictions of Piore and Sabel; that more complex forms of flexible technology would lead to a rescinding of the division between the conception and execution of work, and that this would lead to an upskilling of the workforce.

With regard to perceptions of skill, the dichotomy between practical task knowledge and theoretical knowledge relates to differences in the use of technology and social organisation of work between Nitro-plant, and Project- and Pharma-plants. In terms of the distinction between formal apprenticeship training as skill and on the job training as skill, this is associated with the possession, or lack of possession, of an apprenticeship qualification, thus leading to the argument that apprenticeship training is an important generator of subjective perceptions of skill. With respect to experience as skill, this is widespread and uniform amongst Chemicals UK employees, and relates to long term engagement with a particular trade or job. It is, furthermore, reinforced when this long-term engagement breaks down. Finally, perceptions of discretion and autonomy as skill depend on the scope for meaningful decision making. For those individuals for whom the concepts of discretion and autonomy are defined as the scope to organise work between men, no perceptions of discretion and autonomy as skill are expressed. Where, however, these concepts are defined as the scope to plan and manipulate work, they are perceived as skills.

This chapter, along with Chapters Five and Six, has set out the case study evidence that has formed the empirical foundation of the model put forward in Chapter Four. A variety of patterns and trends relating to perceptions of skill, core and periphery have been identified, and a number of key conclusions have been drawn. These conclusions will now be outlined and discussed in the next, and final, chapter of the book.

8 The Key Conclusions

The empirical evidence presented in the preceding three chapter's lead to the development of a number of key conclusions. These concern the nature of subjective perceptions of skill, core and periphery, and the causal processes that shape them, and also the adequacy of existing sociological theory as an explanatory framework. The key conclusions are as follows:

1. Workforce perceptions of skill are narrowly defined and context dependent.

2. The labour process debates of the 1970s and 1980s remain a useful framework through which to understand the causal processes that shape the perceptions of skill held by many of the production workers interviewed.

3. The organisational structures that help shape subjective perceptions of skill cannot be understood in the context of Fordist and post-Fordist dualisms. This is due to the complex configurations of structural features within firms.

4. The perceptions of workforce skill held by managers are shaped by managers contradictory position in relation to capital.

5. Gender has no direct salience in the generation of workers' perceptions of skill.

6. Workers whose formal position defines them as peripheral express no perception of themselves as forming part of a peripheral workforce.

Workforce perceptions of skill are narrowly defined and context dependent

The first conclusion concerns the nature of perceptions of skill themselves. On the basis of this evidence, it appears that workforce perceptions of skill are narrowly defined and context dependent. In suggesting that workers perceptions of skill are narrowly defined, I am arguing that they are limited to the particular tasks that constitute a specific job. Although interviewees initially define skill in terms of abstract concepts of knowledge, training and experience, closer questioning reveals that these concepts refer to narrow job attributes. Individuals appear unable to move outside their personal experience to consider skill in more abstract generalised terms. In the course of interviews, people were asked to consider skill in general rather than in relation to their own job. When asked to do this, however, the majority launched into a description of the skills needed for their own current or previous occupation. Despite a number of interviewees having shifted between occupations and jobs, when considering the concept of skill they did not draw on the cumulative knowledge gained from these various jobs. Rather, they focused on knowledge gained from either current or previous work.

In comparison with the definitions of skill proposed by sociologists, the perceptions expressed by interviewees are again narrowly defined. Whereas sociologists draw on concepts such as substantive complexity and autonomy control (Spenner 1990), workers perceptions are tied to the specific demands of particular jobs. A further distinction made by sociologists is that between skills that reside in the individual and specific task skills. Workers make no such distinction. Where skills are perceived as an attribute of the individual, they are defined in terms of particular job characteristics. Thus, although perceptions of mechanical competence as skill can be interpreted as a personal attribute, the technological aspects of work shape it. Similarly, whilst knowledge as skill can be interpreted as belonging to the individual, it refers to a narrow job related form of knowledge. A further conclusion relates to the impact of job characteristics on perceptions of discretion and autonomy as skill. Interviewees perceive discretion and autonomy as skill only if their job contains the scope for autonomous decisions regarding the manipulation of work. If these competencies are constrained by the production process or management strategies, workers do not define them as skill. The scope to organise the distribution of tasks within a team does not generate perceptions of discretion and autonomy as skill. This contrasts sharply with the findings of Burchell, Elliot, Rubery and Wilkinson (1994) discussed in Chapter Three. These authors suggest that even low level production and service workers believe their jobs to require a degree of discretion. An explanation of why the sample used by Burchell and his colleagues and my sample should express totally opposing views is beyond the scope of this book. It can be pointed out however, that their research did not attempt to identify the causal processes that shape perceptions. For this reason, no firm comparisons can be made.

It could be suggested that perceptions of skill amongst production workers are best understood in terms of Woods tacit theory of skill. The perceptions of this group are, for example, situation specific and appear to relate to skills that are learned through experience. They are, on the other hand, expressed in a formalised manner, that is as the formal skill requirements of particular jobs. They do not, therefore, correspond with sociological definitions of tacit skill.

The labour process debates of the 1970s and 1980s remain a useful framework through which to understand the causal processes that shape the perceptions of skill held by many of the production workers interviewed

The second key conclusion to be drawn from the case study evidence is that traditional labour process theory remains very useful to an understanding of the processes that shape the subjective perceptions of skill held by many production workers. It might appear that reliving debates that took place during the 1970s and 1980s in order to theorise perceptions of skill in the late 1990s is a retrograde step. Labour process debates have moved on from the preoccupation with deskilling towards analyses of discipline and surveillance, and the impact of flexible, lean (JIT) production systems. Evidence from the three factories indicates, however, that the processes identified by early labour process theorists remain influential in shaping some workers' subjective perceptions of skill.

Braverman and his later supporters (for example, Cooley, Hyman and Streek) argued that deskilling results from an alignment of Taylorism and technology. This alignment ensures management's ability to appropriate workers' wider knowledge of the production process, and facilitates the separation of conception and execution of tasks. The only form of knowledge remaining in the hands of workers is that required for the execution of simplified and fragmented tasks. A detailed discussion of the effects of technology in conjunction with the social organisation of work was given in Chapter Three. The case study evidence put forward here supports the argument that the patterns of skill formation that are associated with particular forms of technology are dependent upon the ways in which labour is organised around machinery (for example, Patrickson 1986, Jones 1988, Lane 1988, Kelley, 1989 and Hendry 1990). Specifically, the extent to which planning, programming and operating functions are combined or divided. Thus, where the amalgamation of management strategy, social organisation of work, and technology results in a separation of conception and execution, workforce perceptions of skill focus on the execution of discrete, and often simplistic, monitoring and operating tasks.

However, as argued earlier in the book, the processes described above cannot be applied to all workers across the three case study firms. Some workers do retain responsibility for conception in the form of planning out tasks. Namely, production workers on Chemicals UK's Project and Pharma-plants, and craft maintenance workers at GlassCo and Chemicals UK. These workers' jobs demand that they imagine the outcome of actions and plan accordingly. This requirement for planning engenders perceptions of skill that focus on theoretical knowledge amongst Project and Pharma-plant operatives, and discretion and autonomy as skill held by craftsmen. Thus, the trends set out by Braverman are not universal or inevitable, they are, however, commonplace.

The assertion that Braverman's deskilling theory remains useful to an understanding of the processes that shape subjective perceptions of skill is not intended to suggest that labour has been completely subjugated to the will of capital. Rather, the changes in the labour process, and corresponding changes in levels of skill, predicted by post-Fordist theorists such as Piore and Sabel, are not apparent in relation to the majority of production workers in the three case study factories. Work, for the majority of interviewees, remains rooted in the Fordist paradigm. In addition, the evidence put forward in this book provides support for those who argue that these changes have been exaggerated, or are old processes dressed up in new theories (Pollert 1988a 1988b 1991, Elger 1991). At the end of the twentieth century, the articulation of managerial strategies and technology continues to facilitate a separation of conception and execution in relation to many workers. This separation results in perceptions of skill that focus on the performance of discrete, demarcated, and often simplified, tasks.

The organisational structures that shape subjective perceptions of skill cannot be understood in the context of a Fordist and post-Fordist dualism. This is due to the complex configurations of structural features within firms

The assertion that perceptions of skill are context dependent requires exploration of the contexts in which they occur. I have demonstrated that the articulation of firm specific structural features has a significant impact on the perceptions of skill held by workers. An important aspect of the research has therefore been to identify the nature and generative properties of these features. An original aim of the research was to identify and explain subjective perceptions of skill, core and periphery in the context of Fordist and post-Fordist organisational structures. Discussion of this issue concentrated on the various forms of flexibility that are generally assumed to characterise the alleged shift to post-Fordism. This is the dichotomy between the traditional Fordist assembly line and the new automated flexible production machinery associated with post-Fordism and neo-Fordism, and also the theory of functional flexibility put forward by Atkinson and Meager. In Chapter Three these purported divisions between Fordism and post-Fordism concentrated on the alleged dichotomy between Taylorist management strategies and patterns of work, and non-Taylorist strategies and work patterns, for example responsible autonomy and teamworking. I have suggested that these dualisms are unsustainable, in particular, the articulation of flexible production technology with Taylorist management strategies and work patterns renders any attempt to categorise firms as Fordist or post-Fordist irrelevant.

The argument that individual firms' organisational structural features cannot be understood in relation to Fordist and post-Fordist dualisms raises two issues. First, Aglietta (1979) and Piore and Sabel (1984) dealt with the impact of new technology on skill formation. For Aglietta the future was bleak, automation would result in a further fragmentation of tasks, and an intensified division between conception and execution. For Piore and Sabel, on the other hand, flexible specialist machinery would result in a rescinding of the separation between conception and execution, and a general upskilling of the workforce. For Atkinson and Meager (1986), changes in the organisation of work would result in functional flexibility and a multi-skilling of the core workforce. I conclude that a number of the above trajectories are in evidence at the three firms. There are however, no distinct patterns between or within firms. Some of the outcomes predicted by Aglietta have been argued to characterise a range of production jobs across the firms. Where technology has taken over the more complex aspects of work, jobs are characterised by a separation of conception and execution. Examples of this process were found at GlassCo, in the Electronics UK Autoinsertion Department and on Chemicals UK's Nitro-plant. It appears, furthermore, that production jobs organised around flexible technology at GlassCo and Electronics UK have not followed the patterns of upskilling proposed by Piore and Sabel. It can be argued, however, that this outcome owes as much to the social organisation of work around technology, namely the division between planning and operating functions, rather than the inherent properties of technology. In terms of the functional flexibility and multi-skilling put forward by Atkinson and Meager, neither are applicable to the majority of production workers at GlassCo or Electronics UK. Even limited functional flexibility in the form of simple task rotation is rare at both firms. In addition, it has been argued that where functional flexibility, in the form of task rotation within a teamwork system, is allied to a production process that contains technological constraints, the effects on perceptions of skill are negligible. An example of this is Chemical UK's Nitro-plant.

The evidence relating to flexibility presented in this book supports authors such as Pollert (1991), Amin (1994) and Elam 1994) who question the validity of Fordist and post-Fordist dualisms. I have demonstrated that each firm retains an integrated mix of Fordist and post-Fordist characteristics that are, on occasions, inseparable. In addition, and it can be argued as a result, the skill trajectories of workers in the three firms display both parallels and deviations to those advanced by post-Fordist theorists. This point leads on to the conclusion that in order to understand perceptions of skill in relation to organisational structures, the specific nature and configuration of firm specific structural features must be examined, and the generative properties identified. It is not possible, for example, to understand perceptions of skill in relation to flexible production technology. Rather, analysis should be made of the ways in which technology and other organisational features interact.

The perceptions of workforce skill held by managers are shaped by managers' contradictory position in relation to capital

Moving on to management perceptions of workforce skill, evidence from managers in the three case study factories   indicates that these focus on attitude and commitment, and the specific task requirements associated with particular jobs. Additional evidence from Electronics UK suggests that management perceptions of skill in the firm are highly gender stereotyped in relation to women workers. For all managers, at all three firms, attitude and commitment are seen as the most crucial of skills. Second, like workers themselves, managers' perceptions of workforce skill are narrowly defined around specific task requirements. I have suggested that management perceptions of workforce skill are closely associated with managers need to exercise agency on behalf of the firm, and to protect their own position in the firm. Managers are responsible for ensuring that workers labour power is transformed into productive labour. That is, for directing and co-ordinating the labour of subordinates. I have shown that a variety of methods for achieving direction and co-ordination are available. Thus, there is the direct control over some production workers and the granting of semi-autonomy to others. It can be suggested however, that whatever managerial model is adopted, this particular function is likely to be made easier if subordinates adopt the correct attitudes, commitment and motivation. Thus, the managerial role of ensuring that labour power is transformed into productive labour shapes managers perceptions of workforce skill as attitude, commitment and motivation. Similarly, if workers perform their tasks accurately, and in accordance with company rules, it is possible that they will be more highly valued than those who view their jobs differently to management. Henceforth the focus on task specific competencies.

The causal processes that shape managers' perceptions of workforce skill can be understood in the context of Savage, Barlow, Dickens and Fielding's (1992) theory of assets and middle-class formation. They argue that different middle-class groups have access to different types of asset, and a distinction is made between the educational credentials held by professionals and the organisational assets, that is assets that arise from an individual's position in the organisation, held by the majority of managers. Although these authors suggest that organisational assets are of a lower value than professional credentials, they also suggest that the value of credentials can only be realised in an organisational context. Regardless of whether managers possess educational qualifications, they need, if they are to secure their position in the firm and realise the value of their assets, to exercise agency on behalf of the firm. The position of managers in relation to the firm is, therefore, contradictory. Whilst, as Armstrong (1989) points out, managers role in the capitalist organisation is one of agency, they are also dependent on the organisation if they are to realise the value of their assets. Thus, I conclude that managers' perceptions of workforce skill are shaped by the need for managers to secure the creation of surplus value in the interests of both the firm and themselves.

A final issue with respect to management perceptions of skill relates to the highly gendered attitudes of the Electronics UK managers who were interviewed. It is difficult to assess whether these gendered attitudes are an outcome of women's position at the bottom of the hierarchical structure, or whether women's positions are an outcome of gender stereotyped attitudes. It can be suggested that managers perceptions of women workers' skills are a possible result of interaction between the above two processes. Comments by the Electronics UK Autoinsertion Manager indicate that he believes women to be less technologically competent than men. This suggests that stereotyped perceptions of women's skills prevent their promotion into higher level jobs. It also fits with Wajcman's argument that women often lack access to technological training and, as a result, lack the power to achieve skilled status, thus reinforcing the identification of technological competence as a masculine attribute.

Gender has no direct salience in the generation of workers' perceptions of skill

Two conclusions relating to the theories of gender and work discussed in Chapter Three are made. First, there are no differences between the work attitudes of men and women in the three factories. This supports arguments put forward by Siltanen (1988), Rowe and Snizek (1995) and Tolbert and Moen (1998), all of whom suggest that women's attitudes to work, like those of men, are best understood in relation to the structural features that characterise particular jobs. Second, at GlassCo and Electronics UK there is a strongly gendered hierarchical and vertical division of labour and women are, in general, located in the lower occupational grades. The structural features associated with these occupations therefore shape the salient reference points from which women consider skill. It appears that gender has only an indirect impact on workers perceptions of skill. Women's perceptions of skill are, like men's, shaped by interaction between the structural features of their employment, and their prior experiences and employment trajectories. The impact of gender is limited to the location of women in lower occupational grades.

Workers whose formal position defines them as peripheral express no perception of themselves as forming part of a peripheral workforce

The final key conclusion is that the majority of individuals whose structural position could be defined as peripheral or secondary have no perceptions of themselves as forming part of a peripheral labour force. Two particular issues arise from this assertion. First, the question of how far the structural position of these workers can be seen as corresponding to the theoretical conceptualisation of the periphery. Second, why is it that these workers have no perception of themselves as peripheral. I have argued that the categorisation of workers into a stable core and an unstable periphery is misleading, and fails to capture the complexities of different types of employment contract. Temporary workers, such as those at Electronics UK, whose temporary status may be a first step into permanent employment, and who enjoy similar occupational benefits as permanent workers, cannot be regarded as peripheral in the same way as short-term agency workers who have no access to these benefits. Similarly, I have questioned whether part-time workers with secure contracts and occupational benefits, and whom managers regard as important to a firm's activities, should be regarded as peripheral. Tam (1997) suggests that the low skilled nature of many part-time jobs limit workers' chances of gaining entry into 'good' jobs. Evidence from GlassCo shows, however, that female full-time workers who occupy similarly low skilled occupations are subject to the same limitations as their part-time colleagues. This supports Pollert's view that workers cannot be neatly divided into distinct core and peripheral categories (Pollert 1988, 1991). I conclude, therefore, that the temporary and part-time workers interviewed during this research do not perceive themselves as peripheral because their employment status cannot be adequately described as such. Had it been possible to conduct interviews with agency workers, perceptions of core and periphery may have differed from those articulated by temporary and part-time workers at Electronics UK and GlassCo. It is suggested, from this evidence, that the core and periphery model is too static and rigid, and needs to be replaced by one which takes account of the possibility of movement between categories over time.

Conclusion

This book began, in Chapter Two, with a theoretical discussion of labour process theory and theories of post-Fordism. In Chapter Three the theoretical discussion concentrated on four specific issues, the first being the subject of skill itself. The chapter then went on to discuss managerial strategies and skill, technology and skill, and gender and skill. Following these theoretical discussions in Chapters Two and Three, Chapter Four outlined the model through which to explain subjective perceptions of skill, core and periphery. In Chapters Five, Six and Seven the case study evidence which informed the construction of the model was presented. Finally, in Chapter Eight, a discussion of the book's key conclusions was made.

The book has focused on a number of key issues. First, it has shifted analysis away from the definitions applied by sociologists towards an understanding of the subjective interpretations of those involved in production. Worker perceptions of skill, core and periphery are largely neglected areas in the literature. If, however, workplace skill, and core and periphery are legitimate areas of sociological study the interpretations and perceptions of workers, and the causal process that shape them, should also be considered. Second, the book draws attention to the strengths and weaknesses of sociological theories. I have demonstrated that traditional labour process analysis remains useful to an understanding of workplace skill, particularly with respect to the continued separation of conception and execution. I have also challenged the alleged shift from the Fordist production paradigm to the post-Fordist paradigm. Evidence has been put forward to support the assertion that organisations cannot be categorised in terms of a paradigmatic shift. The development of organisational structures and the configuration of organisational features are far more complex and uneven that the Fordist-post-Fordist dichotomy allows for.

A further issue in the post-Fordist paradigm is that of Japanisation. It was suggested in Chapter Two that Japanisation is an ambiguous concept, which refers to a range of developments occurring on different levels. On one level Japanisation is conceived as a convergence between Japanese and British economic systems, whilst on another it is defined as a set of management practices copied from Japan. Even at this level however, I have argued that the concept is problematic. For some theorists (for example Clegg 1990), Japanisation as a set of management practices refers to concepts such as teamworking, quality circles and JIT. A review of UK electronics transplants indicates that, with the exception of JIT production (but not JIT supply), these developments are *not* characteristics of the electronics sector. It was further argued in Chapter Two, that whilst Japanese JIT production can be seen as qualitatively different to Fordism, its effects on the labour of workers is to intensify the controls built into Taylorism. In conclusion, exploration of subjective perceptions of skill in the context of Fordist and post-Fordist organisations breaks down in the face of the complex nature and formation of organisational structures.

A further theme of the book has been to argue that the causal processes that shape perceptions of skill are independent of gender. Both men and women perceive skill as a result of interaction between firm specific structural features, and agency mechanisms of prior qualifications and employment trajectories. With respect to theories of core and periphery, evidence has been put forward which questions the usefulness of the core and periphery model as a descriptive framework. I have suggested that the categorisation of jobs in terms of contract type does not take account of the ways in which non-standard employment may be a step into permanent full-time employment.   The shift in focus, from formal core and peripheral categories to the perceptions of core and periphery held by workers, has highlighted the need for a more flexible conceptualisation of employment categories.

Finally, the book demonstrates the value of realist social theory in the analysis of organisations. The overt realist ontology and methodology has enabled an examination of the structural and agency properties and processes that occur on a variety of levels. That is, at the level of the capitalist system, at the level of the organisation, and at the level of the individual agent. The case study approach has also allowed for an analysis of the specific contexts in which perceptions of skill are shaped, whilst the use of three case study organisations has allowed for comparison between different organisational structures. By adopting this approach I have demonstrated that, although perceptions of skill may differ between organisations, the same wider causal processes shape these perceptions.

In conclusion, the principal concern of this book has been to shift the analysis of skill, core and periphery away from sociological definitions towards the subjective perceptions of those involved in production. A further aim has been to construct a model through which to explain the subjective perceptions of skill, core and periphery held by workers and managers in three case study factories, and the causal processes that shape them. I have also demonstrated how perceptions of skill relate to the capitalist system of production. I have argued, on the basis of empirical case study evidence, that the subjective perceptions of skill held by workers are narrowly defined and context dependent. I have also demonstrated that a network of processes that originate in the capitalist system, and which are inextricably linked to the jobs performed shapes perceptions of skill.

Methodology Appendix

The objectives of this research were pursued using a qualitative case study methodology. After gaining access to each case study firm the research was divided into four stages. Stage one aimed to set out the organisational context and to gain a 'feel' for each firm. Stage two dealt with sampling procedures, stage three with topic guide design and interviews, and stage four with analysis of the data.

Stage One: The Organisational Context

Specific research questions and data collection strategies were formulated in order to gain an understanding of how each firm operates.

What is the nature of the product?

In all three firms this question was examined through documentary evidence such as product brochures, and interviews with production managers.

What is the market position of the firm?

At Chemicals UK this information was gained from a number of sources: the 1995 Company Directors Report, interviews with various managers, and newspaper financial reports. At GlassCo and Electronics UK, information was gained from interviews with managers.

What employment patterns exist in the firm?

This question was designed to provide the basis for research into perceptions of core and periphery, for example in terms of the numbers employed and contract types. At both GlassCo and Electronics UK this information was provided in the form of a typed breakdown of employee characteristics, and from interviews with personnel managers.

How is labour recruited, and why are these methods used?

It was hypothesised that recruitment practices would provide an insight into the skill background of the workforce. Information on the issue was gained from personnel managers in each firm. No relationship between recruitment policies and perceptions of skill were uncovered.

What is the overall structure of the firm?

Thee aim of this question was to discover what departments exist, what functions they carry out, and what types of technology are in use. The information was gained from organisational flow charts and interviews with personnel and production managers. Once this information had been collected it was used to make a decision on which departments would be useful research sites. The objective was to interview people involved in a variety of production processes, using different forms of technology, and who have a variety of employment, training and educational backgrounds. At GlassCo the Hot Area (HA) and Cold Area (CA) were selected in order to explore perceptions in the two main production areas, and which contain the two main forms of technology. The Mould Maintenance Workshop was chosen in order to contrast the perceptions of production workers and craft workers. Re-sorters were selected for two reasons. First, these workers are part-time and compare with Atkinson's conceptualisation of the peripheral sector. Second, the work they perform contrasts with HA machinists and sorters in that they do not work with machinery. At Electronics UK the selection of autoinsertion and assembly line staff again facilitated and exploration of perceptions in the two main production areas. Access to craft maintenance staff was denied. However, a small number of technicians in the Autoinsertion Department were interviewed, and these workers did provide a contrast with the craftsmen at GlassCo and Chemicals UK. Finally, at Chemicals UK the selection of Nitro-plant, and Project- and Pharma-plants provided a contrast between continuous and batch production. In addition, interviews with craft maintenance workers provided a contrast between production and maintenance staff and also a point of comparison with the GlassCo craftsmen.

How is work organised?

Once specific research sites were selected this question concerning the social organisation of work was dealt with. For example, whether workers are organised into teams or do they work individually? How closely are they supervised? How much autonomy and discretion are they allowed? Who is responsible for sharing out tasks and deployment of men to jobs; and how is work organised around technology? For example, with respect to the separation of planning, programming and operating functions. The information was gained from interviews with plant/departmental managers, production managers, personnel managers and workers themselves. At Chemicals UK, individual job specification documents were also provided.

What training policies are in operation?

Documentary evidence and interviews with personnel and training managers provided information about each of the three firms training strategy. At GlassCo, training manuals and NVQ manuals were provided, whilst at Electronics UK and Chemicals UK training manuals were accessed.

Stage Two: Research Sites and Sampling Procedures

Research areas in each firm were selected for their theoretical relevance in relation to the production process and technology; the stage of each production process with respect to each firm's overall activities; the organisation of work, and the characteristics of individuals employed on these areas: for example, qualifications and experience. At GlassCo the choice of the HA, CA and Mould Maintenance Workshop were selected for the following reasons. First, the HA and CA represent the two main stages in the production process. These two areas also use differing types of flexible technology, which have variable effects on the nature of work. With respect to the Mould Maintenance Workshop, this area was chosen in order to contrast the perceptions of apprentice qualified men performing skilled craft work with those of unqualified men and women performing semi-skilled and, in the case of re-sorters, unskilled work. Finally, the Re-sorting Department was selected in order to examine the perceptions of core and periphery held by low skilled, part-time workers.

At Electronics UK, production is divided between the Autoinsertion Department and the assembly line areas. The Autoinsertion Department contains flexible automated machinery that can be programmed to produce a variety of circuit boards used in various products. The assembly line areas, on the other hand, use traditional Fordist flow line technology. In terms of workforce characteristics, the Autoinsertion Department contains a mix of apprentice-qualified men and those with no qualifications. In addition to this, a number of individuals have been selected to train as technicians. Whilst Electronics UK does have specialist maintenance departments, these were not accessed due to constraints imposed by the firm.

The three production plants used as research sites at Chemicals UK, Nitro-plant, Project-plant and Pharma-plant, were selected in order to compare and contrast perceptions of skill on a continuous process production plant and batch production plants. Although the technology utilised on each area is fundamentally the same, it is employed in different ways. On Nitro-plant, the chemical process technology is computerised and is used in long run continuous process production. On Project and Pharma-plants control of the technology is manual, and is used to manufacture short run batch chemicals. With respect to workforce characteristics, workers on Nitro-plant have a range of backgrounds, both in terms of qualifications and experience. This includes those with no qualifications, and who have been employed at the firm for a number of years, men with trade qualifications such as joiners, cooks and car mechanics, and recent recruits (less than three years) who have a craft apprenticeship qualification. On Project-plant the workforce divides into Process Chemists with a BSc. Chemistry, and Process Operatives. All the process operatives from Project and Pharma-plants interviewed during this research possess a basic academic qualification. That is, either 'O' level or GCSE Chemistry or the City and Guilds 060 chemical operative qualification. One process operative on Project-plant is an apprentice qualified fitter. As with GlassCo, the Craft Maintenance Workshop was selected in order to provide a contrast with craft apprentice trained men employed as craft maintenance workers, and those with or without qualifications who are employed as process operatives. The Craft workshop also contains men with no qualifications or trade qualifications, and thus facilitates a comparison between apprentice qualified and non-qualified Craft Technicians.

Research at Chemicals UK took place over a six-week period in February and March 1996. The firm allowed unlimited access to individuals and the sample consisted of the following: eleven Nitro-plant Process Operatives (from a total of sixteen) working on three of the four shift teams; one Shift Supervisor; two Day Operations Managers; one Logistics Manager;

the Training Manager; the Technical Manager; the Pharma-plant Manager; the Project-plant Manager; four Project-plant Shift Chemists (from a total of eight); four Project-plant Process Operatives (from a total of eight); four Pharma-plant Process Operatives (from a total of eight); ten Craft Technicians; the Craft workshop Engineering Supervisor; the Assistant Engineering supervisor; two Area Production Managers; the Training Officer and the Personnel Officer. All interviews were taped and conducted on site in restroom or offices.

In contrast to Chemicals UK, Electronics UK placed some constraints on the duration of the research, which was limited to three weeks. The reason for this was the need to keep production running at all times, and the subsequent problem of pulling people off the line. The constraints resulted in a smaller sample size in comparison to the two British firms and, therefore, an imbalanced sample. Fieldwork at Electronics UK took place over a three-week period in July 1996. The final sample was made up of the following: five workers from Autoinsertion; the Autoinsertion Production Manager; six assembly line workers; one Stock Controller one Line Leader; one Production Supervisor; one assembly line Production Manager; the Training Manager and the Personnel Manager. All interviews at Electronics UK were taped.

Finally, fieldwork at GlassCo took place over a five-week period in September and October 1997. As with Chemicals UK, the firm imposed few restrictions, and access was given to all workers. Interviews took place in restrooms and offices and, with the exception of a small number of individuals who refused to speak on tape, the majority of interviews were taped. The GlassCo sample consisted of the following: the Plant Manager; the Personnel Manager; the Cold Area Manager; the Hot Area Manager; the Mould Maintenance Workshop Supervisor and Assistant Supervisor; seven Mould Workshop Engineers (from a total of twelve); five HA Machinists (from a total of eight); ten Sorters (from a total of around 70) and five Re-Sorters (from a total of six). Again, all interviews were taped.

Stage Three: Topic Guide Design and Interviews

The topic guides used in this research adopted a semi-structured approach. This approach was taken for two reasons. First, the multi-site case study nature of the research required systematised topic guides in order to ensure comparability between firms and between areas within firms. Second, a semi-structured interview schedule allows interviewees the freedom to elaborate on clearly defined issues (for example, Pawson 1996 pg. 299). The design also loosely followed principles put forward by Pawson. He proposes that the subject matter of the interview is the researcher's theory. The role of the interviewee is to confirm, falsify or refine theory. In the case of exploratory research such as this, it can be suggested that a further role of the interviewee is to assist in the construction of theory. Thus, the key theoretical issue for this research is to identify subjective perceptions of skill, core and periphery, and the causal mechanisms that shape them within particular institutional contexts. Whilst interviewees posses their own knowledge of skill, core and periphery, which is constructed through their active agency at work, they are, according to the realist position, unlikely to possess a total awareness of why they perceive skill, core and periphery in particular ways. The aim of the interview is, therefore, to elicit information that facilitates the construction of an explanatory model.

Four topic guides were used for the following groups of personnel: personnel managers, production managers, department/plant managers and supervisors, and workers. The personnel guide covered issues such as numbers employed, age, gender and skill profiles, contract type, and reasons for employing workers with particular characteristics. Production managers were questioned on the nature of the product, the organisation of production, technology, the recruitment of skilled labour, and training. Issues covered in the department/plant manager topic guides were the organisation of technology, work and labour; role responsibilities, the nature and distribution of skill, and issues of recruitment, promotion and training. Finally, the workers' topic guide began with a profile of the individual in terms of age, gender, work experience, and qualifications and training. It went on to cover perceptions of skill in general, job characteristics including discretion and autonomy, skill required for particular jobs, and attitudes towards managers and the firm. The topic guide also included a number of questions relating to attitudes to work in general. These questions are based on the speculation that attitudes to work may have some influence on the ways in which skill is defined. The interview data failed, however, to identify any relationship between attitudes to work and perceptions of skill.

I began interviews by informing subjects that I was interested in their views on skills at work, and their definitions of what skill is. I then told them I would begin with general questions about skill, and that these would be followed by questions about their own job. This strategy aimed to elicit interviewees' perceptions of skill in general rather than specifically in relation to their own job. In practice however, the majority of interviewees were unable to distinguish between the two, and immediately launched into a description of their own particular job or previous job.

Stage Four: Data Analysis

Analysis of documentary evidence provided by firms was an ongoing process. Certain types of documentary evidence, for example organisational flow charts, were used to identify the appropriate research areas. Other forms of documentary evidence, for example training documents and job description documents, were analysed during and after fieldwork. Preliminary analysis of interview transcripts was carried out following each case study fieldwork. This began with identification and categorisation of perceptions of skill. With regard to the categorisation process, Marshall and Rossman (1995) discuss two forms of typology. Indigenous typologies reflect the language used by respondents whilst analyst-constructed typologies reflect the assumptions of the researcher (Marshall and Rossman pg. 114). Initial categorisation of the data was based upon the language of respondents and therefore used indigenous typologies. Subsequent analysis of the data employed analyst-constructed typologies that reflect the theoretical concepts applied in the research. An example of this is the perception of knowledge as skill articulated by interviewees at Chemicals UK. Initial categorisation of this perception, that is knowledge as skill, was based upon the language used by interviewees. The sub-categories of theoretical and practical knowledge as skill, on the other hand, are analyst constructs, which were developed to classify the types of knowledge described by interviewees.

In addition to the categorisation of subjective perceptions of skill, core and periphery, categories were developed in relation to possible causal mechanisms. Examples include organisational structural features such as technology, firm specific training policies, job characteristics and contract types, and personal features such as prior qualifications, experience and attitudes to work. These possible causal mechanisms were then cross-referenced with perceptions of skill in an attempt to identify patterns and explanations. Following the completion of fieldwork, comparisons between each firm were made, and the model outlined in Chapter Four was developed.

Bibliography

Ackroyd, S., Burrell, G. and Hughes, M. (1988), 'The Japanisation of British Industry?', *Industrial Relations Journal*, Vol. 19, No. 1, pp. 11-23.

Aglietta, M. (1979), *A Theory of Capitalist Regulation*, London, New Left Books.

Alvesson, M. and Due Billing, Y. (1997), *Understanding Gender in Organizations*, London, Sage.

Amin, A. (1994), 'Post-Fordism: Models, Fantasies and Phantoms of Transition', in Amin, A. (ed.), *Post-Fordism: A Reader*, Oxford, Blackwell.

Archer, M. (1995) *Realist social theory: the morphogenetic approach*, Cambridge, Cambridge University Press.

Armstrong, P. (1989), 'Management, Labour Process and Agency', *Work, Employment and Society*, Vol. 3, No. 3, pp. 307-322.

Atkinson, J. (1984), 'Manpower Strategies for Flexible Organisations', *Personnel Management*, August, pp. 28-31.

Atkinson, J. and Meager, N. (1986), *Changing Work Patterns: how companies achieve flexibility to meet new needs*, London, National Economic Development Office.

Attewell, P. (1990), 'What is Skill?', *Work and Occupations*, Vol. 17, No. 4, pp. 422-448.

Bagguley, P. (1994), 'Post-Fordism and the Enterprise Culture', in Burrows, R. and Leader, P. (eds.), *Towards a Post-Fordist Welfare State*, London, Routledge.

Barker, J. R. (1993), 'Tightening the Iron Cage: Concertive Control in Self Managed Teams', *Administrative Science Quarterly*, Vol. 38, pp. 408-437.

Bendix, R. (1977), *Max Weber: An Intellectual Portrait*, London, Methuen Co. Ltd.

Beynon, H. (1975), *Working for Ford*, Wakefield, EP Publishing.

Bhaskar, R. (1979), *The Possibility of Naturalism*, Hassocks, Harvester.

Blackburn, P., Coombs, R. and Green, K. (1985) *Technology, Economic Growth and the Labour Process*, London, MacMillan.

Blauner, R. (1964), *Alienation and Freedom*, Chicago, Chicago University Press.

Bradley, H. (1989), *Men's Work/Women's Work*, Cambridge, Polity Press.

Braverman, H. (1974), *Labour and Monopoly Capital*, New York, Monthly Press.

Brown, R. K. (1992), *Understanding Industrial Organisations: Theoretical Perspectives in Industrial Sociology*, London, Routledge.

Burawoy, M. (1985), *The Politics of Production*, London, Verso.

Burchell, B., Elliot, J., Rubery, J., and Wilkinson, F. (1994) 'Management and Employee Perceptions of Skill', in Penn, R., Rose, R. and Rubery, J. (eds.), *Skill and Occupational Change*, Oxford, Oxford University Press.

Burns, T. and Stalker, G. M. (1961), *The Management of Innovation*, London, Tavistock.

Burrows, R. (1989), 'Glass in the Year 2000. Can it be done?', *Glass Technology*, Vol. 30, No. 3, pp. 93-97.

Casey, B. (1991), 'Survey Evidence on Trends in "Non-Standard" Employment', in Pollert, A. (ed.), *Farewell to flexibility*, Oxford, Blackwell.

Cavendish, R. (1982), *Women on the Line*, London, Routledge, Kegan and Paul.

Child, J. (1997) 'Strategic Choice in the Analysis of Action, Structure, Organizations and Environment: Retrospect and Prospect', *Organization Studies*, 18:1 pp.43-76.

Clarke, S. (1992), 'What the F---'s name is Fordism', in Burrows, R., Gilbert, N. and Pollert, A. (eds.), *Fordism and Flexibility*, London, MacMillan.

Clegg, A. (1990), *Modern Organizations: Organization studies in the Post Modern World*, London, Sage.

Clegg, S. (1994), 'Power Relations and the Constitution of the Resistant subject', in Jermier, J., Knights, D. and Nord, W. (eds.), *Resistance and Power in Organisations*, London, Routledge.

Cockburn, C. (1983), *Brothers: Male dominance and technological change*, London, Pluto.

Collinson, D. (1994), 'Strategies of Resistance. Power, Knowledge and Subjectivity in the workplace', in Jermier, J., Knights, D. and Nord, W. (eds.), *Resistance and Power in Organisations*, London, Routledge.

Cooley, M. (1987), *Architect or Bee*, Langley Technical services.

Cornaz, R. A. (1992), 'Total Quality Management: opportunity and challenge to the container glass industry', *Glass Technology*, Vol. 33, No. 1, pp. 4-9.

Cotgrove, S. and Vamplew, C. (1972), 'Technology, Class and Politics: The case of the process workers', *Sociology*, Vol 2, No. 6, pp. 169-185.

Coyle, A. (1982), 'Sex and Skill in the Organisation of the Clothing Industry', in West, J. (ed.), *Work, Women and the Labour Market*, London, Routledge.

Cressey, P. and MacInnes, J. (1980), 'Voting for Ford: Industrial Democracy and the control of Labour', *Capital and Class*, Vol. 11, pp. 5-33.

Crompton, R. (1997), *Women and Work in Modern Britain*, Oxford, Oxford University Press.

Davies, F. J. (1993), 'European Container Glass Industry', *Glass Technology*, Vol. 34, No. 1, pp. 4-9.

Deetz, S. (1992), 'Disciplinary Power in the Modern corporation', in Alvesson, M. and Wilmott, H. (eds.), *Critical Management Studies*, London, Sage.

Delbridge, R. and Turnbull, P. (1994), *The Japanization of British Industry? Evidence from Transplants and Emulators*, Working Paper 20, Japanese Management Research Unit, Cardiff Business School.

Delbridge, R., Turnbull, P. and Wilkinson, B. (1992), 'Pushing Back the Frontiers: Management, control and work intensification under JIT/TQM factory regimes', *New Technology, Work and Employment*, Vol. 7, No. 2, pp. 97-106.

Dex, S. (1985), *The Sexual Division of Work*, Brighton, Wheatsheaf Books Ltd.

Dex, S. (1988), *Women's Attitudes towards Work*, Basingstoke, Hampshire, MacMillan Press Ltd.

Dex, S. and McCulloch, A. (1997), *Flexible Employment: The Future of Britain's Jobs*, Basingstoke, Hampshire, MacMillan Press Ltd.

Dohse, K., Jurgens, V. and Malsch, T. (1985), 'From "Fordism" to "Toyotism": The Social Organization of the Labour Process in the Japanese Automobile Industry', *Politics and Society*, Vol. 14, No. 2, pp. 115-116.

Edwards, P. (1988), *Control at Work*, Oxford, Basil Blackwell Ltd.

Elam, M. (1994), 'Puzzling out the Post-Fordist Debate: Technology Markets and Institutions', in Amin, A. (ed.), *Post-Fordism: A Reader*, Oxford, Basil Blackwell.

Elger, T. (1982), 'Bravermania, Capital Accumulation and Deskilling', in Wood, S. (ed.), *The Degredation of Work: Skill, Deskilling and the Labour Process*, London, Hutchinson.

Elger, T. (1991), 'Task Flexibility and the Intensification of Labour in UK Manufacturing in the 1980s', in Pollert, A. (ed.), *Farewell to Flexibility*, Oxford, Blackwell.

Elger, T. and Smith, C. (1993), *Global Japanisation: The Transnational Transformation of the Labour Process*, London, Routledge.

Emslie, C., Hunt, K. and Macintyre, S. (1999), 'Gender or Job Differences? Working Conditions amongst Men and Women in White-collar Occupations', *Work, Employment and Society*, Vol. 13, No. 4, pp. 711-729.

England, P. (1992), *Comparable Worth: Theories and Evidence*, New York, Aldine De Gruyter.

Foucault, M. (1977), *Discipline and Punish: The Birth of the Prison*, London, Allen Lane.

Francis, A. (1986), *New Technology at Work*, Oxford, Clarendon Press.

Francis, B. and Penn, R. (1994), 'Towards a Phenomenology of Skill', in Penn, R., Rose, M. and Rubery, J. (eds.), *Skill and Occupational Change*, Oxford, Oxford University Press.

Fraser Kay, M. (1999), *Same or Different: Gender Politics in the Workplace*, Aldershot, Ashgate.

Friedman, A. (1990), 'Managerial Strategies and the Labour Process', in Knights, D. and Wilmott, H. (eds.), *Labour Process Theory, London*, Basingstoke, MacMillan.

Garrahan, P. and Stewart, P. (1992), *The Nissan Enigma: Flexibility at Work in a Local Economy*, London, Mansell.

Gallie, D. (1996), 'Skill, Gender and the Quality of Employment', in Crompton, R., Gallie, D. and Purcell, K. (eds.), *Changing forms of Employment: Organisations, Skills and Gender*, London, Routledge.

Gallie, D. and White, M. (1993), *Employee commitment and the skills revolution. First findings*, PSI Publishing.

Geary, J. F. (1994), 'Task Participation: Employees Participation Enabled or Constrained?, in Sisson, K. (ed.), *Personnel Management: A Comprehensive guide to theory and Practice in Britain*, Oxford, Blackwell.

Giddens, A. (1994), 'Elements of the Theory of Structuration', in *The Polity Reader in Social Theory*, Cambridge, Polity Press.

Gramsci, A. (1971), *Selections from the Prison Notebooks*, edited and translated by Hoare, Q. and Nowell-Smith, G., London, Lawrence and Wiseheart.

Grint, K. and Woolgar, S. (1997), *The Machine at Work: Technology, Work and Organisation*, Cambridge, Polity Press.

Hakim, C. (1990), 'Core and Periphery in Employers Workforce Strategies: Evidence from the 1987 ELUS Survey', *Work, Employment and Society*, Vol. 4, No. 2, pp. 157-188.

Halle, D. (1984), *America's Working Man: Work, home and politics among blue collar Property Owners*, London, University of Chicago Press.

Hammersly, M. and Atkinson, P. (1983), *Ethnography. Principles in Practice*, London, Routledge.

Hendry, C. (1990), 'New Technology, New Careers: The impact of company employment policy', *New Technology, Work and Employment*, Vol 5, No.1, pp. 31-43.

Herzberg, F. (1968), *Work and the Nature of Man*, London, Staples Press.

Horrel, S., Rubery, J., and Burchell, B. (1994), 'Gender and Skills', in Penn, R. Rose, M. and Rubery, J. (eds.), *Skill and Occupational Change*, Oxford, Oxford University Press.

Hows, U., Hurtsfield, J. and Holmaat, R. (1989), 'What Price Flexibility: The Casualisation of Women's employment', *Low Pay Unit*, Pamphlet 54.

Hyman, R. and Streek, W. (1988), *Trade Unions, Technology and Industrial Democracy*, Oxford, Basil Blackwell.

Isler, E. (1988), 'Job Changes', *Glass Technology*, Vol. 29, No. 1, pp. 8-11.

Jones, B. (1988), 'Work and Flexible Automation in Britain: A review of the possibilities', *Work, Employment and Society*, Vol. 2, No. 4, pp. 451-486.

Keat, R. and Urry, J. (1982), *Social Theory as Science*, London, Routledge, Kegan and Paul.

Kelley, M. R. (1989), 'Alternative Forms of Work Organisation under Programmable Automation', in Wood, S. (ed.), *The Transformation of Work*, London, Hutchinson.

Knights, D. (1990), 'Subjectivity, Power and the Labour Process', in Knights, D. and Wilmott, H. (eds.), *Labour Process Theory*, Basingstoke, MacMillan.

Knights, D. and Vurdubakis, T. (1994), 'Foucault, Power and Resistance and All That', in Jermier, J., Knights, D. and Nord, W. (eds.), *Resistance and Power in Organisations*, London, Routledge.

Knights, D. and Wilmott, H. (1985), 'Power and Identity in Theory and Practice', *Sociological Review*, Vol. 33, No. 1, pp. 22-46.

Knights, D. and Wilmott, H. (1989), 'Power and Subjectivity and Work: From Degradation to Subjugation', *Sociology*, Vol. 23, No. 4, pp. 535-558.

Kumar, K. (1995), *From Post-Industrial to Post-Modern Society*, Oxford, Basil Blackwell Publishers Ltd.

Lane, C. (1988), 'Industrial Change in Europe: the pursuit of flexible specialisation in Britain and West Germany', *Work, Employment and Society*, Vol. 2, No. 2, pp. 141-168.

Layder, D. (1994), *Understanding Social Theory*, London, Sage.

Liepmann, K. (1960), *Apprenticeship: an enquiry into its adequacy under modern conditions*, London, Routledge, Kegan and Paul.

Littler, C. R. and Salaman, G. (1982), 'Bravermania and Beyond: Recent theories of the Labour Process', *Sociology*, Vol. 16, No. 2, pp. 215-269.

Littler C. R. and Salaman, G. (1985), 'The Design of Jobs', in Littler, C. R. (ed.), *The Experience of Work*, Aldershot, Gower Publishing.

McCalman, J. (1988), *The Electronics Industry in Britain: coping with Change*, London, Routledge.

McGregor, A. and Sproull, A. (1992), 'Employers and the Flexible Workforce', *Employment Gaztte*, May Issue.

McKinlay, A. and Taylor, P. (1996), 'Power, Surveillance and Resistance. Inside the "factory of the future"', in Ackers, P., Smith, C. and Smith, P. (eds.), *The New Workplace and Trade Unionism*, London, Routledge.

Marshall, C. and Rossman, G. B. (1995), *Designing Qualitative Research*, London, Sage Publications.

Marx, K. (1846), 'Letter to P. V. Annenkov', in Caute, D. (1967), *Essential Writings of Marx*, New York, Macmillan.

Marx, K. (1976), *Capital: Volume One*, Harmondsworth, Penguin.

Maslow, A. H. (1954), *Motivation and Human Personality*, New York, Harper and Row.

May, T. (1993), *Social Research: Issues, Methods and Proces*, Buckingham, Open University Press.

More, C. (1982), 'Skill and the Survival of the Apprenticeship', in Wood, S. (ed.), *The Degradation of Work: Skill, De-skilling and the Labour Process*, London, Hutchinson..

Morgan, K. and Sayer, A. (1988), *Microcircuits of Capital: Sunrise Industry and Uneven development*, Cambridge, Polity.

Morris, J. and Imrie, K. (1992), *Transforming buyer-supplier relations: Japanese style industrial practices in Western contexts*, Basingstoke, MacMillan.

Mouzelis, N. (1991), *Back to Sociological Theory: The Construction of Social Orders*, London, Macmillan.

Mouzelis, N. (1993), 'The Poverty of Sociological Theory', *Sociology*, Vol. 27, No. 4, pp. 675-695.

Murakami, T. (1997), 'The Autonomy of Teams in the Car Industry: A cross national comparison', *Work, Employment and Society*, Vol. 11, No. 4, pp. 749-758.

Murray, R. (1988), 'Life After Henry (Ford)', *Marxism Today*, Vol. 11, pp. 3-8.

Nichols, T. and Beynon, H. (1977), *Living With Capitalism: Class Relations and the Modern Factory*, London, Routledge, Kegan and Paul.

Oliver, N. and Wilkinson, B. (1988), *The Japanization of British Industry*, Oxford, Blackwell.

O' Neill, J. (1987), 'The Disciplinary Society', *British Journal of Sociology*, No. 37, pp. 42-60.

Patrickson, M. (1986), 'Adaptation by new employees to new technology', *The Journal of Occupational Psychology*, Vol. 59, pp. 1-11.

Pawson, R. (1989), *A Measure for Measures: A Manifesto for Empirical Sociology*, London, Routledge.

Penn, R. (1982), 'Skilled Manual Workers in the Labour Process 1856 - 1964', in Woods, S. (ed.), *The Degradation of Work: Skill, De-skilling and the Labour Process*, London, Hutchinson.

Penn, R. (1990), *Class, Power and Technology: Skilled Workers in Britain and America*, Cambridge, Polity Press.

Penn, R. (1994), 'Technological Change and Skilled Manual Work in Contemporary Rochdale', in Penn, R., Rose, M. and Rubery, J. (eds.), *Skill and Occupational Change*, Oxford, Oxford University Press.

Pettigrew, A. (1985), *The Awakening Giant: Continuity and Change in ICI*, Oxford, Blackwell.

Piore, M. and Sabel, C. (1984), *The Second Industrial Divide: Possibilities for Prosperity*, New York, Basic Books.

Pollert, A. (1988a), 'The Flexible Firm: Fixation or Fact?', *Work, Employment and Society*, Vol. 2, No. 3, pp. 281-316.

Pollert, A. (1988b), Dismantling Flexibility, *Capital and Class*, No. 34.

Pollert, A. (1991), (ed.), *Farewell to Flexibility*, Oxford, Blackwell.

Pollert, A. (1996), 'Team Work' on the Assembly Line: Contradiction and the Dynamics of Union Resilience', in Ackers, P., Smith, C. and Smith, P. *The New workplace and Trade Unionism: Critical Perspectives on work and Organization*, London, Routledge.

Proctor, S. J., Rowlinson, M., McArdle, J. H., and Forrester, P. (1994), 'Flexibility, Politics and Strategy: in Defence of the Model of the Flexible Firm', *Work, Employment and Society*, Vol. 8, No. 2, pp. 221-242.

Rabinow, P. (1986), *The Foucault Reader*, London, Penguin.

Reed, M. (1997), 'In Praise of Duality and Dualism: Rethinking Agency and Structure in Organisation Analysis', *Organisation Studies*, Vol. 18, No. 1, pp. 21-42.

Rolfe, H. (1986), 'Skill, deskilling and new technology in the non-manual labour process', *New Technology, Work and Employment*, Vol. 1, No. 1, pp. 37-49.

Rowe, R. and Snizek, W. E. (1995), 'Gender differences in Work Value', *Work and Occupations*, Vol. 22, No. 2. pp. 399-421.

Sabel, C. (1994), 'Flexible Specialisation and the Re-emergence of Regional Economies', in Amin, A. (ed.), *Post-Fordism: A Reader*, Oxford, Basil Blackwell.

Sakolosky, R. (1992), 'Disciplinary Power and the Labour Process', in Sturdy, A. Knights, D. and Wilmott, H. (eds.), *Skill and Consent: Contemporary Studies in the Labour Process*, London, Routledge.

Savage, M., Barlow, J., Dickens, P. and Fielding, T. (1992), *Property, Bureaucracy and Culture: Middle-Class Formation in Contemporary Britain*, London, Routledge.

Sayer, A. (1992), *Method in Science: A Realist Approach*, London, Routledge.

Scarbrough, H. and Corbett, J. M. (1992), *Technology and Work Organisation: Power, Meaning and Design*, London, Routledge.

Sewell, G. and Wilkinson, B. (1992), 'Someone to Watch over Me: Surveillance, Discipline and the Just-In-Time Labour Process', *Sociology*, Vol. 26, No. 2, pp. 271-289.

Siltanen, J. (1994), *Locating Gender: Occupational Segregation, Wages and Domestic Responsibilities*, London, UCL Press.

Smith, C. (1991), 'From 1960s Automation to Flexible Specialisation: a deja vu of Technical Panaceas', in Pollert, A. (ed.), *Farewell to Flexibility*, Oxford, Blackwell.

Smith, J. H. (1987), 'Elton Mayo and The Hidden Hawthorne', *Work, Employment and Society*, Vol. 1, No. 1, pp. 107-120.

Spenner, K. I. (1990), 'Skill: Meanings, Methods and Measures', *Work and Occupation*, Vol. 17, No. 4, pp. 399-421.

Steinberg, R. L. (1990), 'Social construction of Skill: Gender, Power and Comparable Worth', *Work and Occupations*, Vol. 17, No. 4, pp. 449-482.

Tam, M. (1997), *Part-Time Employment: A Bridge or a Trap*, Aldershot, Avebury.

Taylor, B., Elger, T. and Fairbrother, P. (1993), 'Transplants and Emulators: The Fate of the Japanese Model in British Electronics', in Elger, T. and Smith, C. (eds.), *Global Japanization: The Transnational Transformation of the Labour Process*, London, Routledge.

Thompson, P. (1989), *The Nature of Work*, Basigstoke, Hampshire, MacMillan Press Ltd.

Thompson, P. and Ackroyd, S. (1995), 'All Quiet on the Workplace Front? A Critique of Recent Trends In British Industrial Sociology', *Sociology*, Vol. 29, No. 4, pp. 615-633.

Thompson, P. and McHugh, D. (1995), *Work Organisations: A Critical Introduction*, Hampshire and London, MacMillan.

Tolbert, P. S. and Moen, P. (1998), 'Men's and women's Definitions of Good Jobs: Similarities and Differences by Age and Across Time', *Work and Occupations*, Vol. 25, No. 2, pp. 168-194.

Tomanay, J. (1994), 'A New Paradigm of Work Organisation and Technology', in Amin, A. (ed.), *Post-Fordism: A Reader*, Oxford, Basil Blackwell.

Vroom, V. H. and Deci, E. L. (1992), *Management and Motivation*, Harmondsworth Penguin.

Wajcman, J. (1991), 'Patriarchy, Technology and Conceptions of skill', *Work and Occupations*, Vol. 18, No. 1, pp. 29-44.

Walby, S. (1989), 'Flexibility and the Changing Sexual Division of Labour', in Wood, S. (ed.), *The Transformation of Work*, London, Hutchinson.

Walker, R. (1989), 'Machinery, Labour and Location', in Wood, S. (ed.), *The Transformation of work*, London, Hutchinson.

Weber, M. (1948), *Essays in Sociology*, Routledge, Kegan and Paul, London.
Wedderburn, D. and Crompton, R. (1972), *Workers Attitudes to Technology*, Cambridge, Cambridge University Press.
Westwood, S. (1984), *All Day Every Day*, London, Pluto.
Wickens, P. D. (1987), *The road to Nissan*, London, MacMillan.
Wood, S. (1987), 'The Deskilling Debate, New Technology and Work Organisation', *Acta Sociologica*, Vol. 30, No. 1, pp. 3-24.
Wood, S. (1989), (ed.), *The Transformation of Work*, London, Hutchinson.
Wood, S. (1991), 'Japanisation and/or Toyotaism', *Work, Employment and Society*, Vol. 5, No. 4, pp. 567-600.
Wood, S. and Kelly, J. (1982), 'Taylorism, Responsible Autonomy and Managerial Strategies', in Wood, S. (ed.), *The Degradation of Work: Skill, Deskilling and the Labour Process*, London, Hutchinson.

Index